Neil McDonald

play the Dutch

an opening repertoire for Black based on the Leningrad Variation

EVERYMAN CHESS

Gloucester Publishers plc www.everymanchess.com

First published in 2010 by Gloucester Publishers Limited, London.

British Library Cataloguing-in-Publication Data
A catalogue record for this book is available from the British Library.

ISBN: 978 1 85744 641 8

Distributed in North America by National Book Network,
15200 NBN Way, Blue Ridge Summit, PA 17214. Ph: 717.794.3800.

Distributed in Europe by Central Books Ltd.,
Central Books Ltd, 50 Freshwater Road, Chadwell Heath, London, RM8 1RX.

All other sales enquiries should be directed to Everyman Chess.
email: info@everymanchess.com; website: www.everymanchess.com

Everyman is the registered trade mark of Random House Inc. and is used in this work under licence from Random House Inc.

Everyman Chess Series
Commissioning editor and advisor: Byron Jacobs
Typeset and edited by First Rank Publishing, Brighton.
Cover design by Horatio Monteverde.

Contents

Preface

It is an appealing feature of the Dutch that 1...f5 can be played against virtually any opening move apart from 1 e4.

However, this is slightly misleading if it suggests that you only have to learn one basic sequence of moves after 1...f5 and then you are ready for anything. In reality the Dutch leads to a range of pawn structures, each of which requires its own special treatment. For example, this book is built around the Leningrad Dutch, but in many cases Black will do best to set up a Stonewall centre with ...d7-d5, rather than play the 'characteristic' ...d7-d6 Leningrad move.

Likewise after 2 ♘c3, 2 ♗g5 and other early divergences by White, the pawn structure has little, or sometimes nothing at all, in common with the traditional Leningrad Dutch. Thus at times the centre is characteristic of the Queen's Gambit; at other times the King's Indian; and after 2 ♗g5 it feels like a strange Sicilian Hedgehog!

So more preparation is required to play the opening than is apparent at first glance, when 1...f5 appears such a great labour-saving device. On the plus side you are going to have more fun playing the Dutch – its variety means you aren't going to grow bored of it any time soon.

In view of the range of possibilities after 1...f5, can we say that there is any one strategic theme that runs through the opening? I find the varied adventures of Black's f-pawn the most intriguing aspect of the opening. The pawn is cast forward irretrievably into the world on move one, and ends up performing varied roles, sometimes in the same game: a battering ram when it advances to f4; a pillar of the state in the Stonewall, perhaps supporting a knight on e4; and the destroyer of the white centre when it is exchanged for a pawn on e4. In a less aggressive role it sits patiently on f5, restraining the white centre. Destroyer, restrainer, pillar: the impact of the f-pawn is felt throughout the game, even if it vanishes from the board at an early stage.

The Dutch is a difficult opening for both players to handle, and sometimes it all goes wrong for Black. However, there are also great moments when the f-pawn shows its power. Even the strongest opponents can find their position ripped up by the dynamism of this little pawn.

Let me wish you good luck in your Dutch adventures. Have fun with the f-pawn!

Neil McDonald
Gravesend
September 2008

Introduction

Some Strategical and Tactical Themes in the Dutch

Before we become immersed in sophisticated modern theory, I thought I'd show you one of the very first Dutch games on record.

G.Walker-P.De Saint Amant
London 1836

1 d4 f5 2 c4 ♘f6 3 ♘c3 d6 4 ♘f3 e6?!

Chess history, or at least its terminology, would have to be rewritten if Black had played 4...g6 here, since the Leningrad Dutch wasn't invented until a hundred or so years after this game. Not surprisingly, Black puts his bishop on e7 in Classical Dutch style.

5 e3 ♗e7 6 ♗d3

White is also unable to play in modern style by fianchettoing his king's bishop with 5 g3 and 6 ♗g2.

6...0-0 7 0-0 c6

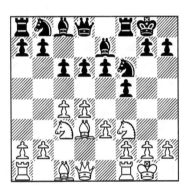

8 ♗c2?!

Nowadays we'd expect 8 e4, seizing space before Black can establish a Stonewall with his next move.

8...d5 9 cxd5 cxd5 10 ♗d2 ♘c6 11 ♕e2 a6 12 a3 ♗d6 13 b4 ♘e4!

A procedure that will be much repeated throughout this book. Black makes use of the 'de facto' outpost on

7

e4. Its effect in 1836 is such that White immediately blunders a pawn.

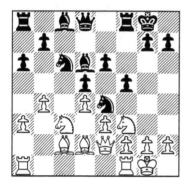

14 b5? ♘xc3 15 ♗xc3 axb5 16 ♕xb5 ♖xa3 17 ♖xa3 ♗xa3 18 ♖a1 ♗d6 19 ♗d3 ♕c7 20 ♗d2 ♗d7 21 ♕b3 ♖b8 22 ♖c1 ♖a8 23 ♘e5 ♗xe5 24 dxe5

Now Black could keep his extra pawn with 24...♕xe5 25 ♕xb7 ♖a7 26 ♕b6 ♖a1 followed by simplifying. However, it seems that Saint Amant wanted to strengthen the f5-pawn against any possible ♗xf5 sacrifice.

24...g6??

The Leningrad Dutch kingside pawn structure is risky enough for Black even when there is a bishop available to guard things on g7. Here the dark squares around the black king are entirely unprotected. Still, even after this positional blunder the wedge of pawns on the light squares acts as a barrier against the white attack.

25 f4 ♕b8 26 ♖b1 ♗c8 27 ♕b6

The manoeuvre 27 ♗e1 and 28 ♗h4 to infiltrate the dark squares on the kingside looks strong.

27...♕a7 28 ♕c7 d4 29 e4 fxe4 30 f5?

A clever attacking idea but with a fatal flaw. He should prefer 30 ♗xe4.

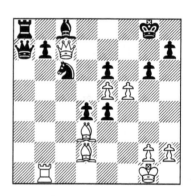

30...♕b8!

Walker was hoping for 30...exd3? 31 f6! b6 (to stop mate on g7) 32 f7+ ♔g7 33 ♗h6+! ♔xh6 34 f8♕+ completing a brilliant career for the f-pawn. Instead he is obliged to exchange queens and after some further adventures was defeated in the endgame by the pretty finishing stroke 40...♘f7.

31 ♕xb8 ♘xb8 32 ♗xe4 gxf5 33 ♗xb7 ♗xb7 34 ♖xb7 ♖a1+ 35 ♔f2 ♘c6 36 ♗h6 ♘xe5 37 ♖g7+ ♔h8 38 h3 ♖a2+ 39 ♔g3 f4+ 40 ♔xf4 ♘f7! 41 ♖xf7 ♖f2+ 42 ♔e4 ♖xf7 43 ♔xd4 ♖f6 0-1

The Dutch pawn-ram

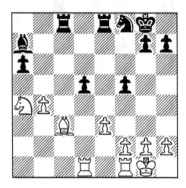

The position was reached in **V.Sergeev-N.Firman**, Alushta 2009. It looks as though Black can't do anything but suffer with 23...♖ed8. However, there came:

23...f4!!

A move of splendid vitality.

24 exf4 ♘e6

What has Black achieved with his ...f5-f4 move that serves him so well in the Dutch?

Firstly, the scope of the bishop on a7 has been increased – it attacks f2 rather than (in Nimzowitsch's memorable phrase) 'biting on granite' against e3.

Secondly, the rook on e8 is granted an open file.

Thirdly, the pawn on d5 is converted into a passed pawn that can advance to d4 where it will be well defended.

Finally, the knight on e6 has been activated with a threat to f4 as 25 ♖xd5 ♘xf4 intending 26...♘e2+ is at least okay for Black.

So a black rook, knight, bishop and

passed pawn have all become important dynamic factors in the position thanks to the sacrifice of the torrent pawn. The upshot is that thanks to the 'Dutch' pawn Black gains activity in what would otherwise have been a dour defensive position for him.

25 ♗e5

It is the black rook on the c-file that profits after 25 g3 d4 26 ♗d2 ♖c2.

25...♖c4 26 ♘c3 d4 27 ♘a2

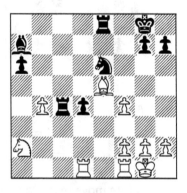

Now Black should have continued generating dynamism with his pawns with 27...g5!, creating a passed pawn and active pieces after 28 fxg5 ♘xg5. Still, he managed to win the endgame anyhow after 22 moves.

Black establishes a pawn wedge in the centre

Sometimes the ...f5-f4 pawn-ram occurs in a closed or static pawn structure after systematic preparation. Often White can be accused of nothing worse than passive play in the Dutch, but ends up in great difficulties before move 20. Here is a typical positional squeeze by Black against passive play, adorned with the pawn-ram.

W.Buehl-L.Reifurth
Chicago 1994

1 d4 f5 2 ♘f3 ♘f6 3 g3 g6 4 ♗g2 ♗g7 5 c4 0-0 6 0-0 d6 7 ♘c3 c6 8 b3 ♕a5 9 ♗b2 e5 10 ♕c2?

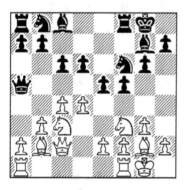

An irresolute move that allows Black to get a grip on the centre. Instead 10 dxe5 dxe5 11 e4 is discussed in Chapter Six.

10...e4 11 ♘e1

From bad to worse. He should play 11 ♘d2 followed by 12 e3 and then try to edge forwards on the queenside.

11...d5 12 cxd5?

The final mistake, giving the black knight the c6-square.

12...cxd5 13 a3 ♘c6 14 ♖d1 ♕d8!

The queen has served her purpose on the queenside and is now needed to support a kingside attack. Black's basic aim is to advance ...f5-f4 at the most favourable moment.

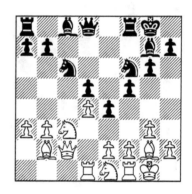

15 b4 ♗e6 16 ♘a4 ♗f7 17 ♕d2

White has no counterplay and so Black hasn't hurried his attack. However, now he decides it is time for violence:

17...♘g4 18 h3 ♗h6! 19 e3

Black provoked this move so that a future ...f5-f4 breakthrough will not only attack e3 but also contain the threat of ...f4-f3, smothering the bishop on g2.

19...♘f6 20 ♗c3 a6 21 ♖b1 b6 22 ♘c2 ♗e8 23 ♖fc1 g5 24 ♗f1 ♘e7!

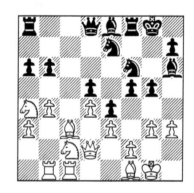

Nicely done. Black wins time to manoeuvre his knight to g6 to support the ...f5-f4 advance by a discovered attack on the knight on a4.

25 ♘b2

The white pieces are grouped on the queenside, but what can they do?

25...f4

The Dutch pawn has the decisive word.

26 exf4 gxf4 27 gxf4 ♘g6 28 ♔h1 ♘xf4 29 ♗g2 ♘g4!

It's not too late for Black to throw it all away with 29...♘xg2? 30 ♕xh6 when 31 ♖g1 gives White a strong attack.

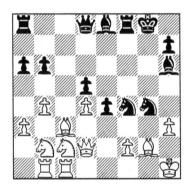

30 ♘e3

It all caves in for White after 30 hxg4 ♕h4+ 31 ♔g1 ♘h3+ 32 ♗xh3 ♗xd2 33 ♗xd2 ♕xf2+.

30...♘xh3 31 ♗xh3 ♕h4 0-1

Either h3 or f2 drops next move with a quick massacre

Black wins through tactical sharpness after a tough defence

In the Dutch White often strives to gain space and/or open lines on the queenside. Black needs to be patient and keep an eye open for favourable tactics. Opportunities may appear suddenly

and have to be grasped!

The following position was reached in **A.Iljushin-E.Berg**, European Championship, Budva 2009.

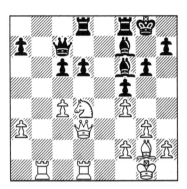

The c6-pawn is attacked twice. If 21...♗e8 then 22 ♘e6 wins the exchange, while 21...♗xd4 22 ♕xd4 gives up Black's important dark-square bishop, and 21...c5 22 ♖b7 ♕c8 23 ♘c6 ♕xb7 24 ♘xd8 ♕c7 25 ♘xf7 ♔xf7 26 ♕xd6 ♕xd6 27 ♖xd6 leaves him a pawn down in an endgame. Berg comes up with a far better solution to Black's travails:

21...d5! 22 cxd5 ♗xd5

Black remains under intense pressure after 22...cxd5 23 ♖dc1.

23 ♘xc6!

Winning a pawn.

23...♗xc6

If 23...♗xg2 24 ♘xd8 ♖xd8 25 ♕b3+ ♔g7 26 ♔xg2 and White wins.

24 ♕c4+ ♔h8 25 ♗xc6 ♖xd1+ 26 ♖xd1 ♖c8 27 ♖c1 ♕d6

White has won a pawn, but the presence of opposite-coloured bishops means he has few winning chances.

28 a4 ♔g7 29 ♔g2 ♖c7 30 ♖c2 ♕d1 31 h3 h5 32 h4 ♕d6 33 a5 ♕d1 34 a6 ♕d6 35 ♕b5 ♔h6 36 ♖c4 ♗d4

Now the exchanges that result from 37 ♗f3 or 37 ♕d5 would leave White with negligible winning chances, but he has lost his sense of danger:

37 ♕a4? ♗xf2!!

The weakness of f2 strikes again.

38 ♔xf2?

White can hold on with 38 ♗f3, for instance if 38...♗c5 39 ♖c2.

38...♕d2+ 39 ♔g1?

White can still draw with 39 ♔f1 ♖e7 40 ♕a1! stopping the mate on e1 and aiming for a perpetual check via

the h8-square: for example, 40...♕d3+ 41 ♔g2 ♕e2+ 42 ♔h3 ♕xc4 43 ♕h8+ ♖h7 44 ♕f8+ ♔g7 45 ♕h8+.

39...♖e7 40 ♗g2 ♕e1+ 41 ♔h2 ♖e3! 42 ♖c1 ♕xc1 43 ♕d4 ♕c3 44 ♕xa7?

Black would still have to prove he is winning after 44 ♕d8! as 44...♖xg3? would only draw after 45 ♕f8+.

44...♕e1! 0-1

A typical advantage for Black in the endgame

Black does surprisingly well in the endgame in the Dutch as White's pawn structure gets worn down. In fact White often wears it down himself, or makes it disjointed, by playing overly sharply. Assuming that e7 remains guarded, the Dutch Leningrad pawn structure is rather solid for Black – the pawn on e7 is a linchpin that is difficult to attack and holds together the black centre.

The following position was reached in **A.Karpov-H.Nakamura**, Cap d'Agde (rapid) 2008.

Black has a couple of advantages:

The white bishop is shut in on g2 by a solid barrier on e4. If f2-f3 is ever played to free it then the white pawn structure and pieces will be exposed to tactical blows from the black pieces that are massed on the e-file and f-files. Here is the paradox of the Dutch e2, f2, g3 and h2 pawn structure: it is incredibly solid, but it can become a tomb for the bishop on g2 – and in some cases for the king on g1. Being behind heavy fortifications is okay so long as you don't want to get out.

In contrast, the black bishop on c4 is active. Unlike its opposite number on g2, it has escaped outside the pawn chain and has a target on e2. Furthermore, and this is an important factor on a board that is so open, it is defended by the pawn on d5 and so is secure from attack.

Whereas the pawn on d5 is soundly defended by the bishop on c4, White has two pawns that are potentially vulnerable. The first is the pawn on e2 – it cramps the white queen's mobility to have to defend it. The second vulnerable pawn is on f2. Its defensive alliance with the bishop on e3 is less secure than that between the black bishop and pawn on d5, because of the possible disruptive move ...d5-d4.

Whereas the white pawn structure is solid but inert, the black pawns control more space and are more dynamic. To have pawns on d5 and e4 versus pawns on e2 and f2 gives Black a lot more potential to expand. He can try to arrange ...d5-d4, whereas White can only make moves with his pieces and wait.

But still, can we really say that the position is anything other than a draw? For the sake of fairness I should point out this was a rapidplay game. On the other hand, the fact that Karpov couldn't defend it shows that it isn't easy. Simple endgame positions are a forte of the great masters, even after their opening knowledge has withered and their tactical sight declined.

25...♛f6!

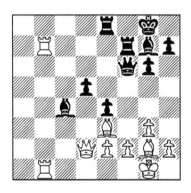

By threatening to mobilize the pawns with 26...d4 Nakamura persuades White to exchange off his active rook.

26 ♖xf7 ♛xf7 27 ♗f1

Intending to unwind with 28 ♗d4 and 29 e3. If all the bishops vanish from the board, Karpov could even try to prove that the d5-pawn is a weakness.

27...♛f6!

Denying Karpov his plan.

28 ♗g5 ♛f5

With the incidental tactical threat of 29...e3! winning instantly as b1, d2, f2 and g5 would suddenly all be hanging!

29 罩b7

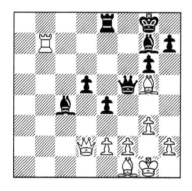

29...罩a8

In principle it would be wrong to hurry the ...d5-d4 push as it deprives the bishop on c4 of its defender. And there is also a tactical reason why: 29...d4 30 罩xg7+! 含xg7 31 彙h6+ (stronger than 31 營xd4+ 營e5 when g5 as well as c4 is hanging) 31...含g8 32 營xd4 營f7 33 彙c1! intending 34 彙b2. Then, notwithstanding being an exchange up, Black can never hope to win because of his dark-square holes.

30 h4

Black's persistence begins to pay off. Karpov secures his bishop but in doing so weakens his kingside pawns. It was simpler to retreat with 30 彙e3! and ask Black 'how can you make progress?'

30...彙e5!

Nakamura straightaway homes in on the g3-pawn. As the bishop also controls b8 and prevents the white

rook checking there, poor Karpov has to worry too about a possible invasion on his second rank with 31...罩a2.

31 罩e7?

The calm 31 彙e3 would still have saved the day: if 31...罩f8 then 32 彙d4 when 32...彙xg3?? allows the killer check 33 罩g7+; and 31...罩a2 32 營b4 threatens 33 營e7 and so prevents Black from continuing his attack.

31...罩f8

With a double threat to f2 and g3.

32 彙f4?!

After 32 彙e3 彙xg3?? 33 營d4!, threatening mate on g7 and defending f2 a third time, turns the tables. But the intermediate 32...營f6! does the trick after 33 罩b7 彙xg3.

32...彙xf4 33 gxf4 營g4+!

The hurried 33...營xf4? allows White counterplay after 34 營d4 罩f6 (34...營f6 is best) 35 彙h3, etc.

34 彙g2 營xh4

Winning a pawn and attacking the white rook...

35 罩c7 營xf4

...and so winning a pawn while

again attacking the white rook. No chance is given to White to counterattack. The rest is fairly straightforward.
36 ♕xf4 ♖xf4 37 e3 ♖f7 38 ♖c8+ ♔g7 39 ♖c5 ♖e7 40 ♖c6 ♗e2 41 ♗h3 ♖a7 42 ♖d6 ♗c4 43 ♔g2 h5 44 ♔g3 ♖a1 45 ♔f4 ♖h1 46 ♗e6 ♖f1 47 ♔g5 ♖g1+ 48 ♔f4 ♖g2 49 ♗xd5 ♖xf2+ 50 ♔xe4 ♗xd5+ 51 ♖xd5 h4 52 ♖d7+ ♖f7 53

♔d4 0-1

White's isolated pawn is no match for Black's connected passed pawns.

Karpov didn't play as well in 2008 as he did twenty years earlier, but I'm pretty sure if he couldn't defend White's position then it won't be easy for your opponents either.

Chapter One

Gambit Lines and Early Oddities

1 d4 f5

In this chapter we'll examine the moves 2 g4, 2 h3, 2 ♕d3 and 2 e4, as we start our journey into the theory of the Dutch Defence by considering those variations in which White aims at the immediate elimination of the f5-pawn. These lines can be tricky and a careless or under-prepared player might well be caught out by them. However, positionally speaking, the move 1...f5 can't be refuted by allowing Black to exchange his f5-pawn for the white e4-pawn, or, even worse, by dislocating the white kingside pawns with g2-g4. That is why the strongest players have shown little interest in these variations for White. In fact only in the Staunton Gambit (2 e4) is the theory developing fairly fast.

The opening period can be a rather anxious time when facing a gambit, as White makes it clear from move two or three that he is out for blood. It may feel that defeat – and an embarrassingly quick one – is only one slight misstep away. But once the initial storm passes over, Black is left in a healthy state. As we will see in the following games, the black pieces easily find good squares – even the bishop on c8. If in doubt, play moves like ...♘f6, ...d7-d5 and ...♘c6, and you can't go far wrong against any of the White gambits.

Part One: 2 g4

1 d4 f5 2 g4

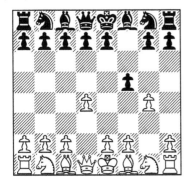

White deflects the pawn from f5 in order to build a centre with e2-e4, or to use the pawn on g4 as a hook to open lines with h2-h3. As long as he plays with a little care, Black is sure to get a good game as White's pawn thrust doesn't have the support of his pieces and loosens his kingside too much. In his work on the Dutch, leading expert Valeri Beim even goes so far as to give 2 g4 a question mark.

2...fxg4 3 e4

After 3 h3, 3...g3! is simplest, returning the pawn to prevent White opening lines on the kingside (you might like to compare this with the line 1 d4 f5 2 ♕d3 d5 3 g4 fxg4 4 h3 g3! given later in the chapter). After 4 fxg3 ♘f6 5 ♗g2 d5 Black can develop with moves like 6...e6, 7...♗d6, 8...0-0 and 9...♘c6. An attempt to throw a spanner in the works with 6 ♘c3 e6 7 e4 is well an-

swered by Kindermann's recommendation of 7...♗b4! 8 e5 ♘e4 9 ♗xe4 dxe4 when White is loose on the light squares, and Black can build up with ...0-0, ...b7-b6, ...♗b7, etc.

Instead 3 ♗f4 is an anti-...g4-g3 measure, but there is nothing to stop Black developing with 3...♘f6 4 h3 d5 5 ♘c3 ♘c6 etc, when we have to ask ourselves what White has got for his pawn. **3...d5!**

Reuben Fine was right when he said that ...d7-d5 is the antidote to all gambits!

4 e5

Now after the natural move 4...♗f5, White can try 5 ♘e2!? e6 6 ♘g3 with the idea of h2-h3 and ♘xf5 at the right moment. I don't like this for Black, as it feels like his pawn structure is being needlessly compromised.

Therefore I would recommend **4...♗e6!?**. If White then plays slowly, the retreat ...♗f7 followed by ...e7-e6 would turn it into a kind of French in which the black bishop is on the good f7-square.

Play could go 5 ♘e2 ♛d7 6 ♘f4 ♘c6 7 ♘xe6 ♛xe6 8 ♗e2 and now 8...♘h6! is an efficient way to defend g4, as 9 ♗xh6 ♛xh6 10 ♗xg4 e6 looks very comfortable for Black. Instead after 9 c4 0-0-0 White stood badly in A.Truskavetsky-V.Romcovici, Dnipropetrovsk 2005.

Part Two: 2 h3

1 d4 f5 2 h3 ♘f6 3 g4

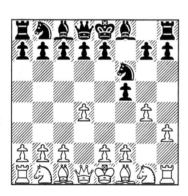

Here simple and good is **3...d5**. If 4 gxf5 ♗xf5 Black is ahead in development and we are left wondering what the pawn is doing on h3. If instead 4 g5 ♘e4 5 ♗f4 e6 6 ♘f3 c5 we have reached the type of set-up for Black that is recommended in Chapter Two against 2 ♘c3, but how inferior has been the play of White! He has gained little from the pawn moves on the g-file and h-file, whereas Black has been steadily increasing his power in the centre. Indeed, after 7 e3 ♛b6 8 ♛c1 ♗d7! (positionally alert, non-routine play: Black intends to exchange off his bad bishop before playing ...♘c6) 9 c3 ♗b5 10 ♘bd2 ♘c6 Black had an excellent position in the game K.Kusnetsov-M.Dzhumaev, Dubai 2001.

More testing is 4 ♛d3, but in the following example Black got a good game with simple consolidating and developing moves: 4...e6 5 gxf5 (against slower play Black can build up with ...♗e7, ...0-0, ...c7-c5, etc) 5...exf5

6 ♗g5 (White decides to eliminate the knight that would become strong in the future after ...♘e4) 6...♗e7 7 ♗xf6 ♗xf6 8 ♗g2 c6 9 ♘d2 0-0 10 c4 ♗e6 11 cxd5 ♗xd5 (the fact that Black

can exchange off the light-squared bishops in a Stonewall set-up is a far from encouraging sign for White) 12 ♗xd5+ ♕xd5 13 ♘gf3 ♘a6 14 ♕b3 ♕xb3 15 ♘xb3 ♖fe8 16 ♖d1 ♖ad8 17 ♖d2 ♖d5 and in B.Heberla-P.Nguyen, Warsaw 2008, Black had achieved a full development without incurring any weaknesses. He possessed the best minor piece in the shape of the dark-squared bishop and had pressure on the white centre. White was rated Elo 2485, Black 2327, but Heberla still had to struggle to draw after his poor opening.

Part Three: 2 ♕d3

1 d4 f5 2 ♕d3
A direct attack on the f5 pawn by Her Majesty. Now **2...d5** with a Stonewall centre looks the best response. After 3 g4...

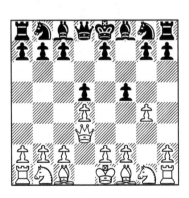

...Black can be very solid with 3...e6, but this to some extent justifies White's play: for example, 4 gxf5 exf5 5

♗f4 ♘f6 6 ♘f3 ♗d6 7 ♘e5 ♘h5 8 e3! and the knight had a strong outpost square on e5 in H.Teske-A.Berelowitsch, Mülheim 2009.

So making it messy with 3...fxg4 looks best. In the following illustrative game, we see a theme characteristic of gambit lines in the Dutch: a white knight on g1 dominated by a black pawn on e4.

**L.Ibarra Chami-
A. Rodriguez Vila**
Mexico City 2007

1 d4 f5 2 ♕d3 d5 3 g4
If White doesn't act quickly then Black can build up with ...♘f6, ...e7-e6, ...c7-c5, ...♘c6, etc, when White has trouble in justifying his queen move – in fact she could become a target of the black pieces.
3...fxg4 4 h3 g3!

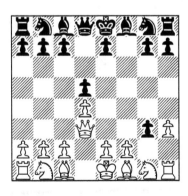

An important strategical device in this type of position. Black doesn't want to take on h3 as 4...gxh3 5 ♘xh3

activates the white knight and opens the h-file for a possible attack on h7. As White also threatens to open the h-file and clear h3 himself by playing 5 hxg4, Black elects to advance the pawn to g3.

5 fxg3

In contrast to 4...gxh3 5 ♘xh3, this recapture does nothing to improve the dynamism of the white pieces. On the contrary, the white pawns are a little bit compromised (one less pawn being in the centre).

The alternative 5 ♕xg3 makes a lot of sense, but I don't think White can claim any advantage. For example, 5...♘f6 6 ♘c3 ♗f5 7 ♗f4 ♘h5 (also possible is 7...♘a6 with ideas of ...♘b4) 8 ♕g5 g6 9 ♗e5, as in G.Welling-J.Bosch, Hertogenbosch 1999, and now 9...♘f6!? is an interesting way to keep the tension, intending 10 ♗g2 (or 10 e3 ♘bd7 11 0-0-0 e6) 10...♘bd7 11 0-0-0 (an important point is that 11 ♘xd5 fails to 11...♘xe5) 11...c6 12 ♘f3 e6 etc.

5...♘f6 6 ♗g2 ♘c6

Note the typical ...♘f6 and ...♘c6 response to White's gambit line. Did White really imagine that with a few flimsy pawn moves he was going to break through the enemy line when there are such powerful 'keepers' opposing him?

7 ♗f4 g6!

Planning to gain time by attacking the queen with 8...♗f5. White's next move stops this but leaves the bishop on f4 undefended – a factor that becomes important as early as move 9.

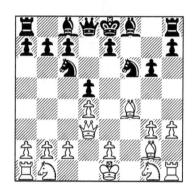

8 g4 ♗g7 9 c3 0-0

With ideas of 10...♘xg4.

10 ♕g3

Chami defends his bishop and attacks the c7-pawn. However, he has fallen too far behind in development and Black is able to exploit this with vigorous play.

10...♘e4 11 ♗xe4 dxe4

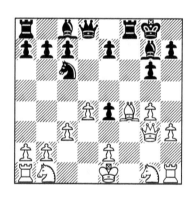

White tried to strike a quick blow in the opening, but has ended up drained of dynamism himself because of the difficulty in developing his knight from g1.

12 ♗xc7 ♕d5 13 ♕e3

After 13 ♘d2 not so clear is 13...e3

14 ♘df3, but Black can keep on attacking with 13...e5.

13...♘xd4! 14 ♘a3

Also hopeless is 14 cxd4 ♗xd4 15 ♕b3 ♗f2+ 16 ♔f1 ♗b6+ 17 ♔g2 ♕xb3 18 axb3 ♗xc7 and wins.

14...♘b5 15 ♘xb5

Or 15 c4 ♕f7! 16 cxb5 ♕f1+ 17 ♔d2 ♕xa1.

15...♕xb5 16 0-0-0 ♕c4 17 ♗g3 ♗e6

If you are wondering why Black's attack is unstoppable, just look at the white knight on g1 and the rook on h1.

18 b3 ♕c6 19 ♔b1 b5 20 ♖c1 a5 21 ♕d2 a4 0-1

White was by no means a bad player – he was rated 2325 – but he was entirely helpless once the lack of cohesion in his position drove him further and further behind in development.

Part Four:
The Staunton Gambit

The Staunton Gambit begins **1 d4 f5 2 e4 fxe4**.

It deserves respect as it is the only system for White in this chapter that has the backing of several top-class players. It has also collected an awful lot of sharp theory, as we shall see.

The modern way to play the Staunton for White is 3 ♘c3 ♘f6 4 ♗g5. This will be analysed in Part Five. Here we'll look at the old-fashioned method which is to stab at the e4-pawn with f2-f3 in an attempt to open lines on the kingside.

In virtually all lines in which White plays f2-f3 without a preliminary d4-d5, it is possible for Black to stand his ground in the centre by defending the e4-pawn with ...d7-d5, and supporting it again if necessary with ...♗f5. It is then a thorn in White's side – or perhaps we should say it is a stone in the hoof of the knight on g1, as it is prevented from going to f3. We have already seen White's problems when the knight is dominated by a black pawn on e4 in the Chami-Rodriguez game above.

B.Predojevic-N.Sedlak
Nova Gorica 2008

1 d4 f5 2 e4 fxe4 3 ♘c3

After 3 f3 the ...d7-d5 recipe already applies: 3...d5 4 fxe4 dxe4 and now 5 ♘c3 ♘f6 6 ♗g5 ♗f5 transposes to our main game, while 5 ♗c4 ♘f6 6 ♘e2 allows Black at least equality with the freeing move 6...e5! when 7 dxe5?! ♕xd1+ 8 ♔xd1 ♘g4 would be bad for White.

3...♘f6 4 f3

We shall discuss ideas of f2-f3 after 3 ♘c3 ♘f6 4 ♗g5 ♘c6 in Part Five.

4...d5!

Black refuses to fall behind in development and give White the initiative after 4...exf3 5 ♘xf3.

5 fxe4 dxe4

The doubled pawns look ugly, but the one on e4 is denying the white knight its natural square on f3. It will require some time and effort for White to regain his pawn, and meanwhile

Black can mobilize all his pieces.

6 ♗g5 ♗f5!

In Queen's pawn openings Black's main strategic problem is usually the development of his queen's bishop. The fact that it here finds a comfortable deployment to f5 is enough on its own to condemn White's opening play.

7 ♗c4 ♘c6!

Black's piece deployment is flowing very smoothly.

8 ♘ge2 e6 9 0-0 ♘a5

A familiar plan: Black hunts down the strong light-squared bishop. It feels that the game is turning in Black's favour, but Predojevic finds a curious drawing variation.

10 ♗d5!

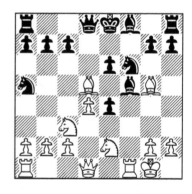

A move that appears to be a typo, as it is surely impossible that the bishop goes to a square defended three times by the black pieces. Alas for Black his control over d5 proves a mirage: the queen dare not take on d5, the knight on f6 is pinned and the pawn on e6 needs to defend f5.

10...♕d7 11 ♖xf5! exf5 12 ♗xf6 gxf6 13

♘f4 h5

Black's king can't run away as 13...0-0-0 loses the queen to 14 ♗e6. It seems that the text move permanently stops the white queen giving a check on h5, but there is going to be another surprise...

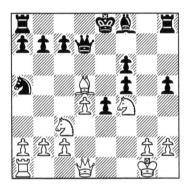

14 ♗e6 ♕d6 15 g3 ♖d8 16 ♘cd5 c6

It appears that White's initiative is coming to an end after 17 ♘xf6+ ♔e7 when, besides the knight on f6, the d4 pawn is hanging with check.

17 ♕xh5+!

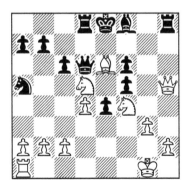

Saving himself. A great move, but I can't bring myself to give it two exclamation marks as it only leads to a draw.

17...♖xh5 18 ♘xf6+ ♔e7 19 ♘g8+ ½-½

A very exciting game. I'm curious to know how much of this was the players' opening preparation, and how much was over-the-board inspiration. I hope they didn't both have the position after 17 ♕xh5+! on their computer screens before the game!

Part Five: The Modern Staunton Variation

1 d4 f5 2 e4 fxe4 3 ♘c3 ♘f6 4 ♗g5

At the time of writing this is the only move respected by very strong players. White undermines e4 by attacking the black knight.

White also sets a positional trap that all Dutch players should be aware of: 4...d5? 5 ♗xf6 exf6 6 ♕h5+ g6 7 ♕xd5 and White has regained his pawn with an excellent game. That means of course that we are deprived, at least temporarily, of our favourite ...d7-d5 move.

But no matter: **4...♘c6** is an attractive alternative.

J.Chauca-L.Rodi
Brasilia 2010

1 d4 f5 2 e4 fxe4 3 ♘c3 ♘f6 4 ♗g5 ♘c6

5 d5

The purpose of this move isn't only to force the knight to e5, where it can be attacked by the white queen. A second objective is to stop Black supporting the pawn on e4 with ...d7-d5. However, if White avoids 5 d5, the ...d7-d5 move remains a motif:

a) 5 f3 d5 6 ♗b5 a6. Now Black had a good game after 7 ♗a4 b5 8 ♗b3 ♘a5 9 ♗xf6 ♘xb3 10 ♗xg7 ♗xg7 11 axb3 0-0 in A.Matviychuk-R.Khaetsky, Evpatoria 2007. Instead 7 ♗xc6+ bxc6 8 fxe4 dxe4 is unclear. In the game A.Schlosser-M.Urban, German League 1994, White decided to get rid of the pesky e4-pawn as quickly as possible, but it turned out to be a bad mistake: 9 ♘ge2 g6 10 0-0 ♗g7 11 ♖f4?! 0-0 12

♘xe4?? ♘xe4 13 ♖xe4 ♕d5! and White was unable to defend both e4 and g5.

b) 5 ♗b5 a6 and now Black has a good version of the 4 f3 gambit style centre after 6 ♗xc6 dxc6!? intending 7...♗f5 etc. So White might retreat the bishop with 6 ♗a4 when 6...b5 7 ♗b3 ♘a5! hunts down the important white bishop, and after, for example, 8 ♗d5 ♘xd5 9 ♘xd5 ♗b7 10 ♘f4 g6 11 h4 ♖g8 12 h5 c5 13 hxg6 hxg6 14 dxc5 ♕c7 Black had good play in R.Cifuentes Parada-V.Malaniuk, Hastings 1994/95.
5...♘e5

6 ♕d4

After 6 f3 Black can't support the e4-pawn, but he can sell its life in return for gaining time to equalize: 6...♘f7 7 ♗e3 (naturally 7 ♗xf6 exf6 8 fxe4 ♗b4 is simply terrible for White) 7...e5! (unfortunately bypassing the f3-pawn with 7...e3 8 ♗xe3 just strikes me as good for White) 8 dxe6 dxe6 9 ♕xd8+ ♔xd8 10 0-0-0+ (or 10 fxe4 ♘g4) 10...♗d7 11 ♘xe4 ♘xe4 12 fxe4 ♗d6 13 ♘f3 ♔e7 with equality.
6...♘f7!

The knight completes a three-move journey to the kingside. What I find most satisfying is that Black gets full value for 1...f5 by utilizing the vacated f7-square for his knight.

7 ♗xf6

White decides to get his pawn back, but now Black's dark-squared bishop will have no rival. The alternative 7 h4 is considered below, while after 7 ♗h4 g5! 8 ♗g3 ♗g7 9 ♘xe4, the fully adequate 9...c6 intending 10...♕b6 has been recommended, but surely Black can trap the white queen with 9...♘xe4 10 ♕xg7 ♘f6 intending 11...♖g8?

7...exf6 8 ♘xe4 f5!

Shades of 1...f5. Black's f-pawn has been reborn and drives the white knight from the centre.

9 ♘g3 g6 10 0-0-0 ♗h6+ 11 ♔b1 0-0 12 h4 ♗g7 13 ♕d2 ♘d6!

The knight will support queenside action from a central post from which it cannot be dislodged.

14 f4

An ugly move is needed to restrain the Dutch pawn, for 14 ♘f3 f4 15 ♘e2

♗xb2! is ruinous for White: 16 ♔xb2? ♘c4+.

14...b5!

15 h5 ♕f6

Other things being equal, it is doubtful that White's attack along the h-file could compete with the diagonal and frontal pressure Black will build up against b2. But what will really kill White here is the combination of the pressure on b2 with the entrance of a black rook along the e-file.

16 c3 ♖b8 17 hxg6 hxg6 18 ♘h3 b4 19 cxb4?

More resistance was offered by 19 c4, but Black should win: 19...♗a6 20 ♖c1 ♖fe8 with the idea of 21...♖e3! in the style of the game (the rook is immune due to mate on b2), and then, once the knight is driven from g3, 22...♘e4 with a crushing initiative.

19...a5! 20 a3 axb4 21 axb4 ♖e8 22 ♘g5 ♖e3!

Once more we have to give credit to the Dutch pawn. If White hadn't felt obliged to stop it in its tracks with 14 f4, the e3-square would never have become available to the black rook. And it is this which breaks the white position – not only is g3 hanging but there is the threat of 23...♖b3.

23 ♘h7 ♕e7 24 ♖h3 ♖xg3! 25 ♖xg3 ♘e4 0-1

After 26 ♕e1 ♖xb4 Black has a winning attack as b2 is collapsing, to say nothing of the hanging knight on h7.

I dare say that White may do better with **1 d4 f5 2 e4 fxe4 3 ♘c3 ♘f6 4 ♗g5 ♘c6 5 d5 ♘e5 6 ♕d4 ♘f7 7 h4!?**.

Here Black can choose between 7...c6 and 7...e5, and we will examine each move in turn.

F.Cirabisi-M.Dzhumaev
Genova 2006

1 d4 f5 2 e4 fxe4 3 ♘c3 ♘f6 4 ♗g5 ♘c6 5 d5 ♘e5 6 ♕d4 ♘f7 7 h4 c6

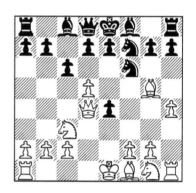

This is the most interesting response, but it is also rather double-edged. The idea is to challenge the white queen with ...♕b6.

8 0-0-0

Play transposes after 8 ♗xf6 gxf6 9 0-0-0 ♕b6.

8...♕b6 9 ♗xf6

Feeble for White is 9 ♕d2?! ♕a5, attacking d5 again and clearing the way for the queenside pawns to advance: 10 ♗c4 ♘d6 11 ♗b3 c5 12 ♘xe4 ♕xd2+ 13 ♘xd2 b5 14 c4 ♗a6. Here Black enjoyed a strong blockading knight on d6, the bishop-pair and active queenside pawns in J.Boguszlavszki-Hoang Thanh Trang, Budapest 2007.

9...gxf6

Having studied various games in this line, I think I need to point out a golden rule for Black:

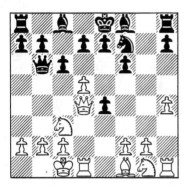

Unless White can reply with ♕h5 mate, you should answer ♗xf6 with ...gxf6! rather than ...exf6.

After ...gxf6, the way is cleared for the bishop on f8 to enter the game. There is often the bonus that ...♗h6 gains time by giving check to a white king castled on c1. Moreover, the black pawn centre is increased in size and forms a hard shell around the black king. And, finally, even if the black centre pawns aren't needed to defend the king, they are a useful positional asset. In contrast, 7...exf6 weakens the black king and leaves the central light squares around it full of holes.

But remember what I said about not being mated by ♕h5 after ...gxf6. If the king is boxed in, make sure you have a move like ...♘f7 available!

10 ♕xe4 ♕xf2

Black has not only gained the f2-pawn, he has also opened up the e3- and f4-squares for co-operation between his queen and dark-squared bishop.

11 ♘f3

If White plays precisely the open e-file may become a useful attacking resource for him. However, everything went swimmingly for Black after the misguided 11 dxc6 bxc6 12 ♗c4 ♗h6+ 13 ♔b1 ♕f4 14 ♕e2 in J.Coleto Calderon-A.Ruiz Saiz, Parla 2008, and now 14...d5, inviting an inadequate sacrifice on d5, was probably even stronger than 14...♖b8.

11...♗h6+ 12 ♔b1 ♕e3 13 ♕a4 ♕f4 14 ♕b3 0-0

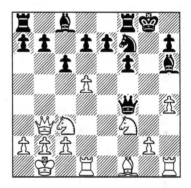

Black decides to evacuate his king from the centre.

15 ♗e2?

Even worse is 15 ♖d4?? which looks like a strong attacking move, because... well, I'll let the reader tell me! We shall discuss the improvement 15 ♗d3! below.

15...c5!

Stopping 16 ♖d4 and threatening to exchange queens if wished with 16...♕b4. Black went on to win in rather straightforward fashion:

16 d6 e6 17 ♘b5 b6 18 ♗c4 ♗b7 19

♖hf1 ♕g3 20 ♘c3 ♔h8 21 ♘e1 ♘e5 22 ♗b5 a6 23 ♗e2 b5 24 ♗f3 ♘xf3 25 gxf3 ♕h3 26 ♖f2 ♖g8 27 ♘e2 ♕xh4 28 ♖f1 ♗d5 29 ♖xd5 exd5 30 ♕xd5 ♖ae8 31 ♕d1 c4 32 f4 ♕h2 33 ♘d4 ♖g1 0-1

Returning to the position after 14...0-0, it seems that White was dazzled by the chance to play 16 ♖d4 and so blocked the e-file with his bishop. Instead 15 ♗d3! would set Black some major problems. The intention is simply 16 ♖de1 to attack e7, possibly followed by 17 ♖e4 to hound the black queen. Black could counter this with 15...a5 when 16 ♖de1 b5! 17 ♖xe7 a4 is bad for White because his queen is smothered after 18 ♕a3 b4. However, 16 ♘d4!...

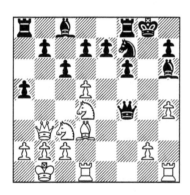

...is a powerful response intending 17 ♘f5 to hit e7 and h6. The knight is immune because of 16...♕xd4 17 ♗xh7+. I can't find a satisfactory line for Black: for example, 16...♔h8 17 ♘f5 b5 18 ♘e2!.

The position leading up to 15 ♗d3 is very interesting and you might like to try to find an improvement for Black.

Assuming the 7...c6 line is under the weather, Black should turn his attention to **7...e5!**.

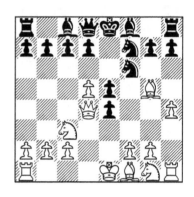

J.Boguszlavszkij-S.Ferkingstad
Budapest 2009

1 d4 f5 2 e4 fxe4 3 ♘c3 ♘f6 4 ♗g5 ♘c6 5 d5 ♘e5 6 ♕d4 ♘f7 7 h4 e5 8 dxe6

Instead 8 ♕a4 was played in G.Mester-F.Grafl, Budapest 2003, but it hasn't attracted any followers at the time of writing.

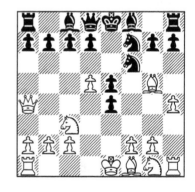

It led to wild complications after 8...c6 9 ♗xf6 gxf6 10 0-0-0 f5! 11 g4 b5

12 ♕b3 b4 13 dxc6! bxc3 14 cxd7+ ♗xd7 15 ♗b5 ♗d6 16 ♕e6+ ♔f8 and now 17 ♗xd7 might be good for White as he doesn't get mated after 17...♕b6 18 b3 ♕b4 19 ♖d5!.

Being more cowardly, I would recommend 8...h6 9 ♗xf6 ♕xf6 10 ♘xe4 ♕b6

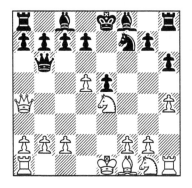

11 0-0-0 ♕b4 12 ♕xb4 ♗xb4 when I don't see any advantage for White.

8...dxe6 9 ♕xd8+ ♘xd8 10 0-0-0

Instead 10 ♗xf6 gxf6 11 ♘xe4 ♗e7 is pleasant for Black, while 10 ♘b5 ♗b4+ 11 c3 ♗a5 defends c7 and leaves White struggling.

10...♗d7

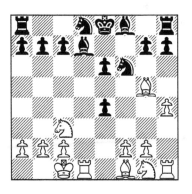

11 ♘b5

After 11 ♘ge2?! Black can defend the e4-pawn with all his minor pieces: 11...♘f7 12 ♘g3 ♘d6 13 ♗e2 (he should swallow his pride and get his pawn back with 13 ♗xf6 gxf6 14 ♘gxe4, although after 14...♘xe4 15 ♘xe4 ♗e7 Black has the two bishops and the superior pawn centre) 13...♗c6 14 ♖he1 ♗e7 15 ♗xf6 ♗xf6 16 ♗g4 ♗xc3 17 bxc3 ♔e7 and it had all gone horribly wrong for White in D.Rensch-G.Antal, Lubbock 2009.

11...♗xb5 12 ♗xb5+ c6 13 ♗c4 ♗c5 14 ♘h3 ♘d5 15 ♖he1 0-0 16 ♖xe4 ♗xf2 17 ♘xf2 ♖xf2 18 ♗xd8 ♖xd8 19 ♖xe6 ♔f7

Instead 19...♖xg2 looks like a draw after 20 ♖e7 b5 21 ♗xd5+ cxd5 22 ♖xa7 ♖c8 23 ♖d2 ♖g1+ 24 ♖d1 ♖g2 with a repetition.

20 ♖e2

If 20 ♖de1, threatening 21 ♖e7+, 20...♔f8 breaking the pin on d5 looks the most precise reply.

20...♖xe2 21 ♗xe2 ♔e7

Black is comfortable and somehow contrived to win the endgame.

Another interesting idea for White in the Staunton Gambit is **1 d4 f5 2 e4 fxe4 3 ♘c3 ♘f6 4 ♗g5 ♘c6 5 d5 ♘e5 6 ♕e2!?**, which has to some extent superseded 6 ♕d4.

6...♘f7

Black retreats his knight to a safe square (kindly provided by 1...f5!) and forces White to choose what to do with his bishop. Now we'll examine 7 h4 towards the end of this chapter, but first we must see what happens if White exchanges:

7 ♗xf6 exf6 8 ♘xe4

Threatening mate in one. After Black blocks the e-file, White intends to

inflict doubled and isolated pawns on him with 9 d6.

We have reached one of the most critical positions in the modern theory of the Staunton Gambit, so we'll take a good look at Black's options. If you wish you can skip straight to 8...♕e7! in Scenario Two which is the move I think Black should play.

Scenario One:
Black plays 8...♗e7 or 8...♗b4+

The immediate **8...♗e7** isn't very promising for Black after **9 d6!**

9...cxd6 10 0-0-0 0-0 and here White can deprive the black knight of e5 with **11 f4!?**, as he did in D.Ortega Hermida-A.Menvielle Lacourrelle, Las Palmas 2009:

11...♕a5?

A poor reaction. Black should try 11...b6 or offer to give back the pawn for some freedom with 11...d5, when White would reply 12 ♘c3, aiming to take on d5 with the knight.

12 ♘c3

It is to stop this move that Black

plays 8...♗b4+ in the variation that follows. Now White now makes full use of Black's weak squares on c4 and d5.

12...♗d8

This position is hardly an advertisement for the power of the bishop-pair!

13 ♘f3 ♖b8 14 ♖d5! b5 15 ♖xb5 ♖xb5 16 ♕xb5 ♕c7 17 ♗c4 ♗b7 18 ♘d5 ♕c6 19 ♕b3 ♗a6 20 ♗xa6 ♕xa6 21 ♘d4 ♔h8 22 ♖e1 ♕a5 23 c3 ♕c5 24 ♕b5 a6 25 ♕xd7!

A pretty combination to put Black out of his misery.

25...♕xd5 26 ♖e8 1-0

If 26...♔g8 then 27 ♘e6 and splat!

Instead Beim and others have recommended the sequence **8...♗b4+ 9 c3 ♗e7 10 d6 cxd6** after which White no longer has the option of ♘c3 to get his knight in contact with the hole on d5. If 11 0-0-0 then the white king's residence is slightly compromised and can be a source of counterplay for Black. Thus the most dangerous move appears to be the quiet **11 ♕d2!?**.

This aims to develop with 12 ♗c4 when the bishop exerts strong pressure. Black stopped this with **11...♕c7** in V.Erdos-V.Sikula, Budapest 2009, but it still led to trouble for him:

12 ♘g3

Not allowing the chance for 12...f5.

12...0-0 13 ♗e2 ♖e8 14 ♗f3 f5

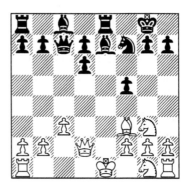

Trying to do something fast before White can play 15 ♘ge2, 16 0-0 and 17 ♘f4, dominating the centre.

15 ♘xf5! ♗g5+ 16 ♘e3 ♕c5 17 ♗d5!

Black is playing without his queenside rook or bishop, so White is going to come out top in the firefight in the centre.

17...g6 18 ♘f3 ♗xe3 19 fxe3 ♖xe3+ 20 ♔d1 ♔g7 21 ♖f1 ♖e7 22 c4

Intending 23 ♘d4 and 24 ♕f4, with a decisive attack along the f-file.

22...♕e3 23 ♕xe3 ♖xe3 24 ♔d2 ♖e7 25 ♘d4 ♖b8 26 ♖ae1 ♘e5 27 ♘b5 b6 28 ♘xd6 ♗a6 29 b4 b5 30 c5 ♘c4+ 31 ♗xc4 ♖xe1 32 ♖xe1 bxc4 33 ♔c3 ♗b7 34 ♘xb7 ♖xb7 35 ♔xc4 ♔f7 36 a4 ♖b8 37 b5 ♖c8 38 ♔d5 1-0

The leading Dutch expert Vladimir Malaniuk also came a cropper in this variation when he tried **11...♕a5 12 ♗c4 ♕e5**, aiming to do something fast before White can develop and castle kingside:

13 ♗d5! ♘g5

Now instead of the slow 14 f3 in S.Drazic-V.Malaniuk, Milan 2009, the clever 14 ♘f3!? looks stronger:

a) 14...♘xf3+ 15 gxf3 intends 16 0-0-0 and 17 ♖de1. Black can't respond 15...f5 as 16 f4 traps the queen.

b) 14...♘xe4 15 ♕d3! (a neat point) 15...♘c5+ (to exchange queens, as 15...♘xf2+ 16 ♔xf2 followed by 17 ♖ae1 is horrible for Black) 16 ♘xe5

♘xd3+ 17 ♘xd3 and Black has a very poor endgame. As usual, White's idea would be to apply pressure along the e-file after, say, 18 0-0-0 and 19 ♖he1 perhaps followed by doubling rooks.

So the conclusion is that Black has a hard life after both 8...♗e7 and 8...♗b4+ 9 c3 ♗e7.

Scenario Two:
Black plays 8...♕e7!

V.Erdos-P.Nikolic
German League 2010

1 d4 f5 2 e4 fxe4 3 ♘c3 ♘f6 4 ♗g5 ♘c6 5 d5 ♘e5 6 ♕e2 ♘f7 7 ♗xf6 exf6 8 ♘xe4 ♕e7!

I think this is the best remedy for Black.

9 d6 ♕e6!

If you play through the variations of the previous scenario, you'll understand why Nikolic is keen to avoid the doubled pawns and light-square weakness that result from 9...♘xd6 10

♘xd6+ cxd6. White could continue 11 0-0-0 or even 11 g3!? planning 12 ♗g2.

10 dxc7 ♗b4+

This is Nikolic's idea: Black will re-capture the c7-pawn with his bishop. Instead 10...d5 give White the chance to attack the d5-pawn with 11 ♘c3! (better than the 11 ♘d2 of I.Nemet-A.Cherniaev, Biel 2006), such as with 11...♗b4 12 ♕xe6+ ♗xe6 13 ♘ge2 ♔d7 14 0-0-0.

11 c3 ♗a5 12 ♘c5!

Forcing Black to unwind the white kingside by capturing on e2.

12...♕xe2+ 13 ♗xe2 ♗xc7 14 ♘f3 b6 15 ♘a6!

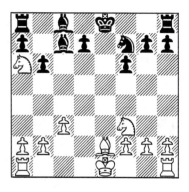

If the knight retreats Black will have a comfortable game with 15...♗b7. In fact, the bishop-pair would allow him to play for an advantage.

15...♔d8 16 0-0-0 ♗b7 17 ♘d4

After 17 ♘xc7 ♔xc7 Black is in no danger as the isolated pawn is soundly defended. He could even try to increase the pressure along the a8-h1 diagonal.

17...♗f4+ 18 ♔b1 ♖e8 19 ♗f3 ♗xf3 20 ♘xf3 ♖c8 21 ♘b4 ♗d6!

Nikolic sees the chance for counter-play against the f2-pawn with moves like ...♗c5 and ...♖e2, so White is compelled to go on the defensive.

22 ♘d5 ♖e2 23 ♖hf1 ♗c5 24 ♘d4 ♗xd4 25 ♖xd4 ♖c5 26 ♘f4 ♖e7 27 ♘d5 ♖e2 28 ♘f4 ♖e7 29 ♘d5 ½-½

The active black rooks persuade White to agree to a repetition.

That wasn't the most exciting game ever in the Dutch, but Nikolic achieved a fairly comfortable draw as Black against one of the most promising young Hungarian Grandmasters. And if White had played one or two inaccurate moves, the veteran Bosnian Grandmaster could have tried for the advantage.

We now turn our attention to another sub-variation in which White delays recouping his pawn.

L.Rosko-D.Semcesen
Olomouc 2008

1 d4 f5 2 e4 fxe4 3 ♘c3 ♘f6 4 ♗g5 ♘c6

5 d5 ♘e5 6 ♕e2 ♘f7 7 h4!?

Again we see this bold advance.

7...c6!

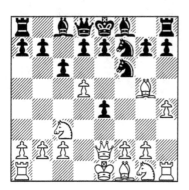

Freeing the black queen for action on a5 or b6, and preparing to complete the liquidation of the white pawn centre which began with 2...fxe4.

8 0-0-0 cxd5 9 ♘xd5

After 9 ♗xf6 gxf6 10 ♘xd5 Black can transpose with 10...e6.

I can sympathize if you find this position rather scary for Black, but let's not forget that White no longer has a battering ram in the shape of a centre pawn. Unless Black blunders, there's no good reason why White should be able to break through his defensive line.

9...e6!

Here's a way for Black to blunder and lose: 9...b6?? 10 ♗xf6 gxf6 (or 10...exf6 11 ♕xe4+ ♗e7 – 11...♘e5 11 f4 – 12 ♘xe7, attacking a8) 11 ♕xe4 ♗h6+ (if 11...♗b7 it's mate in one) 12 ♔b1 and Black has no defence to the double threats of 13 ♘xf6+ and 13 ♘xe7, uncovering an attack on a8.

Instead Black returns the extra pawn to strengthen his centre.

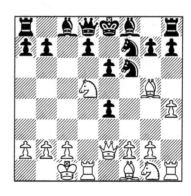

10 ♗xf6

If 10 ♘xf6+ gxf6 and Black will build a massive centre with ...d7-d5.

10...gxf6 11 ♕xe4 ♗h6+ 12 ♘e3 f5 13 ♕b4 ♕e7

Securing the right to castle, as the endgame is poor for White after 14 ♕xe7+ ♔xe7.

14 ♕b3 0-0

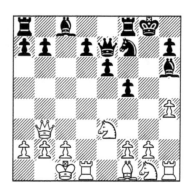

Black has a big centre and the bishop-pair, including the dark-square monster on h6.

Realizing that his position was going to go gradually downhill if he didn't do anything fast, White tried to attack along the g-file, but the black king proved to be safe on h8. The remaining moves were:

15 ♘f3 b6 16 ♗b5 a6 17 ♗e2 b5 18 g4 fxg4 19 ♖hg1 ♚h8 20 ♖xg4 ♛f6 21 ♘g5 ♘e5 22 ♘e4 ♛e7 23 ♛c3 ♗g7 24 ♖xg7 ♛xg7 25 ♖f1 d5 26 ♘g3 ♘c4 27 ♛xg7+ ♚xg7 28 ♘h5+ ♚h8 29 ♘g4 e5 30 ♘gf6 ♗e6 31 b3 ♘d6 32 ♖d1 ♖ad8 33 ♗g4 ♗xg4 34 ♘xg4 ♘e4 35 ♘xe5 ♖xf2 36 ♘d3 ♖h2 37 ♘hf4 ♖c8 38 ♘e1 ♘c3 39 ♖d3 ♘xa2+ 40 ♚b2 ♘b4 41 ♖g3 ♘xc2 42 ♘f3 ♖f2 43 ♘d3 ♖e2 44 ♘f4 ♖e4 45 ♘xd5 ♘d4 46 ♘g5 ♖e2+ 47 ♚a3 ♖f8 48 ♚b4 ♖e5 49 ♘c7 h6 50 ♘h3 ♘c6+ 51 ♚c3 a5 52 ♘g1 ♖c8 53 ♘a6 ♘b4+ 0-1

Part Six: The Staunton Gambit with g2-g4

V.Gerber-A.Panchenko
Kyiv 2008

1 d4 f5 2 e4 fxe4 3 ♘c3 ♘f6 4 g4

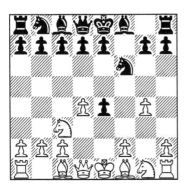

An aggressive move planning to drive back the knight with 5 g5.

4...d5!?

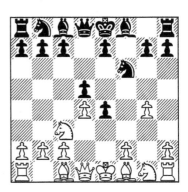

The normal move is 4...h6, securing the knight on f6, but it would be great if Black could just ignore the threat. There now begins an extremely long forcing line:

5 g5 ♗g4

Not allowing White the initiative he is looking for after 5...♘g8 6 f3!.

6 ♗e2 ♗xe2 7 ♛xe2

If 7 ♘gxe2? then Black has the reply 7...♘h5.

7...♘g8 8 ♛b5+

White should prefer 8 f3: for example, 8...♘c6 9 fxe4 (Black is doing nicely after 11 ♗e3 e6 12 fxe4 ♗b4) 9...♘xd4 10 ♛d3 e5 11 ♘f3 ♗c5 with unclear play.

8...♘c6!

The only good move. A couple of players have fallen for the traditional Staunton ♛h5+ and ♛xd5 trick in a different form after 8...♛d7 9 ♛xb7 ♛c6 10 ♛c8+ ♚f7 11 ♛f5+ ♚e8 12 ♛xd5.

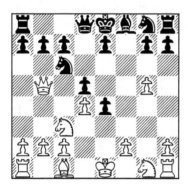

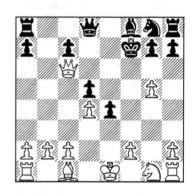

9 ♘xd5

If this is White's best move then the opening has gone wrong for him.

Black also stands well after 9 ♕xd5 ♕xd5 10 ♘xd5 0-0-0, but the key line is 9 ♕xb7 ♘xd4 10 ♘xd5 ♘xc2+ 11 ♔d1 ♘xa1 12 ♕xa8 ♕xa8 13 ♘xc7+ ♔d7 14 ♘xa8 e5. However, this also looks excellent for Black as the knight on a8 is easier to trap than the one on a1: for example, 15 ♗e3 ♘e7 16 ♘e2 (or 16 ♗xa7 ♔c6 planning 17...♔b7) 16...♘d5 17 ♘c3 ♘xe3+ 18 fxe3 ♗b4 with winning chances for Black.

9...e6?

A serious mistake. He should play 9...♕d7! intending 10...0-0-0 when White looks busted as 10 ♕xb7 ♖b8 11 ♘xc7+ ♔d8 costs him a piece.

10 ♕xb7 exd5

The best chance is 10...♔d7, but simply 11 ♘c3 should be winning for White.

11 ♕xc6+ ♔f7

And now White has a good game after 12 f3, but absolutely crushing was 12 ♘h3! with the threat of 13 g6+ hxg6 14 ♘g5+. If Black stops it with 12...g6, both 13 f3, to open the f-file for the attack, and 13 ♘f4 are killing. However, in the game White gradually lost his way and ended up dropping a piece:

12 ♗f4 ♘e7 13 ♕c3 ♘g6 14 ♗e3 ♗d6 15 h4 ♕d7 16 h5 ♘e7 17 0-0-0 ♖hf8 18 g6+ hxg6 19 h6 gxh6 20 ♗xh6 ♖h8 21 ♘e2 ♕g4 22 f3 exf3 23 ♖df1 ♘f5 24 ♕xf3 ♕xf3 25 ♖xf3 ♗f8 26 ♘g3 ♗xh6+ 27 ♔d1 ♗g7 28 ♖hf1 ♗xd4 29 c3 ♗e5 30 ♘xf5 gxf5 31 ♖xf5+ ♔e6 0-1

So is this line playable for Black? Was IM Panchenko following some analysis he prepared years ago and forgot what to do after the inferior 9 ♘xd5? Or was he feeling inspired at the board, and the inspiration ran out after eight moves? I can't answer those two questions, but 4...d5!? looks to be in good shape from what I can see!

Chapter Two

White Plays 2 ♘c3

1 d4 f5 2 ♘c3

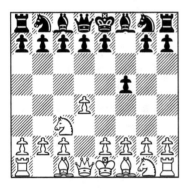

In the Queen's pawn opening, after 1 d4 d5, the move 2 ♘c3 (The Veresov Opening) has never become particularly popular for White. It is well known that he gains the most profit by attacking the black pawn centre with 2 c4 or 2 ♘f3 and then 3 c4, and putting the horse on c3 gets in the way of this plan. Of course White doesn't stand worse after 2 ♘c3; it merely means that his strategic options are more limited. He can't cause Black as much grief as with 2 c4.

Let's now turn to 1 d4 f5 2 ♘c3. Once again White has blocked in his c2-pawn. On the other hand, he is threatening to seize space with 3 e4 – if he can play this unopposed then there can be no criticism of 2 ♘c3. For example, after 2 ♘c3 d6?! 3 e4 fxe4 4 ♘xe4 we have a kind of mirror image of the Sicilian Defence with 1 e4 c5 2 ♘f3 e6 3 d4 cxd4 ♘xd4. In the Sicilian version Black's queen and bishop on f8 have open lines, and he can challenge the white knight on d4 with 4...♘c6. Things are much poorer for Black in the Dutch version due to the fragility of his king and the fact that his queen and dark-squared bishop are still passive.

Therefore, in contrast to the Sicilian, after 1 d4 f5 2 ♘c3 *it is important that Black put up an obstacle to White's 3 e4 advance.*

Which variation to choose?

One obvious method of stopping 3 e4 is 2...♘f6. The knight is bound to go to f6 at some point, so why not play it there straightaway? A typical sequence is 3 ♗g5 d5 4 ♗xf6 exf6 5 e3.

White might then engineer c2-c4 after all with ♗d3 and ♘ce2, or try for an attack as Black often castles queen-side. Black has a lot of resources in these variations, and many strong Grandmasters have defended them with success. The bishop-pair and a solid centre are not to be sneezed at, and I gave 2...♘f6 my support in *Starting Out with the Dutch*.

However, in this book the emphasis is on dynamism. I find the positions after the exchange ♗xf6 and the recapture ...exf6 a little static for Black. The pawn break ...c7-c5 would leave the d5-pawn weak after d4xc5, while advancing the kingside pawn clump is problematical. We occasionally see a game in which Black manages to arrange ...f5-f4 to get the pawns rolling, but it requires some help from White!

So after 2...♘f6 Black has a reduced capacity to make effective pawn breaks. Therefore I want to recommend **2...d5** in this chapter, and after **3 ♗f4** the little pawn move **3...a6!**.

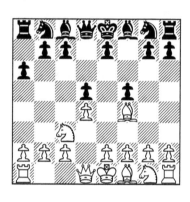

In contrast to White's 2 ♘c3, Black avoids blocking in his c-pawn with ...♘c6. He intends to build up with ...♘f6, ...e7-e6, ...c7-c5 and only then ...♘c6. If he succeeds he has a bigger centre than White.

Such a strategy, with its multiple pawn moves, looks risky. However, Black is trusting in the solidity of the Stonewall centre and the fact that White cannot easily arrange a pawn break. The move 3...a6 actually makes the black centre safer as it rules out an attack on it based on ♘b5 followed by c2-c4.

A word on the Stonewall Formation

In this book I've referred to any structure as a Stonewall in which Black advances ...d7-d5 so that his pawns on d5 and f5 give him a grip on the central light squares. In particular, White's e2-e4 space-gaining move is prevented or made difficult to arrange. White's light-squared bishop is also reduced in scope, as on g2 it would be staring at a wall on d5, or on d3 at a wall on f5. So White's attacking chances are on the whole reduced.

So the good news for Black is that he has equal space in the centre and is solidly entrenched on the light squares. The main drawback is that Black has renounced setting up a mobile pawn centre with ...d7-d6 and ...e7-e5. Instead the e5-square is a hole in the black centre, a perfect post for a white knight, and has to be carefully watched over by the black pieces.

Perhaps the fundamental strategic decision Black has to make in the Dutch is: should I set up a Stonewall centre (with ...d7-d5) or a mobile centre (with ...d7-d6 and ...e7-e5). Black doesn't always have a choice – as in the 2 ♘c3 variation, where he is virtually obliged to set up a Stonewall to prevent White gaining space with an 'easy' e2-e4.

White's strategy

Turning to the specific position after 2 ♘c3 d5, Black is planning to seize a large share of space in the centre and, if left alone, will complete his development with a safe and active game. The weakness of the e5-square isn't enough on its own to cause him any trouble. White therefore has to devise a plan of action to undermine the black centre. From a strategic point of view he has two options: play a violent e2-e4 breakthrough or else arrange c2-c4 after all.

The Immediate Gambit: 3 e4

1 d4 f5 2 ♘c3 d5 3 e4 dxe4 4 f3 e5!

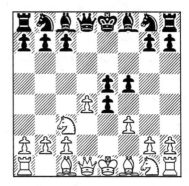

Black is at least equal after this freeing move, which explains why highly-rated players prefer to play 3 ♗f4 to rule it out and only after 3...a6 go 4 e4 (not that it does them much good in the games in this chapter).

5 dxe5

Black has opened the centre at a bad time for White, as his knight on g1 is denied the f3-square. In fact this has proved the downfall of White in all the gambit games discussed here – he sacrifices a pawn to speed up his development, only to find that it has made it harder, not easier, to mobilize his kingside pieces.

5...♛xd1+ 6 ♚xd1

After 6 ♘xd1 ♘c6 7 f4 ♘b4!...

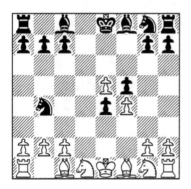

...Black already had the initiative in S.Tikhomirov-M.Grunberg, Bucharest 2002.

6...♘c6! 7 ♗f4 ♘ge7 8 ♘h3 ♗e6! 9 fxe4 0-0-0+

Black has responded to White's pawn sacrifice with a double-pawn offer in order to speed up his development and embarrass the white king.

10 ♗d3 h6!

Threatening 11...g5 when the e5-pawn is sure to drop.

11 exf5 ♘xf5 12 ♖e1 ♘h4!

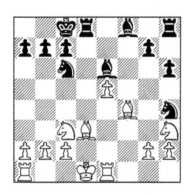

And suddenly White's position is collapsing as there is no good way to defend g2: for instance if 12 ♖g1 ♗c5, etc. In P.Raineri de Luca-F.Peralta, Castelldefels 2005, White gave up the exchange but eventually lost after 13 ♖e2 ♗g4 14 ♘f2 ♗xe2+ 15 ♔xe2 when 15...♘xg2 was simplest.

A curious point: after the move order 1 d4 f5 2 ♘c3 d5 3 e4 dxe4 4 ♗f4 should Black play 4...a6, or find a more 'productive' move? I think we should stick with 4...a6. After all, in the games that follow it helps Black destroy a couple of top players in the move order 3 ♗f4 a6 4 e4.

The Delayed Gambit: 3 ♗f4 a6 4 e4

V.Malakhatko-N.Firman
German League 2008

1 d4 f5 2 ♘c3 d5 3 ♗f4 a6 4 e4

White tries to prove that 3...a6 is an irrelevant, self-indulgent move by starting a fight in the centre. However, as we shall see, in a fast-moving battle the fact that 3...a6 prevents ♘b5 or ♗b5 proves valuable.

4...dxe4

Every Dutch player needs to know that in this type of position 4...fxe4? runs into 5 ♕h5+ and 6 ♕xd5, leaving the black centre ruined.

5 f3 ♘f6!

Very sensible. Having taken a liberty with 3...a6, we shouldn't push our luck too far. Rather than speed up White's development with 5...exf3 6 ♘xf3, Black brings his own knight into the game.

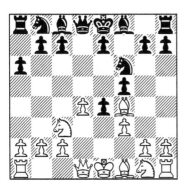

6 fxe4 fxe4

The black pawn on e4 looks ugly, but just as ugly is the fact that the white knight on g1 can't go to f3. And ugliest of all from a strategic perspective is the fact that White has granted an easy development to the bishop on c8, Black's worst piece in 1 d4 openings for the past 500 years.

7 ♗c4 ♘c6!

Preparing to hunt down White's excellent light-squared bishop. You will notice this plan is possible due to the service of the a6-pawn in preventing ♘b5.

8 ♘ge2

The alternative 8 ♗e5 is examined in the next game.

8...♘a5 9 ♗b3 ♘xb3 10 axb3 ♗f5

This bishop always seems supercharged once the obstruction on f5 is removed. Perhaps it is because White has had to soften up his light squares

in disposing of the f5-pawn, making the path more smooth for the bishop that follows in its wake.

11 ♕d2 e6 12 0-0-0

Malakhatko has made a lot of aggressive moves, but it is Firman who has the more dynamic chances thanks to his steady and precise play.

12...♗b4 13 h3 0-0 14 g4 ♗g6 15 ♕e3 a5!

Black already has an excellent game thanks to his grip on the centre. Now the wonderful a-pawn is called on to lead the attack against the white king.

16 ♕g3 ♕d7 17 h4 h5!

A crucial move to break up the

white attacking front and prevent the bishop being driven backward with 18 h5.

18 gxh5 ♗xh5 19 ♖dg1

It appears at first glance that White's assault is as promising as Black's queenside play. However, he can't conquer the g7-point, whereas Black can break through along the a-file where the attackers far outnumber the defenders.

19...a4

This is not even a sacrifice as both 20 ♘xa4? ♗xe2 and 20 bxa4 ♗xe2 21 ♘xe2 ♖xa4 (but not 21...♕xa4??) are bad for White.

20 ♗e5 axb3 21 cxb3 ♗xe2 22 ♘xe2 ♘h5!

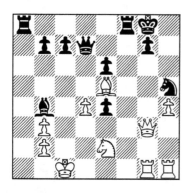

The knight takes over the defence of g7 to free the black queen for decisive action on the queenside.

23 ♕g2 ♕c6+ 24 ♘c3 ♖f3 25 d5 exd5 26 ♔b1 ♗xc3 27 ♗xc3 ♖xc3

Simultaneously destroying White's hope of an attack g7 and wrecking his king's defences.

28 bxc3 ♕xc3 29 ♕b2 ♕d3+ 30 ♔c1

Of course if 30 ♕c2, then 30...♖a1+ 31 ♔b2 ♖a2+ wins the white queen.

30...♖a6 31 ♖g2 ♖c6+ 32 ♖c2 ♘g3!

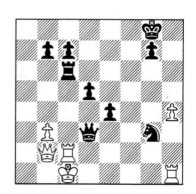

The entry of the knight decides matters. If now 33 ♖e1 Black can get a king and pawn endgame three pawns up: 33...♘e2+ 34 ♖exe2 ♕xe2 35 ♖xc6 ♕xb2+ 36 ♔xb2 bxc6.

33 ♖xc6 ♘e2+ 34 ♕xe2 ♕xe2 35 ♖xc7 ♕a2 36 ♖h3 d4 37 ♖g3 ♕a1+ 0-1

I.Lysyj-M.Narciso Dublan
European Championship,
Plovdiv 2008

1 d4 f5 2 ♘c3 d5 3 ♗f4 a6 4 e4 dxe4 5 f3 ♘f6 6 fxe4 fxe4 7 ♗c4 ♘c6 8 ♗e5

White defends his d4-pawn with his bishop as he is evidently unhappy about 8 ♘ge2 ♘a5! as in the game above. If now 8...♘a5 White could always keep his bishop with 9 ♗e2!? – not that there is anything great for him in the resulting position. Instead Narciso Dublan prefers to increase the pressure on the white centre:

8...♘g4!

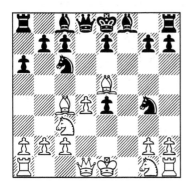

And why not? Black has just as much dynamism as White in this position – he doesn't have to be awed by his opponent's attacking gestures. Now besides the double capture on e5 White has to watch out for a fork on e3. Indeed, 9 ♘ge2?? ♘e3 would win a piece.

9 ♗d5 ♗f5!

Black develops simply and leaves White to sort out his mess. Once again the plan of kingside development with 10 ♘ge2? falls apart: 10...♘xe5 11 dxe5 ♘e3 12 ♕d2 ♘xg2+ 13 ♔f1 e6! and the bishop on d5 is pinned.

10 ♕e2 ♘gxe5 11 dxe5 ♘d4

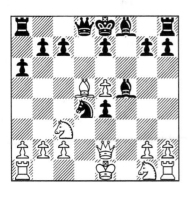

12 ♕c4?

Black would have a useful initiative after 12 ♕d2 e6!. Therefore White tries to continue in attacking vein, but with disastrous results.

12...♘xc2+ 13 ♔e2 e6!

Also good enough was 13...♘xa1, but Black didn't want to give White an attack after 14 ♗f7+ ♔d7 15 ♘h3.

14 ♗xb7 ♕g5!

Decisive, as 15 ♗xa8 ♕xg2+ 16 ♔d1 ♘e3+ wins the white queen.

15 ♗c6+ ♔f7 16 ♗xe4 ♖d8!

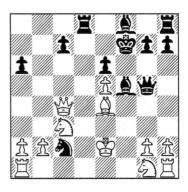

So that if 17 ♖d1 ♕e3+ and mate in two moves.

17 ♗xc2 ♕xg2+ 18 ♔e1 ♕xh1 19 ♗xf5

White is now threatening mate in one so Black has to play with a little care.

19...♕xg1+ 20 ♔e2 ♕xh2+ 21 ♔f3 ♕xe5 22 ♖f1 ♗e7 23 ♘e4 ♗f6 24 ♔g2 ♖d4 25 ♘g5+ ♗xg5 26 ♗xe6+ ♔e7 27 ♖f7+ ♔d8 28 ♕xa6 ♖d2+ 29 ♔f1 ♖d1+ 30 ♔f2 ♕e3+ 0-1

In these last two games we have seen players rated 2633 and 2595 lose with White against players rated 2525 and 2509 respectively. The problem for White is that he can't develop his knight to f3, while ♗c4 and ♘ge2 runs into the awkward ...♘a5! exchanging off the important bishop.

White Plays ♘e5

We shall now consider games which feature a more positional approach by White. After **3 ♗f4 a6 4 e3 ♘f6 5 ♘f3 e6** he has two strategic strings to his bow: the hole on e5 and the possibility of undermining the black pawn structure along the c-file.

K.Sakaev-A.Volokitin
European Club Cup,
Ohrid 2009

1 d4 f5 2 ♘c3 d5 3 ♗f4 a6 4 e3 ♘f6 5 ♘f3

White can also delay developing his knight in favour of immediate kingside action with 5 h3, whereupon after the routine 5...e6?! the pawn lever 6 g4! worked out well in V.Epishin-V.Malaniuk, Tashkent 1987. In a later game Bartel struck back with the immediate 5...c5: 6 dxc5 ♘c6 7 ♘f3 e6 8 g4 (the consistent move, though it seems to leave White's position too loose; perhaps he should play 8 ♘a4 when 8...♘d7 9 c4 ♘xc5 is balanced) 8...♗xc5 9 gxf5 exf5 10 ♘e5 (White's

knight manoeuvre is decidedly suspect – he spends two moves to exchange it on c6, which merely strengthens Black's centre and opens the b-file for Black's heavy pieces; still, White is already in an awkward situation as after say 10 ♖g1 0-0 he has to reckon with a ...d4 pawn advance) 10...0-0 11 ♕d2 ♖e8 12 ♘xc6 bxc6 13 ♗e2 ♗d6 (securing b8 for his rook) 14 ♗xd6 ♕xd6 15 0-0-0 ♖b8 and Black had the attack in T.Reiss-M.Bartel, Wattenscheid 2009. **5...e6 6 ♘e5**

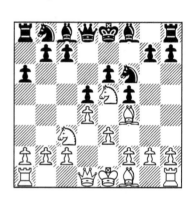

At the first opportunity the white knight takes possession of the hole on e5.

Instead White can play solidly with 6 ♗d3 c5 7 dxc5 ♗xc5 8 0-0, aiming to hit the d5-pawn with a quick c2-c4. Incidentally, this is the approach advocated by Richard Palliser in *Play 1 d4!*. After 8...♘c6 9 ♘e2 0-0 10 c4, Glenn Flear recommends 10...♘b4!? with unclear play.

6...♘bd7!

Immediately challenging its opposite number. Now Volokitin intends

...♗d6 and ...0-0, which would leave White in a positional dead-end. After all, how can he improve his position, as f2-f3 can be answered by ...♘h5, harassing the bishop on f4? Perhaps the best chance would be ♘b1, ♘d2 and ♘df3, but this convoluted manoeuvre is hardly a vote of confidence in 2 ♘c3.

Instead Sakaev tried to force matters:

7 g4 ♘xe5 8 dxe5 ♘xg4 9 h3 ♘h6 10 ♗xh6 gxh6 11 ♕h5+ ♔d7 12 0-0-0

Threatening 13 ♘xd5!.

12...♕g5! 13 ♕f3 c6

Formerly speaking, White has a huge lead in development, but there is no good way to break through. In the Dutch we often see the resilience of the Stonewall centre and the feebleness of the white pawns as an attacking force.

14 ♘e2 ♔c7

Black has managed to flee with his king, after which his dark-squared bishop, solid centre and fairly useful extra pawn give him the advantage. Volokitin was eventually able to exchange down into a winning rook and pawn endgame. For the record here are the remaining moves:

15 ♖g1 ♕e7 16 ♕f4 ♗d7 17 ♘d4 ♕f7 18 c4 ♖g8 19 ♖xg8 ♕xg8 20 cxd5 cxd5 21 ♔b1 ♕g5 22 ♕h2 ♖c8 23 h4 ♕g7 24 ♗d3 ♔b6 25 ♖g1 ♕e7 26 h5 ♕b4 27 f4 ♔a7 28 ♕f2 ♕b6 29 ♕d2 ♗e8 30 ♗e2 ♗b4 31 ♕d1 ♗c5 32 ♕d2 ♗a4 33 ♗d1 ♗xd4 34 ♕xd4 ♕xd4 35 exd4 ♗xd1 36 ♖xd1 ♖g8 37 ♔c2 ♖g4 38 ♖f1 ♔b6 39 ♔d3 ♖g3+ 40 ♔d2 ♖g2+ 41 ♔c3 ♔b5 42 ♖c1 ♖h2 43 ♔b3 ♖xh5 44 ♖c7 ♖h3+ 45 ♔c2 ♖h4 46 ♖xb7+ ♔c4 47 ♖a7 ♖xf4 48 ♖xa6 ♖f2+ 49 ♔b1 ♖xd4 50 ♖xe6 ♖e2 51 a4 ♖xe5 52 ♖f6 ♔e3 53 ♔c2 d4 54 b4 d3+ 55 ♔c3 f4 56 ♖d6 ♔e2 57 ♖xd3 ♖e3 58 ♖xe3+ fxe3 0-1

So the immediate 6 ♘e5 got nowhere. But we should see what happens if White waits a move with **6 ♗d3** and only after 6...c5 plays **7 ♘e5**.

Then 7...♘bd7!? still seems okay: for example, 8 0-0 ♘xe5 9 ♗xe5 ♗d6 looks equal or critically 9 dxe5 ♘d7. The black centre seems to be holding firm as 10 ♗xf5? doesn't work for White

after 10...exf5 11 ♘xd5 ♘b6!. That means that Black will have time for 10...♗e7 and 11...0-0 with a good game.

Instead White can try 6 ♗d3 c5 7 0-0 ♘c6 8 ♘e5, but 8...♘xe5 transposes to the 7...♘bd7 8 0-0 ♘xe5 line above. White could also play **6 ♗e2** (rather than 6 ♗d3) but I don't think this helps him. For example, 6...c5 7 ♘e5 (7 0-0 will be seen in our next illustrative game) 7...♘bd7 8 ♗h5+ g6

9 ♗e2 (if 9 ♘xg6 hxg6 10 ♗xg6+ ♔e7 11 dxc5 ♘xc5 and the Stonewall centre protects the black king) 9...♘xe5 10 ♗xe5 (after 10 dxe5 ♘d7 the pawn on e5 can be assailed with ...♗g7) 10...♗d6 and playing ...g7-g6 doesn't really seem to have hurt Black.

Incidentally, in my book *Starting Out: the Dutch* I was rather dismissive of the plan of 2...d5 because I was too impressed by the game F.Ljubicic-M.Zelic, Split 2000, where White was allowed to weaken the black pawns after 6 ♗d3 c5 7 ♘e5 ♘c6?! 8 0-0 ♗e7 9 b3 0-0 10 ♘xc6 bxc6 11 ♘a4! etc, although in fact Black is probably still

okay in this position. However, 7...♘bd7!? makes me feel a lot more confident about Black's chances.

Thus it appears that White can't get lasting benefit through putting his knight on e5.

White Tries for Queenside Action

F.Elsness-M.Bartel
European Team
Championship, Novi Sad 2009

1 d4 f5 2 ♘c3 d5 3 ♗f4 a6 4 ♘f3 ♘f6 5 e3 e6 6 ♗e2 c5 7 0-0 ♘c6

Black has almost completed the plan of development he envisaged with 3...a6. However his centre is still somewhat fragile. Elsness hopes to exploit this by lashing out at the c5-pawn.

8 ♘a4 cxd4

Instead 8...c4 looks sounder, but 9 b3 gave White some edge and he managed to win in I.Sokolov-M.Bartel,

European Championship, Warsaw 2005. In his preparation for the present game Bartel had come up with a more dynamic plan for Black.

9 exd4 ♘e4 10 ♘e5

Even so, the position looks awkward for Black. After 10...♘xe5 11 ♗xe5 he has to reckon with the disruptive 12 ♗h5+ (as 12...g6 drops h8). Meanwhile f2-f3 is hanging over his head: once the knight is driven back from e4, the energy in Black's set-up would begin to fade and his positional weaknesses come to the fore – a backward pawn on an open file on e6, and dark-square holes on c5 and e5.

10...♗d6!

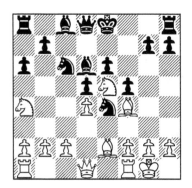

Bartel plays the move he wants to play, even though it costs him a pawn.

11 ♘xc6 bxc6 12 ♗xd6 ♕xd6 13 ♘b6 ♖b8 14 ♘xc8 ♖xc8 15 ♗xa6 ♖b8

The pawn sacrifice has increased the size of Black's centre and removed from the board his passive bishop on c8. The white knights that were putting pressure on the c5 and e5 dark squares have also vanished.

16 ♖b1 ♖a8 17 ♕e2 ♔f7!

The decision of a seasoned Dutch Defence player. The obvious move was 17...0-0, but Bartel sees it is a good idea to set the king to work in defending the e6-pawn. In doing so he frees the black queen for aggressive action, whereas otherwise she would have been tied to e6 by White's latent threat of f2-f3, driving away the knight, followed by ♕xe6.

18 ♗d3

Giving back the pawn. Instead the game might have ended 18 f3 ♘f6 19 b4! ♘h5! 20 g3 (20 a4? ♘f4 wins the bishop) 20...♘xg3 21 hxg3 ♕xg3+ 22 ♔h1 ♕h3+ 23 ♔g1 ♕g3+ and Black gives perpetual check, as intervening with the queen costs White the bishop.

18...♖xa2

Black now has a clear edge and wrapped up the endgame with some sharp moves.

19 ♗xe4 dxe4 20 c3 ♖b8 21 f3 exf3 22 ♖xf3 g6 23 ♕f2 c5 24 dxc5 ♖bxb2! 25 ♕xb2

Instead 25 ♖xb2 ♖a1+ 26 ♕f1

Wxc5+ is similar to the game, and after 25 cxd6 Rxb1+ 26 Wf1 Rxf1+ 27 Kxf1 Ke8 Black will pick up the d6-pawn with a winning endgame.

25...Wxc5+ 26 Kh1 Rxb2 27 Rxb2 e5 28 Rb7+ Kf6 29 Rxh7 e4 30 Rf1 e3 31 Rb7 e2 32 Re1 Wf2 33 Rbb1 Ke5 34 c4 Kd4 0-1

White has had enough of his paralysed position, and resigned before Bartel had the chance to demonstrate the win by advancing his kingside.

I'm most impressed by Bartel's move 17...Kf7!. It is all too easy to get carried away with an attack and forget about the weakness of e6. Your author had the following bitter experience:

The diagram position was reached in **Hoang Thanh Trang-N.McDonald**, Budapest 2003. White played **29 Kh2** whereupon I confidently replied **29...Rfc8?** doubling up rooks on the c-file. I was convinced I had a good position and that there was no danger facing me – I took 29 Kh2 as an indication that White had run out of constructive

moves. In fact, it was preparation for a nasty trap as **30 f4!** followed.

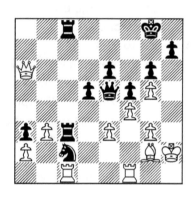

After **30...Wxe3 31 Rf3! Wxc1 32 Wxe6+** the e6-pawn, the linchpin of the black pawn structure, had collapsed. White grabbed a lot of pawns before regaining the rook:

32...Kf8 33 Wf6+ Ke8 34 Wh8+ Kd7 35 Wxh7+ Kd8 36 Wg8+ Ke7 37 Wg7+ Kd8 38 Wf8+ Kd7 39 Wf7+ Kd8 40 Wxd5+ Ke7 41 We5+ Kd8 42 Wd6+ Ke8 43 Wxg6+ Kd8 44 Wf6+ Ke8 45 Rxc3 Rxc3 46 Wxc3 Wb2 47 Wc8+ Ke7 48 Kh3 Nd4 49 Wc7+ Ke6 50 We5+ Kd7 51 g6 Ne6 52 Wxf5 Ke7 53 Bd5 Ng7 54 We5+ 1-0

Instead I should have played the 'Bartel' move 29...Kf7! defending the e6-pawn, and only then thought about doubling rooks along the c-file. The Dutch is an opening that is unforgiving of natural moves. Black pushes so many pawns that he has to keep his eyes open for sudden tactics. Of course, the same problem faces White – he also pushes a lot of pawns, and so is vulnerable to sudden tactics.

White Plays
2 ♘c3 d5 3 ♗g5

We should now consider what to do if White plays 3 ♗g5, hoping to transpose to the 2 ♘c3 ♘f6 3 ♗g5 d5 variation.

S.Huerta-A.Graf
Merida 2006

1 d4 f5 2 ♘c3 d5 3 ♗g5 h6

Played in the spirit of 2 ♗g5 h6 as seen in Chapter Three. But in those lines the intention is to build a small centre with ...d7-d6, whereas here we are committed to a Stonewall centre with ...d7-d5. The upshot is that once White's bishop is chased to g3, it will enjoy an open diagonal and access to the e5-square. Do we care? Let's see how Graf, a 2600-rated player, makes it work for Black.

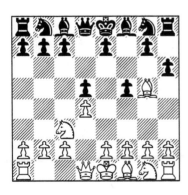

4 ♗f4

Or 4 ♗h4 g5 5 e3 ♘f6 (instead 5...gxh4 6 ♕h5+ ♔d7 7 ♘f3 looks risky for Black, though it might be worth a try) 6 ♗g3 ♗g7 7 ♘f3 0-0 8 ♘e5, transposing to the note to White's 6th, below.

4...♘f6 5 e3 g5

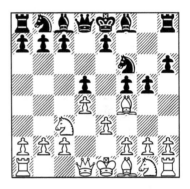

6 ♗e5

A challenging move. The threat is 7 ♗xf6, doubling our pawns, which would be bad enough anyway without the disruptive queen check after 7...exf6 by 8 ♕h5+.

If White had played more peaceably with 6 ♗g3 I assume that Graf would have developed his kingside normally: 6...♗g7 7 ♘f3 0-0 8 ♘e5, but now, despite being an advocate of ...♘e4 in the Stonewall set-up, I have to say that 8...♘e4 is premature and bad, as White had an obvious advantage after 9 ♘xe4 dxe4 10 ♗c4+ e6 11 ♕d2 ♕e8 12 h4 in R.Geisler-K.Renner, German League 1994.

More appropriate is the immediate advance 8...c5 to attack the white centre.

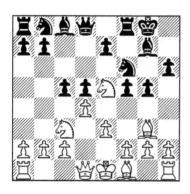

For example, 9 dxc5 ♕a5 10 ♕d2 ♘c6 intending ...♕xc5 or ...♖d8 as appropriate, and Black is active. Alternatively, if 9 h4 we can counterattack with our favourite centre-busting move: 9...f4!? 10 exf4 (10 hxg5 fxg3 11 gxf6 gxf2+ 12 ♔xf2 ♖xf6+ is also good for Black, so the best of a bad lot is the meek 10 ♗h2) 10...cxd4 11 ♕xd4 gxf4 12 ♗xf4 ♘g4! with an awkward pin on e5, including ideas of ...♖xf4 followed by ...♗xe5.

In the above analysis both ...c7-c5! and ...f5-f4! ate away at the white centre. Whereas after 8...♘e4? in the Geisler-Renner game the black pawns became a static clump in the centre. Maintaining the vitality of his pawns is essential for Black – you might call it guarding the dynamic health of the black position.

6...e6 7 ♘b5 ♖h7!

An economical move as it breaks the pin on f6 and defends c7.

8 ♗e2 ♗d6 9 ♘xd6+

It makes a bad impression to rid Black of the hole on e5, but White had

no good way to strengthen his attack.

9...cxd6 10 ♗xf6 ♕xf6

Black has a huge centre that protects his own king and can power forwards to cause problems for the white monarch.

11 ♗d3 ♘c6 12 ♕h5+ ♔e7 13 c3 e5 14 ♕d1 ♗e6 15 ♘e2 e4 16 ♗c2 f4 17 f3 exf3 18 gxf3

Black has dangerous passed pawns for the exchange after 18 ♗xh7 fxg2 19 ♖g1 fxe3 (threatening mate on f3) 20 ♖xg2 ♕f3! 21 ♘f4! ♕xd1+ 22 ♔xd1 gxf4.

18...♖g7 19 ♕d2 fxe3 20 ♕xe3 ♖f8

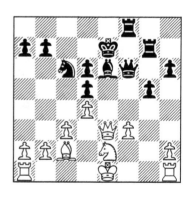

Black stands well as f3 is weaker

than his doubled centre pawns.

21 ♖f1 ♔d8 22 0-0-0 ♗h3 23 ♖f2 ♖e7 24 ♕d2 ♕e6 25 ♘g1

It is only Chapter Two of this book, and already we have seen a white knight sitting passively on g1 in a remarkable number of games.

25...♗f5 26 ♖e2 ♕g6 27 ♗b3 ♖xe2 28 ♕xe2 ♕f7 29 ♖e1 ♗g6 30 ♕d2 ♘a5 31 ♕e3?

He had to keep the bishop with 31 ♗c2.

31...♘xb3+ 32 axb3 ♔d7!

So that the king can go to c6 to stop the exchange of queens that occurs after the immediate 32...♕f5 33 ♕e7+ ♔c8 34 ♕e6+.

33 ♔d2 ♕f5

The queen-and-bishop battery is now decisive.

34 ♖c1 ♖e8 35 ♕f2 ♕d3 mate (0-1)

An upbeat moment to end our examination of the 2 ♘c3 variation!

Chapter Three

White Plays 2 ♗g5

1 d4 f5 2 ♗g5

going to happen to the black king.

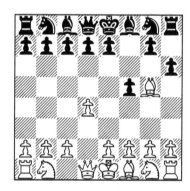

In this chapter we'll look at the most radical response to White's 2 ♗g5, namely **2...h6!?**. At first glance this seems like an insane move: Black has already weakened his kingside with 1...f5, and now he plays 2...h6, just asking to be mated on the light squares! Well, I hope the shock isn't too much when I tell you that his third move is 3...g5. In reality, so long as we avoid a couple of beginner's mates, nothing is

In fact, Black's play is based on solid strategic considerations, not an urge to commit hari-kari. He is planning to utilize his kingside pawns before developing any pieces. This means that he is going to have dynamic chances, even if the pawns are somewhat fragile. Incidentally, he is playing according to the precepts of Philidor, who taught that in the opening the pieces should always play second fiddle to the requirements of the pawns. Black's set-up might be described as a dynamic hedgehog. He builds a strong but flexible structure on d6 and e6, and only then tries to lash out with ...f5-f4 on the kingside.

A good practical feature of 2...h6 is that it allows Black to dictate the opening variation, whereas after 2...g6 White can choose between a sharp battle in the centre with 3 ♘d2 ♗g7 4 e4 or solid play with 3 e3.

The Solid 3 ♗h4 g5 4 e3

G.Kasparov-Leigh Interest PLC
London simul' 1993

1 d4 f5!

A good choice by the business people in this simul' game. The dynamic properties of the Dutch seem to make Kasparov uncomfortable even when he isn't being distracted by other games.

2 ♗g5 h6 3 ♗h4 g5 4 e3 ♘f6 5 ♗g3 d6 6 c4!?

Kasparov wants his own torrent pawn on the c-file to counter the force of Black's battering ram on the f-file. A c4-c5 advance would fit in nicely with the bishop on g3. The alternative, 6 h4, will be seen in the next game.

6...e6 7 ♘c3 ♕e7

The consulting team go about the business of mobilizing their pieces with a view to a future queenside castling,

but they are careful to delay ...♘c6 until the last moment, so that no target is presented for a centre-splitting d4-d5 advance by White. At the same time, the natural move ...♗g7 is held back – after all, why weaken the d6-square by moving the bishop away from its defence when c4-c5 is looming?

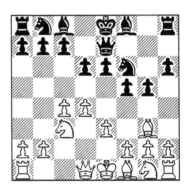

8 ♘f3 ♗d7 9 ♕c2

The white queen clears the way for 0-0-0 and gives the c4-c5 pawn push at least moral support. After ♗d3 next move she adds extra power to a d4-d5 advance in reply to ...♘c6, as the f5-pawn would become a target.

9...♗g7

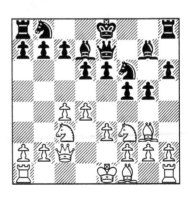

The Black players decide it is time to develop their other minor pieces.

10 ♗d3 ♘c6

Very tempting, as 11...♘b4 is a threat. Nonetheless, 10...♘h5!? should have been preferred: for example, 11 d5? ♘a6 or 11 ♕b3 (a change of front) 11...♘c6 12 d5 (if 12 ♕xb7 ♖b8 13 ♕xc7 ♘xg3 14 hxg3 and Black has a at least a draw with the repetition 14...♖c8 15 ♕b7 ♖b8 etc, as 16 ♕a6? ♘b4 forks a6 and d3) 12...♘a5 13 ♕b4 b6 14 ♘b5 ♔d8!? with unclear play.

11 a3

A simple move that puts Black into difficulties.

11...♕f7

Fighting against 12 d5, but allowing White's other pawn advance:

12 c5! dxc5 13 dxc5 ♖c8

14 ♗b5?

Instead 14 ♘b5! attacking c7 would be very awkward for Black, as the natural reply 14...♘d5 allows the tactic 15 ♗xc7! threatening a fork with 16 ♘d6+. There is little doubt that Kasparov would have seen this in a one-to-one game, but in a simul' he makes a natural move that aims to win control of the e5-square.

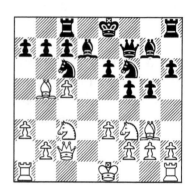

14...♘g4!

Suddenly the dynamism of the black set-up exerts itself. If 15 h3 Black can apply a pawn-ram with 15...♘ge5 and then 16...f4.

15 0-0-0 a6 16 ♗xc6 ♗xc6 17 h3 ♗xf3 18 gxf3 ♘e5 19 f4 ♘c6

Black has an excellent bishop on g7 and pawns that cover key squares in the centre.

20 ♖hg1 ♕e7 21 ♕b3 ♖b8 22 ♔b1 0-0 23 fxg5 hxg5 24 ♖d2 ♖f7

Directed against an invasion attempt on d7 after 25 ♖gd1.

25 ♘e2 ♘a5

Satisfied that they have neutralized the pressure from the World Champion, the consulting team become ambitious.

26 ♕c2 b5!

Planning a knight invasion on c4.

27 ♘d4 ♖e8 28 b3

Keeping out the enemy knight, but now things begin to look shaky for White along the a1-h8 diagonal.

28...f4 29 exf4 gxf4 30 ♗h2 e5 31 ♘f5 ♕e6 32 ♘xg7 ♖xg7 33 ♖xg7+ ♔xg7

The simplification has eliminated Black's powerful bishop, but on the other hand White has weak pawns on b3 and h3, as well as an entombed bishop on h2.

34 ♔b2 ♖h8 35 ♕c3 ♕xb3+!

Forcing White into an unpleasant endgame.

36 ♕xb3 ♘xb3 37 ♔xb3 ♖xh3+ 38 f3

Uncovering a defence of his bishop. Here Kasparov was astute enough to offer a draw, as after 38...♖xf3+ 39 ♔b4 ♔f6 40 c6 e4 he would be hard pressed

to save himself. But then World Champions are very resourceful so – **½-½**

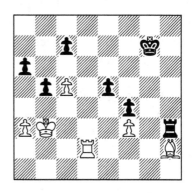

R.Hille-V.Malaniuk
Münster 1995

1 d4 f5 2 ♗g5 h6 3 ♗h4 g5 4 e3 ♘f6 5 ♗g3 d6

No routine 5...♗g7 please. As we saw in the game above, there are sound strategic reasons to delay the development of the bishop for a considerable number of moves.

6 h4 ♖g8

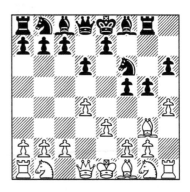

This seems more precise than 6...g4,

which, although it closes the kingside, lessens Black's control over the f4-square. Instead Malaniuk is prepared to cede an open h-file to the white rook in order to keep the chance of a dynamic ...f5-f4 advance – see his 14th move.

7 hxg5 hxg5 8 ♘d2

The 2 ♗g5 variation has been under a cloud because of the space-gaining line 8 ♘c3 e6 9 f3 ♕e7 10 ♕d2 ♘c6 11 0-0-0 ♗d7 12 e4 fxe4 (a key point is that 12...f4, our favourite move, fails after 13 ♗f2 ♗g7 – or 13...a6 14 e5! – 14 ♘b5 with a dangerous initiative for White) 13 fxe4 which Kasparov used against Illescas Cordoba at Dos Hermanas in 1996.

That game continued 13...0-0-0 14 d5 exd5 15 exd5 ♘e5 16 ♖e1 ♔b8 17 ♔b1 ♗g7 18 a3 ♖h8 19 ♖xh8 ♖xh8 20 ♗xe5 dxe5 21 ♘f3 e4 22 ♕xg5 and White had won a pawn, although I wonder whether White has any real advantage after, say, 18...♘fg4!? when 19 ♘f3 ♘xf3 20 gxf3 ♘e5 is nothing for White.

This is confirmed in a tacit way by the later game Y.Kuzubov-D.Swiercz Polanica Zdroj 2008, in which White rated 2578, declined to play Kasparov's 14 d5 and only drew after 14 ♔b1 ♗g7 15 ♘ge2 ♘g4 16 d5 exd5 17 exd5 ♘ce5 18 ♘d4 a6 19 ♗e2 ♔b8 20 ♖he1 ♕f7 21 ♖f1 ½-½.

So it seems there's not much to fear here for Black. Furthermore, Illescas Cordoba has played an interesting variant on his game with Kasparov 10...a6!? (rather than 10...♘c6) 11 0-0-0 ♘c6 12 e4 and here, because ♘b5 has been ruled out, we can play 12...f4!.

Only after 13 ♗f2 is the bishop developed to d7. The game M.Gurevich-M.Illescas Cordoba, Spanish Team Championship 2004, continued 13...♗d7 14 e5 ♘d5 15 exd6 ♕xd6 16 ♘e4 ♕e7 17 ♗c4 0-0-0 and Black went on to win in a hair-raising fight.

Finally, in the game E.Atalik-M.Muzychuk, Dagomys 2010, White tried a different way to attack in the centre: 8 ♗d3!? (rather than Kasparov's 8 ♘c3 e6 9 f3) 8...e6 9 ♘c3 ♘c6 10 d5!?.

After 10...♘e7 11 dxe6 ♗xe6 12 ♘f3, rather than 12...c5 as played, I would recommend the simple 12...♕d7 and if 13 ♘d4 0-0-0 Black is very active – the exchange 14 ♗xe6 ♕xe6 increases his initiative.

8...e6

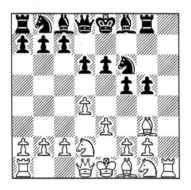

Malaniuk clears the way for the queen to galvanize the black position from the second rank.

9 c3

Hille's moves aren't forceful and they allow Black to mobilize without any problems. Not that there is anything exactly wrong with playing like this as White. In fact many players with a pronounced positional style are happy to defer the main struggle to the middlegame.

9...♕e7 10 ♕c2 ♘c6

Further to the previous comment, it's something of a luxury for Black not to be in any danger of being hit over the head with d4-d5. If that threat had existed Malaniuk might have employed the move order ...♗d7 and only then ...♘c6, to lessen the impact of a d4-d5

break – see, for example, the Kasparov game above.

11 ♗d3 ♗d7 12 ♘e2 ♕f7 13 f3 0-0-0

Black has built up his game in impeccable style. His pawn chain contains no weaknesses and controls a lot of squares. His queenside pieces have been developed in good order and his king is safely castled. He has been astute enough to leave his bishop on f8 to deter pressure by White against d6. A crass example: put the bishop on g7, move the white knight from d2 on c4, and already White has ♗xd6! winning a pawn due to a possible knight fork. Of course, this tactic could be easily avoided by Black, even if he had played ...♗g7 – the real danger to d6 comes from a c4-c5 pawn advance. In this game Hille has made no effort to arrange c4-c5, but Malaniuk wasn't to know that his opponent was going to be in a peaceful mood.

Malaniuk has also been clever enough to put his queen on f7, where she supports moves like ...♘h5 and the pawn-ram ...f5-f4. Meanwhile White's cental pawns moves have been too solid, without any bite. If he had carried on solidly with 14 0-0-0 chances would have remained about equal. Black might then have tried a different pawn advance: 14...♘d5 15 ♗f2 g4!? as 14...f4? is ineffective after 15 exf4 gxf4 16 ♗h4! with a much superior version of the actual game for White.

14 b4

White suddenly wants to attack the black king, but the quiet 14 0-0-0 was required.

14...f4! 15 exf4 gxf4

16 ♗h4!

Instead 16 ♗xf4 ♖xg2 is just good for Black, so Hille pins f6 and prepares to take on f4 with his knight.

16...♖xg2?

And now it is Black's turn to be in too much of a hurry. The subtle 16...♖e8! was stronger. It breaks the pin on f6 and prepares to answer 17 ♘xf4 with 17...e5! opening the centre to get at the white king. If 17 0-0-0 then 17...♘d5 sets up a fork on e3 – Black suffers so much with the hole on e6 in

the Leningrad that it is nice to see White get some of his own medicine. Or 17 b5 ♘e7 18 ♘xf4 ♗h6 and, with the white bishop denied access to the g6-square, Black has a strong initiative.

17 ♘xf4 ♖g8

18 ♘g6?

After 18 ♗g6 ♕g7 19 0-0-0 the white pieces appear rather loose on the kingside, but 19...e5 20 dxe5 dxe5 21 ♘e4! is unclear, perhaps good for White, so Black would have to make do with a solid alternative such as 19...♘e7.

18...♘e7!

The exchange of knights removes

the dynamism that compensated for the weaknesses in the white pawn structure.

19 ♘xf8 ♖dxf8 20 c4

White is understandably reluctant to let the black knight into the centre with 20 0-0-0 ♘ed5, attacking his weak squares on e3 and f4. On the other hand, his pawn structure is becoming even flimsier.

20...♘c6 21 ♕c3 e5 22 d5 ♘d4 23 ♗f2?

He should have castled, although Black has huge pressure on the kingside after 23...♘h5 intending 24...♘f4, etc.

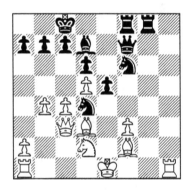

23...♘xf3+!

Black has such a huge amount of firepower on the f-file that a combination was always going to appear.

24 ♘xf3 ♘g4 25 ♗xa7

Losing quickly, but if 25 ♗e2 ♘xf2 26 ♔xf2 e4 or 25 ♗e4 ♗f5, in either case breaking down the resistance along the f-file.

25...♕xf3 26 ♔d2 ♕g2+ 27 ♗e2 ♘f2 28 ♗xf2 ♖xf2 29 ♕e3 ♗g4 30 ♖he1 ♖h8 31 ♔d1 ♗xe2+ 32 ♖xe2 ♖xe2 0-1

White loses a rook after 33 ♕xe2 ♖h1+.

White Plays 3 ♗f4

1 d4 f5 2 ♗g5 h6 3 ♗f4

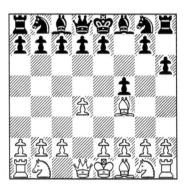

The thing most noteworthy here is 3...♘f6 4 e4 – a gambit line in the style of the Staunton. As usual, sound developing moves, a refusal to remove the pawn from e4, and hunting down White's light-squared bishop are the perfect recipe for Black: 4 e4 fxe4 5 ♘c3 d5 6 f3 ♗f5 (it's not a good sign for White's strategy when Black is able to develop his light-squared bishop so easily) 7 fxe4 dxe4 8 ♗c4 e6 9 ♘ge2 ♘c6 10 0-0 ♕d7 11 ♕d2 ♘a5 12 ♗b3 ♘xb3 13 axb3 ♗b4 14 ♘g3 0-0 15 ♖ae1 ♖ad8 and Black had a clear advantage in S.Ghane Gardeh-M.Mahjoob, Teheran 2002.

However, if White plays a solid move, say 4 e3, we are left wondering why the bishop went to f4 rather than h4.

J.Demina-A.Muzychuk
St Petersburg 2009

1 d4 f5 2 &g5 h6 3 &f4 ♘f6 4 e3 d6 5 h4 g6!

Preparing the fianchetto and also preventing an encroachment with 6 h5.
6 ♘d2 &g7 7 &c4 e6 8 c3 ♕e7 9 ♘gf3 ♘c6

Muzychuk follows the system of development outlined above versus 3 &h4. White hasn't any counterplay along the h-file, as Black wasn't required to play ...g7-g5 to drive away the bishop – it went to f4 of its own accord.
10 ♕a4 &d7 11 ♕a3 a6

Do you recall the Philidor comment about how the pieces shouldn't get in the way of the pawns in the opening? It explains what has gone so wrong with White's position.

The problem is that the white pieces have been developed in a clumsy manner without any thought about pawn breaks. For example, the bishop on c4

gets in the way of the c4-c5 advance that Kasparov arranged versus the consultants, and the knight on f3 gets in the way of the f2-f3 move to support e3-e4, which he played versus Illescas Cordoba, as we saw above.

A position that can't be strengthened with pawn moves is on the way downhill. It's no wonder that the white pieces flounder around helplessly until they are caught by a crushing attack.
12 ♘b3 ♘d8!

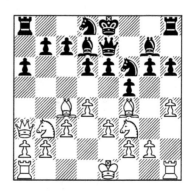

A fine manoeuvre by the strong lady player. The knight goes to f7 where it can support pawn breaks with ...e6-e5 or ...g6-g5. Black is also refraining from castling as she wants to see what her opponent is going to do with her king.
13 ♘c1 ♘f7 14 ♘d3 ♘e4 15 0-0-0?

If White had castled kingside, or kept her king in the centre – the most sensible thing to do – Black would have began an attack with 15...g5. But now the white king is too tempting a target on the queenside.
15...b5! 16 &b3 a5 17 ♘d2 0-0 18 ♘xe4 fxe4 19 ♘e1 ♖fb8

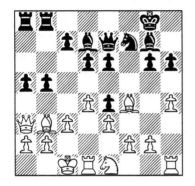

White has no counterplay at all to offset the attack on her king. That's what happens when you don't prepare any pawn advances in the opening.

20 ♗c2 b4 21 cxb4 axb4 22 ♕b3 ♗c6 23 d5 ♗xd5 24 ♖xd5 exd5 25 ♕xd5 ♕f6 26 ♕b3 c5 0-1

The Bold 3 ♗h4 g5 4 e4

V.Shishkin-V.Malaniuk
Mielno 2007

1 d4 f5 2 ♗g5 h6 3 ♗h4 g5 4 e4

Threatening mate, so keep your hands off the bishop.

4...♘f6

The best reply. Dubious is 4...♗g7 5 ♗g3 f4 6 ♗xf4! gxf4 7 ♕h5+ ♔f8 8 ♕f5+! ♘f6 (or 8...♔e8 9 ♗e2! ♘f6 10 e5) 9 e5 d6 10 ♕xf4 and Black is busted. I've seen GM Chris Ward win games like this a couple of times in tournaments.

5 e5 e6!

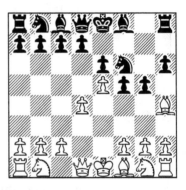

Only thus. If instead 5...gxh4 6 exf6 is abysmal for Black.

6 exf6

Or 6 ♗g3 f4 7 ♗xf4 gxf4 8 exf6 ♕xf6 9 ♘c3 ♘c6 10 ♘b5 ♔d8 11 ♘f3 a6 12 ♘c3 d5! (a characteristic move by Black in this variation when his king is on d8; he plays ...d7-d5 to control the e4-square and block the advance of the white d-pawn) 13 ♕d2 ♗d6 (now the bishop comes to a strong central square where it guards f4 and controls e5) 14 0-0-0 b5!, restraining any pawn break with c2-c4 which White might have arranged. Black is rock-solid in the centre and his king is completely free from danger. He went on to win in C.Bauer-M.Santo Roman, Toulouse 1995.

6...♕xf6!

Here we have to take the pawn to stop mate on h5. But never mind: White's bishop won't escape the clutches of the black pawns.

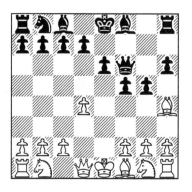

7 ♗g3

If instead 7 ♕h5+ Black has the added option of exchanging queens with 7...♕f7, but I would suggest 7...♔d8 8 ♗g3 f4, transposing back to the mainline.

7...f4

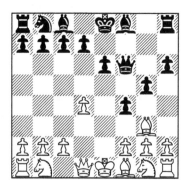

8 ♕h5+

Alternatively 8 ♗d3 ♘c6 9 c3 (see below for 9 ♕h5+) 9...d5!? (highly sharp is 9...e5!? 10 ♘e2 d5 11 dxe5 ♘xe5 12 0-0 as in E.Postny-F.Grafl, Pardubice 2003, and now Postny recommends 12...♗d6 13 ♗c2 ♗e6 'when Black is at least not worse') 10 ♘e2 h5!? (this looks outrageous, but it achieves the desired effect of provoking or panicking White into a blunder) 11 h4? (11 ♕c2 ♖h6!? is unclear) 11...fxg3 12 ♘xg3 gxh4 13 ♘xh5 ♕g5 and the double attack on h5 and g2 left White in trouble in T.Meynard-V.Sikula, Villeneuve Tolosane 2006.

Instead after 8 ♗d3 ♘c6 White can give a check on h5 after all:

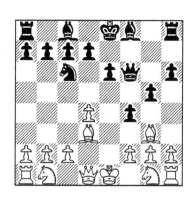

9 ♕h5+ ♔d8 10 c3 d5 11 ♘f3 fxg3 (he could delay this with 11...♗d7, when 12 ♘bd2 e5!? speculates in the style of the Postny game as the white king is a useful target for a check on e1; but if 12 0-0 I would recommend a transposition with 12...fxg3 13 fxg3 ♕g7) 12 fxg3 ♕g7 13 0-0 ♗d7 14 ♘bd2 ♗d6. A characteristic position for this line has emerged. Black has the two bishops, an imposing

wedge of centre pawns, and control over the e5-square. Positionally it is far from perfect for White, but that won't matter if he strikes a deadly blow against the black king. In D.Orzech-V.Malaniuk, Barlinek 2006, Black's king managed to edge away to safety, after which his more compact pawns became the important factor: 15 ♖ae1 a6 16 ♔h1 ♔c8 17 c4 ♗b4 18 ♖f2 ♔b8 19 ♘e5 ♘xe5 20 dxe5 ♔a7 21 a3 ♗xd2 22 ♖xd2 ♗c6 and Black went on to win the positional battle.

8...♔d8

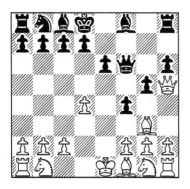

The black king is usually safe on d8 in these variations. The pawns on d7 and e6 are a hard nut to crack, and remain solid even if Black chooses to advance ...d7-d5, as we saw in the Bauer-Santo Roman game above. Meanwhile, after he captures on g3, Black will have an unopposed dark-squared bishop.

So much for the good points in Black's position. The question is whether White can organize an attack to take advantage of a lack of coordination among the black pieces caused by

having the king on d8. For this reason Malaniuk doesn't hurry to capture on g3, as he doesn't want to clear any lines for the white attack.

9 ♘c3 ♗b4 10 ♘ge2 fxg3 11 hxg3 b6

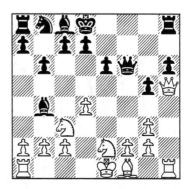

12 0-0-0

Gambiting the f2-pawn for a breakthrough after 12...♕xf2 13 d5.

12...♗b7 13 f4?

This leads to weaknesses in White's own king's defences. The forceful 13 d5! ♗xd5!? 14 ♘xd5 exd5 15 f4! would give White attacking chances, though Black's king looks safe enough and can run away to b7 if necessary.

13...gxf4 14 ♘xf4 ♗xc3 15 bxc3 ♗e4!

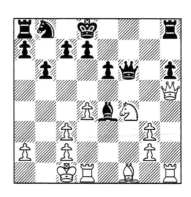

Clearing the way for the king to go to b7 and preventing White's methodical development with ♗d3 and ♖df1 save at the cost of exchanging bishops, which lessens the power of his onslaught.

16 ♗d3 ♗xd3 17 ♘xd3 ♘c6

18 ♖df1 ♛e7 19 ♖f7 ♛a3+ 20 ♔d2 ♔c8 21 g4 ♘a5 22 ♘e5 d6 23 ♘g6 ♖d8 24 ♛xh6 ♔b7 25 ♛g7 ♖ac8

Black's king has reached safety and he is fully developed. White's passed pawn isn't any compensation for the attack that Malaniuk is about to unleash against the exposed king.

26 ♘e7 ♘c4+ 27 ♔d3

To hold onto the c3-pawn.

27...♘e5+!

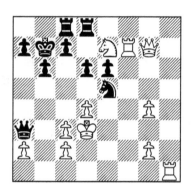

28 ♔d2

After 28 dxe5 dxe5+ 29 ♔e2 ♛xc3 the white pieces are too far away to defend their king: e.g., 30 ♘xc8 ♛xc2+ 31 ♔e3 ♖d3+ 32 ♔e4 ♛e2 mate.

28...♘xf7 29 ♘xc8 ♘e5 30 ♘e7 ♘c4+ 31 ♔d3 d5 32 g5 ♛d6 33 ♖h3 ♛f4 0-1

The finish could be 34 ♔e2 (to stop mate on d2) 34...♖f8 35 ♖f3 ♛d2+ 36 ♔f1 ♘e3+ and mate next move.

Chapter Four

White Avoids an early g2-g3 against a Leningrad Set-up

1 d4 f5

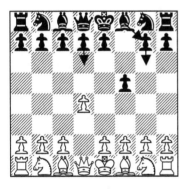

If White avoids putting the bishop on g2 versus the Leningrad Dutch set-up, it might mean one of three things:

1. He doesn't know much theory and is happy with simple, albeit passive, development in the opening.

2. He is a subtle positional master who has spent years developing a pet system with ♗e2 and b2-b4.

3. He knows a lot of sharp theory and wants to destroy his opponent with 2 c4 and 3 ♘c3.

In other words, you can't take anything for granted. In this chapter we'll have a look at the mixture of systems and pawn structures that might arise when White avoids g2-g3 and ♗g2, but allows Black a Leningrad set-up.

After 1 d4 f5 we'll explore:

Part One – White plays e2-e3 and ♗e2 or ♗d3;

Part Two – 2 c4 ♘f6 3 ♘c3;

Part Three – 2 ♘f3 ♘f6 3 ♗g5;

Part Four – White plays b2-b3.

Part One: White Plays e2-e3

At club level, games with ♗e2 or

♗d3 are common. If White wants a non-theoretical game that avoids putting the bishop on g2 the best way is probably **1 d4 f5 2 ♘f3 ♘f6 3 c4 g6 4 ♘c3 ♗g7 5 e3 d6 6 ♗e2 0-0 7 0-0...**

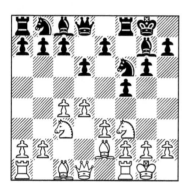

...after which White plans to develop queenside pressure with 8 b4.

Putting the bishop on e2 (or d3) certainly doesn't have the same bite as deploying it to g2, where it stares menacingly down the long diagonal and causes Black problems in mobilizing his queenside pieces. Nor has White made any saving in time, as g2-g3 and ♗g2 takes no longer than e2-e3 and ♗e2.

On the other hand, Black mustn't go thinking that ♗e2 is harmless, or that he should be able to seize the initiative after this 'inferior' move. White hasn't made any mistake: he has avoided the sharpest line, that is all. In the diagram above White has more space on the queenside, and can try to exploit this. I expect that a Kramnik would be able to grind down most top GMs as White from this position, or at least cause them some trouble.

Fortunately (or unfortunately) we don't get to play Kramnik that often; so how can we create dynamic chances as Black from the above position?

White's premature 6 b4

It's worth knowing that after **1 d4 f5 2 ♘f3 ♘f6 3 c4 g6 4 ♘c3 ♗g7 5 e3 d6**, the immediate **6 b4** is ineffective because of 6...c5! as played in N.Sulava-V.Malaniuk, Montecatini Terme 1995.

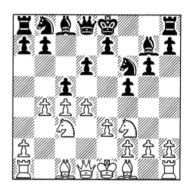

That game continued 7 a3 0-0 8 ♗b2 ♘c6 9 d5? (Beim prefers 9 b5! but Black is already doing well) 9...cxb4! 10 ♘b5 bxa3 11 ♗xf6 ♗xf6 12 dxc6 ♕a5+ 13 ♘d2 ♗xa1 14 cxb7 ♗xb7 15 ♕xa1 a2 and Black had good winning chances before blundering and losing.

Instead White could try the 'impossible' move 7 dxc5, based on the trick 7...♘e4 8 ♗b2 ♘xc3 9 ♕b3 when he regains his piece. However, the simple 7...0-0 looks good for Black after 8 cxd6?! ♘e4.

More challenging is 7 b5! Then 7...0-0 is sensible, but I'd like to play 7...♕c7 8 ♗b2 ♘bd7 to put pressure on c4 with ...♘b6. For example, 9 ♗e2 ♘b6 and now White has a choice:

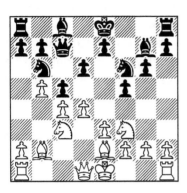

a) 10 ♕b3 cxd4 11 exd4 ♗e6 12 d5 ♗f7 and the c4-pawn is a target.

b) 10 d5 e6 11 dxe6 ♗xe6 12 ♘g5? (or 12 ♕b3 h6 when Black can aim for ...d6-d5, e.g. 13 a4?! ♕f7 14 ♘d2 d5!) 12...♗xc4 13 ♗xc4 ♘xc4 14 ♘e6 ♕e7 15 ♘xg7+ ♕xg7 and White's position is falling apart.

c) A tricky move is 10 dxc5!? ♕xc5 11 ♘d5, threatening to trap the black queen with 12 ♗d4. However, Black has 11...e5!? and it appears that White has overreached himself. The tactical 12 ♗a3 fails to 12...♕xa3 13 ♘c7+ ♔d8 14 ♘xa8 b6 and the knight will be trapped by ...♗b7.

White plays 7 0-0 and Black stops b2-b4

N.Wright-D.Sharma
Canberra 2010

1 ♘f3 d6 2 d4 f5 3 c4 ♘f6 4 ♘c3 g6 5 e3

♗g7 6 ♗e2 0-0 7 0-0 a5

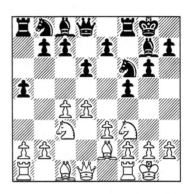

A very logical move. White's pieces and pawns aren't geared up for operations in the centre or on the kingside, so why not make it hard for him to expand on the queenside?

8 a3

If 8 b3 ♘a6 9 ♗b2 ♕e8 when after 10 ♘d2 e5 in M.Sefeloge-R.Huss, Bad Homburg 2006, or 10 a3 ♗d7! 11 ♕c2 e5 in M.Tietze-G.Wiege, Alfeld 2005, Black had equalized. Note the importance of 10...♗d7 in this second variation: the rook on a8 is defended so that White can't advance on the queenside, whereas after 10...e5, 11 b4! is possible due to the potential pin on the a-file.

Meanwhile 8 ♕c2 can be answered by 8...♘a6 9 ♖d1 ♕e8, intending 10...e5, but the game move shows a desire to expand after 8...♘a6? 9 b4!.

8...♘c6!?

With the idea of advancing 9...e5 and creating mobile pawns in the centre.

Suppose White had played 8 b3 rather than 8 a3. In that case 8...♘c6 would be less effective as White could fight against the ...e7-e5 advance with 9 ♗b2, or try to profit from it with ♗a3. Likewise if White had played 8 ♕c2, he would be in a position to impede the ...e7-e5 advance with 9 ♖d1. That is why a6 was the preferred square for the knight in the variations given in the previous note: with c7 defended, the black queen is free to go to e8 to support ...e7-e5 without Black being bothered by an attack on c7 by ♘b5 or ♘d5.

9 d5 ♘e5

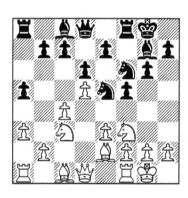

10 ♘d4

Black has his pawn centre after 10 ♘xe5 dxe5. He could then attack d5 with 11...e6, after which White would really regret having his bishop on e2 rather than g2.

10...c5

Now White is obliged to give up his pawn wedge on d5 in order to keep his knight in the centre.

11 dxc6 ♘xc6

With the bishop on e2 rather than g2, White is far less able to exploit the weakness of the d5-square. Meanwhile

Black has activity not dissimilar to that which he achieves in the 7 ♘c3 ♘c6 8 d5 ♘a5 variation of Chapter Seven.

12 ♘db5?

A pointless decentralization. He should play the consolidating 12 b3.

12...♗e6 13 ♕b3 ♘d7 14 ♕c2 ♘b6 15 ♘a4 ♘e5 16 ♘d4 ♗f7 17 ♘xb6 ♕xb6 18 b3 ♖fc8

So that if 19 a4 d5! conquers the c4-pawn.

19 ♕d2 a4

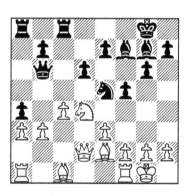

Now White's structure on the queenside collapses and he soon loses material.

20 f4 ♘c6 21 ♗b2 ♘a5 22 bxa4 e5 23 ♘b5 ♘b3 24 ♕c3 ♘xa1 25 ♗xa1 ♖xa4 26 ♖d1 ♖c6 27 ♖xd6 ♖xd6 28 c5 ♖c6 29 cxb6 ♖xc3 30 ♗xc3 exf4 31 ♗d2 fxe3 32 ♗xe3 ♖e4 33 ♔f2 f4 34 ♗c5 ♖xe2+ 35 ♔xe2 ♗c4+ 36 ♔f3 ♗xb5 37 ♔xf4 ♔f7 38 h4 h6 39 g4 ♔e6 0-1

White plays 7 b4

1 d4 f5 2 ♘f3 ♘f6 3 c4 g6 4 ♘c3 ♗g7 5 e3 d6 6 ♗e2 0-0 7 b4

Getting in the b2-b4 advance before Black can play the restraining move 7...a5. The drawback is that the tactics of the position permit Black to make his own desired pawn advance without any preparation:

7...e5! 8 dxe5 dxe5

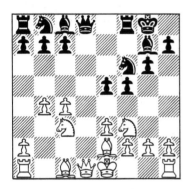

Now White has to avoid 9 ♕xd8 (or 9 ♘xe5?? ♘e4!) 9...♖xd8 10 ♘xe5?? ♘e4! 11 ♘xe4 ♗xe5 when he drops a piece.

9 ♕b3!

A testing move. I only have five games with this position in my database, but remarkably five GMs and a couple of other titled players were involved in these games.

9...e4 10 ♘d4 c5?!

We examine 10...♘c6! below.

The game move is attractive as it breaks up the white pawns, but it seems we have to reject it as too risky, based on the game **R.Kempinski-F.Nijboer**, European Championship, Warsaw 2005:

11 bxc5 ♘c6 12 ♗b2! f4

Black trusts in the celebrated ...f5-f4

pawn-ram, but after his next move the white king is whisked away. Instead Black could make a thematic exchange sacrifice for a pawn with 12...♘xd4 13 exd4 ♕xd4 14 ♘d5 ♕xc5 15 ♗a3 ♕a5+ 16 ♗b4 ♕d8 17 ♗xf8 (or 17 ♖d1) 17...♕xf8 18 ♖c1. Black has a fine dark-squared bishop, but I think he is a bit worse because getting rid of the knight on d5 with 18...♘xd5 19 cxd5 grants White a passed pawn and an open file for his rook.

13 0-0-0!

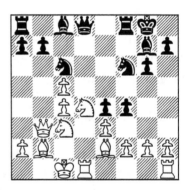

Slightly unexpected as White's queenside pawns are wrecked. But on the queenside the white king is surrounded by defenders, whereas after 13 0-0?? he would be almost on his own, and facing the prospect of a further advance of Black's Dutch pawn with ...f4-f3.

13...♘xd4

Black wants to get his kingside pawns rolling, but straightening out White's queenside pawn structure is a high price to pay. On the other hand, he can't go after the c5-pawn with

13...♕e7 as 14 exf4 is a simple and good reply.

14 exd4 ♗f5 15 f3

15...♖c8

If 15...e3 then 16 g4! is excellent for White. The e3-pawn is going nowhere and meanwhile White can...

16 ♘b5

...head for d6. Nijboer managed to save himself with some resourceful play, but we have to conclude that White's extra pawn – in the centre the balance is 4-2 in White's favour – means he has good winning chances. Returning to move 10, the most reliable move is **10...♘c6!**.

It's understandable that Black should have misgivings about taking on doubled and isolated c-pawns, but the white b-pawn, which stands on an open file, is just as much a target. For example:

a) 11 ♘xc6 bxc6 12 0-0 ♗e6 (other moves such as 12...♕e7 are also interesting), and Black can utilize his a-pawn to attack b4: 13 ♗b2 a5, or 13 ♗a3 ♘d7 14 ♖ad1 ♕f6 15 ♘a4 a5 16 bxa5?! ♖fb8, or 13 ♘a4 a5 14 ♘c5 ♗f7 (14...♕e7!?) 15 ♘b7 a4! and in all cases Black has queenside pressure to compensate for the fracturing of his c-pawns.

b) Alternatively S.Grebennikov-A.Sofieva, Leningrad 1990, went 11 c5+ ♚h8 12 ♘xc6 bxc6 13 ♗b2 ♕e7 14 0-0 a5! 15 b5 ♗e6 and White was already on the defensive due to the fragile queenside pawns.

White plays ♗d3

In the games with ♗e2 above, we saw that one of Black's main ideas is to advance ...e7-e5 and create a mobile pawn centre. By this reasoning, the plan of ♗d3, which encourages Black to advance further with ...e5-e4, which might fork the bishop and a knight on f3, already feels dubious.

The game **N.Giffard-N.Legky**, Cannes 1992, is the long-established model of how Black gets maximum value out of the poor placement of the bishop on d3:

1 ♘f3 g6 2 c4 ♗g7 3 d4 f5 4 ♘c3 ♘f6 5

e3 d6

Move order! Notice that it is important that Black plays 5...d6 rather than 5...0-0 as he needs to set up his next move.

6 ♗d3 e5!

An excellent pawn sacrifice.

7 dxe5 dxe5 8 ♘xe5

Any slower move that stops the 8...e4 fork would admit the opening has gone wrong for White.

8...♘e4!

The point. If the white knight retreats from e5 then c3 drops. Now 9 ♘xe4 fxe4 loses a piece, as does 9 ♕a4+ though in a more sophisticated manner: 9...b5! 10 ♕xb5+ (or 10 ♘xb5 c6 11 ♗xe4 fxe4 when two white knights are hanging) 10...c6 11 ♘xc6 ♘xc3 12 ♘xd8+ ♘xb5 13 cxb5 ♔xd8 and White's extra pawns are no match for a piece.

9 ♗xe4 ♕xd1+ 10 ♘xd1 fxe4 11 f4 exf3 12 ♘xf3 ♗e6

Black has a splendid initiative for the pawn. First the c4-pawn is attacked, and the rook that comes to help it becomes a target of the black knight, which makes the white king flee the centre to avoid a fork on d3. This in turn allows the black rook to infiltrate along the d-file.

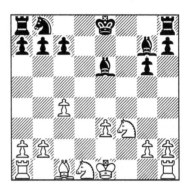

13 ♗d2 ♘d7 14 ♖c1 ♘c5 15 0-0 ♘e4 16 ♗e1 0-0-0 17 b3 ♖d3 18 ♘f2 ♖xe3 19 ♘xe4 ♖xe4 20 ♗c3 ♗xc3 21 ♖xc3 ♗f5

Black has regained his pawn with the better chances due to his superior minor piece. He managed to convert the win on move 63.

Perhaps White would have been able to survive the endgame if he had been the GM rather than Black, but in any case this is hardly an advertisement for 6 ♗d3.

It is curious that there are only two games on my database with 6...e5. Both are wins for Black (in the other game White played the sorry 8 ♗e2), and the computer also likes it for Black. Perhaps the plan of 6 ♗d3 is so rare that most players of the Dutch have never got around to studying it and so are unaware of 6...e5.

Part Two:
2 c4 ♘f6 3 ♘c3

1 d4 f5 2 c4 ♘f6 3 ♘c3

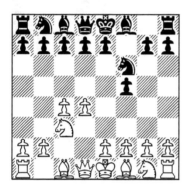

Don't be fooled by White's unobtrusive-looking move order. If you play 3...g6, he is ready to hit you with 4 h4! and 5 h5. This attacking line has done very well for White, so rather sadly I have to recommend the alternative 3...d6. With no target on g6, White is obliged to change plans.

The game could easily transpose to familiar territory; e.g. if White plays 4 ♘f3 then 4...g6 5 g3 ♗g7 6 ♗g2 reaches our standard Leningrad Main Line. Here we'll look at two ways in which White can exploit the move order to carry out a specific plan.

The Sämisch approach: 4 f3

1 d4 f5 2 c4 ♘f6 3 ♘c3 d6 4 f3

White tries to play in the style of the King's Indian Sämisch, in which 1 d4

♘f6 2 c4 g6 3 ♘c3 ♗g7 4 e4 d6 5 f3 constructs a formidable skeleton of pawns on the light squares. The drawbacks remain the same: White is left somewhat loose on the dark squares and his knight is denied its natural square on f3.

Here I want to suggest **4...♘bd7!?**.

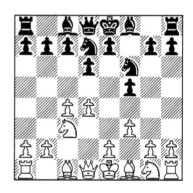

An unusual but flexible move that keeps the options of ...c7-c5, ...e7-e5 or ...g7-g6 according to circumstances.
5 e4

He might have tried 5 ♘h3 as Black's e6-square is undefended. Then 5...e5 should be okay for Black, but 5...c5 is critical:

a) 6 d5 ♘e5 gives us a centre familiar from ♘h3 lines in Chapter Five.

b) 6 e3 e5! stops ♘f4 and fights for the centre. Black can resist an invasion by the white knights: e.g. 7 ♘g5 ♕e7 8 ♘b5 ♘b6, followed by ...a7-a6 as needed, when he has the better game since White's centre is shaky.

c) 6 ♘g5 cxd4 7 ♘e6 ♕a5 8 ♕xd4 ♘c5! also proves ineffective for White.
5...fxe4 6 fxe4 c5

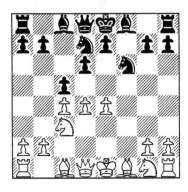

7 d5

White sticks to his pre-game plan of seizing the light squares. Maintaining the pawn on d4 doesn't promise much: for example, 7 ♗e3 ♕a5 8 ♗d3 (or 8 ♕d2 ♘g4) 8...cxd4 9 ♗xd4 ♘c5. Alternatively, 7 ♘f3 cxd4 8 ♘xd4 (Black has a solid centre after 8 ♕xd4 e5 9 ♕e3 ♗e7) 8...♘c5 and then ...g7-g6. In all these lines Black has active play in an unclear and unusual position – exactly what we are aiming for when we play the Dutch.

7...g6 8 ♘f3 ♗g7

White has more space and can try to exploit the hole on e6. Meanwhile Black can try to utilize the e5-square. And who is most likely to benefit from the open f-file? That will depend on the skill of the players.

9 ♗e2 0-0 10 0-0

How is Black to unwind his game? The knight on d7 is looking clumsy as it blocks in the bishop on c8.

The e5-square is a fine central post for a knight from which no white pawn can drive it away. For that reason

10...♘e5?? 11 ♘xe5 fxe5 would be plain ridiculous for Black. He wants a knight on the square, not a weak pawn. So a more methodical rearrangement of the black pieces is called for: first ...♘g4, so that ...♘de5 can be played without suffering doubled pawns; then ...♗d7 develops the bishop; and finally ...♘f7 retreats the knight so that ...♘ge5 can be played. Black thus consolidates his grip over the e5-square and frees his bishop on c8.

And Black has to give thanks to 1...f5 that this plan is possible, as otherwise there wouldn't be a base for the knight on f7.

10...♘g4!

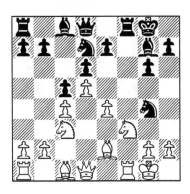

In **M.Dambacher-S.Van Blitterswijk**, Leeuwarden 2004, White was worn down after a series of exchanges, some of which he carelessly arranged himself:

11 ♗g5

For 11 ♔h1, see the next game.

11...♘de5 12 ♔h1 ♗d7 13 ♕d2 ♘f7

Casting doubt on White's 11th move, as the positional threat of

14...♘xg5, eliminating the 'good' white bishop, means that Black gains time to carry out his thematic knight retreat.

14 ♗f4 ♕a5

The queen probes the queenside and makes way for the rook on a8 to be centralized.

15 a3 ♖ae8 16 ♘e1 ♘ge5 17 ♘c2 a6 18 ♗e3

Moving the bishop for a third time. The only move consistent with his previous play was the space-gaining 18 b4, answering 18...♕c7 with 19 ♘e3 to bolster the c4-pawn. The game would then be balanced.

18...♕c7 19 ♖f2 ♘g4!

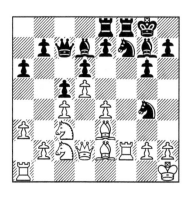

Black has two knights, but only one brilliant central base on e5, so it's good to get rid of one of them.

20 ♗xg4 ♗xg4 21 ♖af1 ♘e5

The exchange on g4 has also left the white pawn on c4 undefended.

22 ♖xf8+

If White wants to attack on the kingside he should speculate with 22 ♗h6! ♘xc4 (or 22...♖xf2!?) 23 ♕g5.

22...♖xf8 23 ♖xf8+ ♔xf8 24 ♗h6?

White completes his quartet of bishop moves on the long diagonal: ♗g5, ♗f4, ♗e3 and now ♗h6. The problem is that after the series of exchanges White no longer has enough pieces to defend his queenside pawns.

24...♗xh6

But not 24...♘xc4? 25 ♕f4+ when White wins a piece.

25 ♕xh6+ ♔g8 26 ♘e3

The best chance to hold things together was 26 ♕h4! ♕b6 27 b4.

26...♕b6

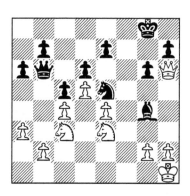

Now White is suddenly unable to defend his b2-pawn.

27 ♘xg4 ♕xb2 28 h3 ♘xg4 29 hxg4 ♕xc3 30 ♕f4 ♕xa3 31 ♔h2 ♕c3 0-1

Dambacher is an IM but he couldn't find a plan that suited the unusual pawn structure.

P.Lagowski-M. Bartel
Polish Team
Championship 2006

1 d4 f5 2 c4 ♘f6 3 ♘c3 d6 4 f3 ♘bd7 5

e4 fxe4 6 fxe4 c5 7 d5 g6 8 ♘f3 ♗g7 9 ♗e2 0-0 10 0-0 ♘g4

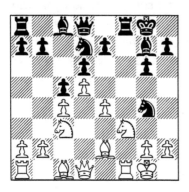

(In fact this game actually began with the 3 ♘c3 g6 move order: namely 1 d4 f5 2 c4 ♘f6 3 ♘c3 g6 4 f3 c5 5 d5 d6 6 e4 fxe4 7 fxe4 ♗g7 8 ♘f3 ♘bd7 9 ♗e2 0-0 10 0-0 ♘g4.)

11 ♔h1

Rather than 11 ♗g5 as in the game above. Lagowski is preparing an interesting plan of attack which requires a pawn sacrifice.

11...♘de5

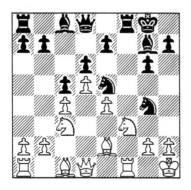

12 ♕e1

The white queen heads for g3 or h4.

12...♗d7

Intending 13...♘f7 and 14...♘ge5, but White's next move forces Black to change his plan.

13 h3!? ♘xf3 14 gxf3 ♘f6 15 f4 ♗xh3

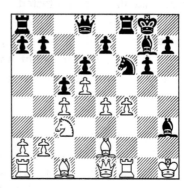

At the price of a pawn, White has much altered the centre structure: the black knight base on e5 has vanished and White has a mass of mobile pawns.

16 ♖g1

If left in peace, Lagowski can build up an initiative with moves like ♕h4 and f4-f5, with ♗h6 thrown in as appropriate, or ♕g3 and e4-e5.

16...e5!!

To play the Dutch successfully, Black has to master the art of transforming the pawn structure. The fluid nature of the opening means that there are usually interesting pawn thrusts available to both players, and choosing the right one and playing it at the right moment is never easy.

The game move is excellent because it:

1. Prevents the advance e4-e5;

2. Doesn't allow White time to prepare f4-f5 in a favourable manner;

3. Opens the f-file for counterplay from his rook on f8; and

4. Allows the black queen to become an attacking or defensive force.

But what about the protected passed pawn that White acquires on d5? It is a factor, of course; but the game is going to be decided in a dynamic fight, and so long-term endgame advantages are of less importance.

17 fxe5

Perhaps the best way to continue the attack is 17 f5 gxf5 18 ♕g3 ♗g4 19 exf5 h5! 20 ♗g5, though 20...♔f7 looks good for Black – it is the white king which will be in the most danger if exchanges on g4 open the h-file.

17...dxe5 18 ♗g5 ♕b6!

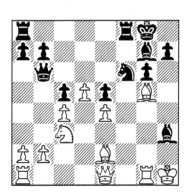

The queen escapes the pin, clears the way for the rook on a8 to enter the game, and attacks b2.

19 ♕h4 ♗d7 20 ♖af1 ♖f7

If Black hadn't played 16...e5 the knight on f6 would be hanging now.

21 b4

White doesn't have enough power to conclude the game with a violent king-side attack. He should have played the calm 21 b3. He is then a pawn down with no compensating dynamism after 21...♖af8, but he still has well-placed pieces and the strong pawn on d5.

21...cxb4 22 c5 ♕xc5 23 ♖xf6 ♖xf6!

White was hoping for 23...♗xf6? 24 ♗xf6 when 24...bxc3 allows 25 ♖xg6+! ♔f8 (or 25...hxg6 26 ♕h8 mate) 26 ♕h6+ ♔e8 27 ♖g8+ ♖f8 28 ♗h5 mate.

So here Black would have to bail out with a draw after 24...♖xf6 25 ♕xf6 bxc3 26 ♖xg6+ hxg6 27 ♕xg6+ ♔f8 28 ♕f6+ ♔g8 etc, with perpetual, as 28...♔e8? allows 29 ♗h5 mate.

24 ♗xf6 bxc3

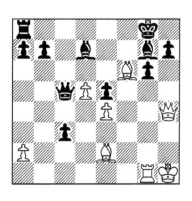

25 ♗g4

There's no way forward for the white attack after 25 ♗xg7 ♔xg7 26 ♕g5 ♕d6. The attempt to complicate just speeds up the end.

25...♗xg4 26 ♗xg7

There's no hope either in 26 ♖xg4 c2.

26...♗f3+ 27 ♔h2 ♔xg7 28 ♕g3 ♖f8 29 ♕xe5+ ♖f6 30 ♖f1 ♕e3 31 ♕e7+ ♖f7 32 ♕e5+ ♔h6 0-1

Rapid development: 4 ♗g5

1 d4 f5 2 c4 ♘f6 3 ♘c3 d6 4 ♗g5

This is an attempt to avoid the usual variations as 4...g6 5 ♗xf6 exf6 is unfavourable for Black (in the variation 1 d4 f5 2 ♗g5 ♘f6 3 ♗xf6 exf6 Black would play ...d7-d5 to equalize the space in the centre, and maybe ...♗d6; whereas here he is committed to the inferior moves ...d7-d6 and ...g7-g6).

Therefore Black normally plays **4...♘bd7** once again.

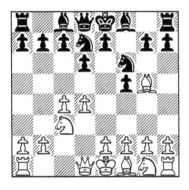

Now White has to choose between a central break with ♕c2 and e2-e4, or else stabilize things with e2-e3, after which he can castle kingside or queenside according to preference.

J.Berkvens-D.Reinderman
Dutch League 2006

1 d4 f5 2 c4 ♘f6 3 ♘c3 d6 4 ♗g5 ♘bd7 5 ♕c2 g6 6 e4

White decides on immediate action in the centre.

6...fxe4 7 ♘xe4 ♗g7 8 ♘f3 c5!

The most aggressive riposte. Black strikes at the d4-point which has been weakened by both e2-e4 (because e2-e3 can no longer defend it) and ♕c2.

9 ♘c3

Castling queenside allows Black dynamic chances after 9 0-0-0 ♕a5. The a2-pawn is hanging and if White defends it with 10 ♔b1 then ideas of a pin with ...♗f5 appear.

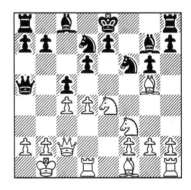

For example, 10...cxd4 11 ♘xf6+ ♘xf6 12 ♖xd4 0-0 13 ♗d3 e5! 14 ♖xd6 (White could stay in the game with 14 ♖h4! e4 15 ♗xf6 exd3 16 ♕c3) 14...e4 15 ♖xf6 (if 15 ♗xe4 ♘xe4 16 ♕xe4 ♗f5

and wins) 15...♗xf6 16 ♗xf6 exd3 17
♕c3 ♕xc3 18 ♗xc3 ♗h3 19 ♘e5 ♗xg2
20 ♘g4 ♖f4 (but not 20...♗xh1 21 ♘h6
mate!) 21 ♘h6+ ♔f8 22 ♖g1 ♖xf2 0-1
F.Ladron de Guevara-J.Lopez Martinez,
Donostia 2008.

Alternatively, 9 ♘xf6+ ♘xf6 10 d5
(Black is comfortable after 10 dxc5
♕a5+ 11 ♗d2 ♕xc5 12 ♗d3 0-0)
10...0-0 11 ♗d3 e6! (liquidating the
strong pawn on d5) 12 dxe6 ♗xe6 13
0-0, as in D.Sutkovic-B.Kovacevic, Zadar
2007, and now after 13...♕d7 14 ♖ae1
♖ae8 I can't see any advantage for
White. On the contrary, Black can try to
take the initiative by preparing ...d6-d5
or starting some action down the f-file.
9...♕a5

Now White has to reckon with
10...cxd4, when 11 ♘xd4? would drop
the bishop on g5.
10 d5 b5!

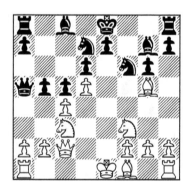

Undermining the d5-pawn gives
Black good counterplay as 11 cxb5
♘xd5 leaves White clearly in trouble
due to his smashed pawns.

After **1 d4 f5 2 c4 ♘f6 3 ♘c3 d6 4
♗g5 ♘bd7 5 ♕c2 g6**, instead of 6 e4,
White can keep things solid with **6 e3
♗g7 7 ♘f3** (another move order is 4
♘f3 g6 5 ♗g5 ♘bd7 6 e3 ♗g7 7 ♕c2).

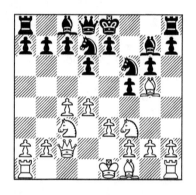

Here I like the idea of **7...c6!?**. Now 8
♗e2 0-0 9 0-0-0 ♕a5 or 9 0-0 e5 looks
perfectly okay for Black.

Instead after **8 0-0-0 ♕a5** Black gen-
erates queenside counterplay without
having loosened his centre with ...e7-
e5. In the game **A.Bitalzadeh-F.Nijboer**,
Wijk aan Zee 2009, Black went on to
outplay his opponent:
**9 h4 h6 10 ♗xf6 ♘xf6 11 h5 g5 12 ♗d3
0-0**

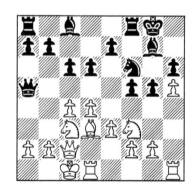

13 ♔b1

Or 13 ♘d2 ♘g4 14 ♖hf1 e5 – only now! – and Black was active in L.Polugaevsky-V.Malaniuk, USSR Championship, Moscow 1983

13...♗d7 14 c5 ♖f7 15 e4

Black has plenty of play for the pawn after 15 ♗xf5 ♗xf5 16 ♕xf5 ♘d5 17 ♕c2 ♘xc3+ 18 bxc3 ♖af8 with ideas of 19...g4.

15...fxe4 16 ♘xe4 ♘xe4 17 ♗xe4 ♗e6 18 a3 ♕b5 19 ♖d2 ♕b3 20 ♕xb3 ♗xb3 21 ♖e1 ♖f6 22 ♖e3 ♗f7 23 g4 ♖f8 and White's position was wobbling due to his loose pawns.

Another approach for White after **1 d4 f5 2 c4 ♘f6 3 ♘c3 d6 4 ♗g5 ♘bd7** is that of **5 e3 g6**

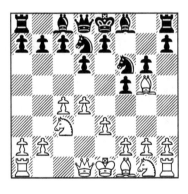

and then **6 ♘ge2**.

Here White can also castle kingside, but Black has little to fear after 6 ♗d3 ♗g7 7 ♘ge2 e5 8 f3 0-0 9 0-0 c6. After all, Black has an equal share of space in the centre, and the plan of advancing with g2-g4 is only appropriate if White has castled queenside. Not that this

stopped White from playing 9 0-0 c6 10 g4? in O.Poisson-C.Philippe, Noyon 2008. He was predictably crushed: 10...fxg4 11 f4 (he should at least get the pawn back with 11 fxg4, though that means he has needlessly weakened his kingside) 11...♕e8 12 fxe5 dxe5 13 ♕c2 b6 14 ♘g3 ♗b7 15 ♖f2 exd4 16 exd4 ♘h5! (a nicely-calculated tactic allows the Dutch bishop to conquer d4) 17 ♘xh5 (the last chance to hold things together was 17 ♖xf8+) 17...♗xd4! 18 ♘f4 ♕e5! 19 ♘e4 ♖xf4 20 ♗xf4 ♕xf4 21 ♔f1 ♗xf2 22 ♘xf2 ♘e5 23 ♖e1 ♖f8 0-1. Two pawns down and facing a big attack, White called it a day.

6...e5

Black sets up the typical Dutch mobile pawn centre.

7 ♕c2 ♗g7

Now we'll follow the game **S.Feller-M.Bartel**, European Team Championship, Novi Sad 2009:

8 0-0-0 0-0 9 h3

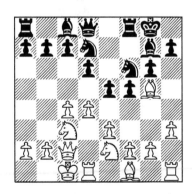

White has taken on a rather defensive stance in the centre. He is content if things remain quiet there so that he can stab from the wings with g2-g4, etc.

9...exd4

An interesting decision. Black concedes his pawn centre in order to generate counterplay. Either he will get e5 for his knight or an open e-file for his rook.

10 ♘xd4

After 10 exd4 c6 11 f3 ♖e8 12 g4 ♘f8 13 d5 (instead 13 ♘g3 ♘e6 is awkward for White, seeing that 14 ♗h4? loses to 14...g5) 13...h6 it is dynamically balanced.

10...♘e5 11 ♗h4

Or 11 c5 d5 12 c6 ♕d6!?.

11...c6 12 f3 ♕e8!

Breaking the pin and preparing the development of the bishop on e6.

13 ♗e2 ♗e6 14 ♘xe6 ♕xe6

Normally White would be happy to have the bishop-pair and a possible target on d6, but here the black pieces are very compact in the centre and the c4- and e3-pawns are both vulnerable.

15 g4?!

After 15 ♕b3 (with the threat of 16 ♖xd6! ♕xd6? 17 c5+ winning the black queen) 15...♖ae8! White should make do with 16 ♕b4 ♘f7 17 ♗f2, with a defensible game, as 16 ♕xb7 ♘fd7, planning 17...♘c5, gives Black a huge initiative for the pawn.

15...fxg4 16 hxg4 ♘xf3! 17 ♗xf6

If 17 ♗xf3 then 17...♕xe3+ regains the piece with an extra pawn or two.

17...♗xf6 18 ♘e4 ♘g5

Here 18...♗e7! defends everything whilst keeping an extra pawn.

19 ♘xd6 ♕xe3+ 20 ♔b1 ♖ad8?

A routine move. Instead 20...c5! would deny White the attacking resource of ♗c4+ and ♕h2.

21 c5 b6 22 cxb6 axb6 23 ♗c4+ ♔g7 24 ♕h2 h5!

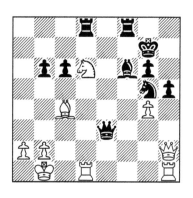

Realizing he has misplayed things Bartel is wise enough to force simplification to kill off the white attack.

25 gxh5 ♕e5 26 hxg6 ♕xh2 27 ♖xh2 ♗e7 ½-½

After 28 ♖hd2 ♘f3 29 ♘f5+ ♖xf5 30 ♖xd8 ♗xd8 31 ♖xd8 ♘e5 Black will pick up the g6-pawn.

Even if White establishes a winning position in the Dutch, there are often huge obstacles to be overcome.

Part Three:
2 ♘f3 ♘f6 3 ♗g5

M.Armstrong-T.Rendle
Liverpool 2007

1 d4 f5 2 ♘f3 ♘f6 3 ♗g5

A slightly irritating move for fans of the Leningrad. Black was gearing up to push his g-pawn and suddenly finds that 3...g6 allows 4 ♗xf6 exf6. Not that this is so bad for him; but White is a bit better and, besides, putting the bishop on g7 ceases to be a good idea as the f6-pawn would shut it in. Hence 3 ♗g5 has ruled out the Leningrad.

And so we have to play a Classical Dutch style move:

3...e6 4 ♘bd2 ♗e7 5 c3

After 5 ♗xf6 ♗xf6 6 e4 it's important that Black doesn't concede the centre, as 6...fxe4 7 ♘xe4 is rather pleasant for White. Correct is 6...0-0! 7 ♗d3 (if 7 e5 ♗e7 White has more space, but Black has the bishop-pair) 7...d5 8 exf5 exf5 9 0-0 ♘c6 10 c3 ♕d6 11 ♖e1 a6 (to rule out ♗b5 and ♗xc6 as an option in the fight for control of the e5-square) 12 b4 g5! and Black was active in O.Kirsanov-N.McDonald, London 2001.

5...b6!?

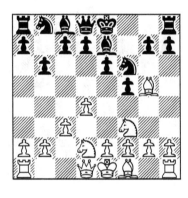

A natural but rather underestimated move.

6 e3

Critical is 6 ♗xf6 ♗xf6 7 e4, but Black can stand his ground in the centre with 7...0-0 8 ♗d3 d5 9 exf5 exf5. After 10 0-0 he can try to justify the ...b7-b6 move with 10...c5 and then ...♘c6 with pressure against d4. Black has the best minor piece on the board in the shape of the dark-squared bishop.

If this seems too shaky for Black, he could avoid ...c7-c5 and consolidate with 10...♕d6, ...♘c6 and ...♗d7. The ...b7-b6 move might not be relevant, but Black is solid anyhow. Also note that if White attacks f5 with ♕c2 at any point, ...g7-g6 looks secure enough.

6...♗b7 7 ♗d3 ♘e4

The exchange of bishops eases Black's game. The question is whether White will be able to claim any advantage once he evicts the knight from e4 and advances e3-e4.

8 ♗xe7 ♕xe7 9 0-0 0-0 10 ♕c2 ♘xd2 11 ♘xd2 ♕g5 12 e4 f4!

Bypassing the e4-pawn. A good point of this is that it prevents White gaining space himself with 15 f4.

Instead your author once tried 12...fxe4? 13 ♘xe4 ♕h6, thinking he could do some attacking down the f-file, but it was White's rook that did the attacking after 14 ♖ae1! ♘c6 15 ♖e3 g6 16 ♖h3 in S.Conquest-N.McDonald, British League 2000.

13 f3

A good positional move is 13 e5, but unfortunately for White it allows mate in one.

13...e5

Stopping 14 e5 and increasing his

influence over the dark squares.

14 a4

The old game S.Dittmann-L.Alster, Dresden 1957, saw instead 14 ♖fd1 ♘c6 15 ♕a4 ♕e7 16 ♗a6 ♗xa6 17 ♕xa6 ♔h8 18 ♘b3 exd4 19 cxd4 d5 20 ♖ac1 (or 20 exd5 ♘b4 21 ♕c4 ♕d6 and 22...♘xd5 gets the knight on to a brilliant square) 20...♘b4 21 ♕b7 ♖fc8 22 a3 ♖ab8 23 ♕xa7 ♖a8 ½-½.

14...a5 15 ♘c4 d6 16 ♖fd1 ♘d7

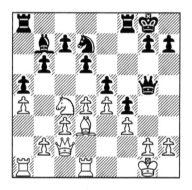

17 dxe5

The opening has gone well for Black, but now he becomes rather careless.

17...dxe5?

I assume that IM Thomas Rendle, the stronger player, was keen to avoid the variation 17...♘xe5 18 ♘xe5 ♕xe5 19 ♗c4+ ♔h8 20 ♗d5 when after the exchange of bishops he would have few winning chances. And so he retook on e5 with the pawn, to keep two minor pieces on the board. At first glance, this seems a good idea as he has 18...♘c5 next move. But White crossed this plan with a devastating tactic:

18 ♘xa5! ♗c8

White has won a clean pawn and has a rook on the seventh rank to boot after 18...Rxa5 19 Bc4+ Kh8 20 Rxd7. The text at least keeps some tension.

19 Bc4+ Kh8 20 Nb3 Nf6 21 a5

Black is utterly lost on the queenside, and the only open file in the centre is controlled by White. The only hope of creating counterplay is the Dutch pawn on f4.

21...bxa5 22 Rxa5 Bb7 23 Rxa8 Bxa8 24 Nc5 Qh5 25 Nd7!

Instead White could have played a slow move such as 25 b4, keeping all his advantages, but the game move is objectively best.

The exchange of knights would kill off all Black's counterplay. Therefore he tries his luck with a piece sacrifice to mobilize the Dutch pawn:

25...Bxe4!?

This should lead to a quick defeat, but as a practical try it can't be bettered.

26 fxe4 Ng4

Threatening h2 as well as a fork with 27...Ne3. But Black is already a

piece down, and his rook is hanging – surely it must all end in disaster?

27 h3

White is mated in six moves after 27 Nxf8? Qxh2+ 28 Kf1 Qh1+ (actually Black just needed to see 28...Ne3+ when he can win the white queen with check) 29 Ke2 Qxg2+ 30 Ke1 Qg1+ 31 Ke2 (or 31 Bf1 Qg3+ 32 Kd2 Qe3 mate) 31...Qf2+ 32 Kd3 Qe3 mate.

27...Ne3 28 Qe2?

A natural reply as the exchange of queens wins at once for White. There was a cast-iron win, but it required a bit of tactical calculation: 28 Nxf8! Nxc2 29 Rd8 (threatening discovered checkmate) 29...h6 30 Ng6+ Kh7 31 Bf7!. The killer. Black can only stop checkmate with 32 Rh8 by giving up his queen with 31...Qxg6 when 32 Bxg6+ Kxg6 leaves him with no hope at all in the endgame.

28...f3!

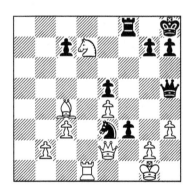

The Dutch pawn breaks through the white defences.

29 Qxe3??

After 29 gxf3 Rxf3 intending

30...♖g3+ Black has a dangerous initiative, while if 29 ♖f1 (pinning the pawn) 29...♘xf1 30 ♕xf1 ♖d8 Black also has enough fight for a practical game.

29...f2+ 30 ♔h2 ♕xd1 31 ♘xf8

White had calculated this far, and saw that he remains a piece and a pawn up after 31...f1♕ 32 ♗xf1 ♕xf1 33 ♕f3. But Black had seen further:

31...♕g1+ 32 ♔g3 f1♘+! 0-1

The discovered attack wins the white queen after 33 ♗xf1 ♕xe3+.

Two paradoxes:

1. If Black hadn't blundered with 17...dxe5? he probably wouldn't have won the game, as the correct 17...♘xe5 would have led to a very drawish position.

2. If White hadn't played the incisive move 25 ♘d7! he would probably have won the game.

Was this simply a lucky win for Black, with the opening having no bearing on the result? No: Black's aggressive play with 11...♕g5 and 12...f4 showed his aggressive intent. He then proved tactically the stronger.

Part Four: An Early b2-b3

1 d4 f5 2 b3

I think that most players would underestimate this odd-looking move, which makes it rather dangerous. Also, there is hardly any theory on it. It might

surprise you that the six highest-rated Elo players on my database who have faced 2 b3 have all lost! I guess that's not so surprising when fans of 2 b3 include Topalov and two other players rated over 2600.

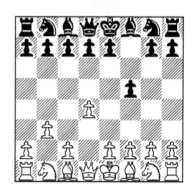

Well, Black can develop in normal Leningrad style with **2...♘f6 3 ♗b2 g6** when White might transpose to familiar lines; the only thing that makes me anxious is **4 e3 ♗g7 5 ♗e2!? d6 6 h4** with a quick advance against g6 with 7 h5. But we can respond to the wing attack in classic style by seeking counterplay in the centre:

6...♘e4!?

If now 7 ♘d2 c5! 8 ♘xe4 fxe4 and Black has more space as the e4-pawn stops White developing with ♘f3.

Critical is 7 h5 when 7...♘c6?! 8 ♘d2 ♘xd2 9 ♕xd2 e5 10 d5 ♘e7 11 f4! looked good for White in A.Fier-J.Alonso-Moyano, Sabadell 2009, due to the awkward pin on e5.

Instead 7...c5! appears the best way to get counterplay. Black can increase the pressure on d4 with ...♘c6 and maybe try a disruptive ...♛a5+. For example, 8 ♘h3 (or 8 ♘d2 ♛a5, while 8 hxg6 hxg6 9 ♖xh8+ ♗xh8 doesn't give White anything) 8...♘c6 9 ♘f4 ♛a5+ 10 ♔f1 cxd4 11 exd4 e5! and Black takes the initiative in the centre.

White might also fianchetto with **1 ♘f3 f5** (more on this move order in Chapter Eight) **2 b3 d6 3 d4**.

J.Kraai-H.Nakamura
Foxwoods 2007

1 ♘f3 f5 2 b3 d6

Nakamura aims to set up a mobile centre with 3...e5, 4...♘f6, 5...g6 and 6...♗g7. So GM Jesse Kraai establishes a foothold on d4.

3 d4 g6 4 ♗b2 ♗g7

Black plays Leningrad Dutch moves, but White isn't interested in a transposition to familiar lines, which could be reached after, say, 5 g3 ♘f6 6 ♗g2 0-0 7 c4 c6 8 0-0 ♛a5.

5 e3 ♘f6 6 ♗c4 e6 7 0-0 0-0 8 ♘bd2

♔h8 9 ♛e2 ♘c6 10 ♖ad1 ♛e7 11 ♖fe1

An exceptionally solid development by White, whose initial aim seems to be to restrain the tactical talent of his opponent. Only once all his pieces are centralized does he try to edge forwards slowly on the queenside.

11...♗d7 12 a3 ♖ae8 13 b4 ♘h5!?

Black is provoked by his opponent's restrained play into a sharp attacking bid on the kingside.

On the other hand, after the centralization 13...♘e4! it seems to me that Black has a good game with no risk: for example, 14 b5 ♘d8 15 ♗b3 (15 ♗d3 ♘c5, exploiting the pin on b2, is a nuisance for White, due to ideas of 16...♘xd3 or 16...♘a4) 15...♘xd2 16 ♖xd2 ♘f7 17 ♖dd1 e5, expanding in the centre.

14 ♗b3 g5 15 ♘e5!

Uncovering an attack on h5.

15...♘xe5?

Critical was 15...dxe5! 16 ♛xh5 when Black gets blown away if he tries to grab a pawn in the centre: 16...exd4?! 17 exd4 ♘xd4? 18 ♘c4! (very powerful)

18...♘xb3 19 ♘e5! (the point – d7 and 20 ♘g6+ are threatened) 19...♗xe5 20 ♗xe5+ ♔g8 21 ♖xd7! ♕xd7 22 ♕xg5+ ♔f7 23 ♕g7 mate!

However, here 16...g4! is much stronger, so that if 17 dxe5? ♖d8! threatens to trap the white queen with 18...♗e8. Instead there are complications after 17 h3 ♖f6 (again threatening to reap the queen, but this time with 18...♖h6) 18 ♕h4 gxh3 19 dxe5 ♖g6 20 ♕xh3 ♘xe5. In this way Nakamura might have justified his 13th.

16 dxe5 ♕f7 17 ♘c4!

A fine move. Black can't give away the e5-square to a white piece, and now that b2 is defended, 18 exd6 is a threat. Therefore Black has to make a positional concession.

17...d5

After 17...b5 18 ♘a5 dxe5?! 19 ♖xd7! ♕xd7 20 ♕xh5 White has won two pieces for a rook.

18 ♘d2

Back again. Now that the e5-point has been secured by White, the black knight finds itself paralysed on h5, unable to advance to f4 or retreat to f6.

18...b5 19 ♖f1 g4 20 ♗d4 ♖g8 21 g3!

Not only stopping any pawn thrust with 21...f4, but also the first step in a plan to seize the initiative with an attack down the h-file.

21...a5 22 c3 a4 23 ♗c2 ♕g6 24 ♗d3 ♖b8 25 ♔g2 ♗f8 26 ♖h1 ♘g7

Black has evacuated his knight from the dangerous h5-square, but can't prevent a breakthrough there by White.

27 h3 gxh3+ 28 ♖xh3 h5 29 ♖dh1 ♗e8 30 ♔f1 ♗e7 31 ♘f3 ♕g4 32 ♗c5 ♗xc5 33 bxc5 ♖f8 34 ♖h4 ♕g6 35 g4 ♕h6 36 g5 ♕g6 37 ♖g1 ♔g8 38 ♘d4 ♔f7

Instead 38...c6 would secure the queenside, but White could always target h5 by putting his queen on d1, bishop on e2 and knight (via e2) on f4.

39 c6!

Nakamura probably allowed this move hoping to get at least a semblance of counterplay, rather than waiting for White to pile up on h5. But Kraai kept his cool and eventually ground out the win:

39...♖b6 40 ♗xb5 ♔g8 41 f4 ♗f7 42 c4 dxc4 43 ♕xc4 ♖d8 44 ♕xa4 ♗e8 45 ♔f2 ♕f7 46 ♖c1 ♕e7 47 ♖c3 ♖d5 48 ♕c4 ♕d7 49 a4 ♖b8 50 ♕b4 ♔h7 51 ♔g3 ♗g6 52 ♖h2 ♗e8 53 ♔h4 ♔g6 54 ♖d2 ♗f7 55 ♖c4 ♖a8 56 ♘f3 ♖b8 57 ♖cd4 ♕e8 58 ♖xd5 exd5 59 ♘d4 ♗e6 60 ♕c5 ♖a8 61 ♖a2 ♗f7 62 ♗d3 ♕f8 63 ♕xf8 ♖xf8 64 a5 ♖a8 65 a6 ♗e6 66 ♖b2 ♗c8 67 ♖b7 1-0

An impressive game by White once his opponent had fallen into a bind. However, Black also had his chances.

Chapter Five

Sidelines in the Leningrad Variation

1 d4 f5 2 g3 ♘f6 3 ♗g2 g6

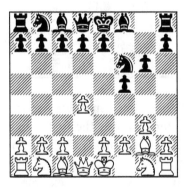

0-0 0-0 6 b4

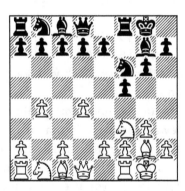

In this chapter we look at four ways in which White avoids the main line of the Leningrad Variation, broadly speaking by going b2-b4, b2-b3, c2-c3 or opting for ♘h3 rather than ♘f3.

Part One:
White plays b2-b4

1 d4 f5 2 g3 ♘f6 3 ♗g2 g6 4 ♘f3 ♗g7 5

The idea of a quick b2-b4 versus the Leningrad became popular for White in tournaments of the early 2000s. It initially caused Black some problems, and in many games he was squashed on the queenside before he could generate any counterplay elsewhere on the board. This seems to have got players questioning the value of trying to establish a d6- and e5-pawn centre against it.

The Stonewall System comes to the rescue

As a result of this soul searching, the strongest Dutch experts such as Nakamura and Bartel have been championing the Stonewall-style set-up – and with considerable success. The Stonewall, in which Black puts a pawn on d5, is a clear and easy system to learn here. White is denied any space advantage in the centre, and his control of territory on the queenside is challenged by the active black pieces.

There are two distinct preludes to playing ...d7-d5 as Black, depending on whether White plays an early c2-c4:

a) 1 d4 f5 2 g3 ♘f6 3 ♗g2 g6 4 ♘f3 ♗g7 5 0-0 0-0 6 b4 ♘c6!; and

b) 1 d4 f5 2 g3 ♘f6 3 ♗g2 g6 4 ♘f3 ♗g7 5 c4 0-0 6 b4 c6!.

In either case Black will soon play ...d7-d5.

One of the good things about the Stonewall for Black is that it is comparatively easy to choose the right squares for the pieces – you can't go too far wrong if you use them either to defend the hole on e5 or to support the pawn on d5.

Scheme One: 5 0-0 0-0 6 b4 ♘c6!

L.Fressinet-C.Renner
German League 2008

1 d4 f5 2 g3 ♘f6 3 ♗g2 g6 4 ♘f3 ♗g7 5 0-0 0-0 6 b4

A sound space-gaining move, but it might help our understanding of Black's plan, and certainly our morale, if we frame this move as a positional mistake which leaves a gaping hole on the c4-square. After all, White has already removed two potential defenders of c4 with 1 d4 and 3 ♗g2, so isn't the third 'desertion' with 6 b4 showing a lack of respect for a key central square?

6...♘c6!

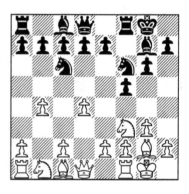

I like this energetic move that threatens b4. It is the first step in getting the knight in contact with c4.

7 b5

In the next game we examine 7 c3.

7...♘a5 8 ♕d3

With the positional threat of 9 c4, getting rid of the hole on c4, to say nothing of 9 ♗d2, hitting the black knight.

8...d5!

This is a vital part of Black's strategy. He leaves himself with a hole on e5, but in return he gets a grip on the light squares and an equal share of space in the centre.

9 ♘bd2 ♗e6

Reaffirming his hold over the contested c4-square. If Black had played 9...♗d7, the bishop could be hit by 10 ♘e5. On e6 the bishop will be attacked by ♘g5, but it retreats to d7 – and then what is the white knight doing on g5?

10 ♗a3 a6

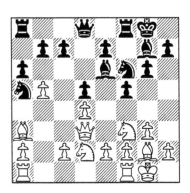

Continuing to undermine White's queenside pawns.

11 ♘g5 ♗d7 12 ♕e3 ♗h6?!

Instead 12...♘e4 looks fine for Black.

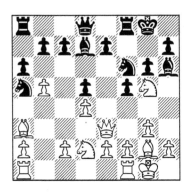

13 f4

He should have tried 13 ♗xe7 ♗xg5 14 ♕a3!: for example, 14...♕e8 15 f4 ♗h6 16 ♗xf6 ♖xf6 17 ♕xa5 when

White has a loose position, but also an extra pawn.

13...♖e8 14 bxa6

After various delaying tactics White has to concede the a6-square to the black rook.

14...♖xa6 15 c4

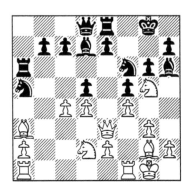

Fressinet plays for complications rather than risk being worn down on the light squares.

15...dxc4 16 ♗b4 ♘c6 17 ♗c3 ♘g4 18 ♕f3 ♗g7 19 ♔h1 h6 20 ♘h3 b5!

The c4-square still maintains its magic. White can only regain his pawn at the cost of letting the black knight into e3.

21 ♕d5+ ♔h7 22 ♕xb5 ♖b6 23 ♕c5

Instead 23 ♕xc4 ♘e3 wins the exchange, or even better 23...♘xd4! 24 ♗xd4 ♗b5, intending 25...♗xd4. A similar trick occurs in the game.

23...♘e3 24 ♘xc4 ♘xg2

The exchange of a knight for White's light-squared bishop is a strategical coup for Black, which is immediately followed by a tactical one:

25 ♔xg2 ♘xd4!

One of the little known rules of chess strategy is that when a player is weak on a complex of squares of one colour, the winning tactical breakthrough often comes on a square of the other colour.

26 ♘e5

Black has a decisive attack against the white king after 26 ♘xb6 cxb6 27 ♕b4 ♗c6+ 28 ♔f2 ♕d5.

26...♘xe2

Now besides all his problems with his king, White is also a pawn down.

27 ♖fd1 ♕a8+ 28 ♔f2 ♘xc3 29 ♕xc3 ♗e6 30 ♘g1 ♕a7 31 ♔f1 ♖d6 32 ♘e2 ♖ed8 33 ♖dc1 ♖d2 34 ♖c2 ♖d1+ 35 ♖xd1 ♖xd1+ 36 ♔g2 ♗d5+ 37 ♔h3 ♕f2 38 ♘c1 ♗g2+ 0-1

The final triumph of Black's light-square strategy that began with 6...♘c6 (or was it with 1...f5?). Moreover, it would have been unjust if the bishop which has sat at g7 since move four got all the glory after 39 ♔h4 ♗f6 mate! Though to be fair it was this bishop that supported 25...♘xd4.

It's for moments like this that we play the Dutch. All the horrible defeats fade from memory when we can scalp one of the best players in the world. A player rated 2422 doesn't often win, especially with Black, against a 2676-rated opponent.

V.Anand-H.Nakamura
Wijk aan Zee 2010

1 d4 f5 2 g3 ♘f6 3 ♗g2 g6 4 ♘f3 ♗g7 5 0-0 0-0 6 b4 ♘c6 7 a3

World Champions know a thing or two about strategy. In contrast to the 7 b5 ♘a5 of the previous game, Anand stands his ground on the queenside, rather than letting the black knight come into contact with the hole on c4.

7...d5 8 ♗b2 ♘e4

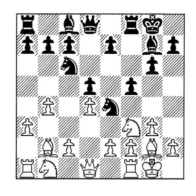

Black continues his light-square strategy. Formerly, the e4-square isn't an outpost square, as White can chase the knight away with f2-f3. But how difficult it is for White to arrange this! If the knight leaves f3 then Black would be able to seize space with ...e7-e5.

9 ♘bd2 ♗e6

The final link in Black's light-square opening strategy. Note that rather than support his pawn centre with ...c7-c6 and ...e7-e6, as typically occurs in the Stonewall, Black has occupied these squares with a knight and bishop. He therefore has what might be called an ultra-dynamic Stonewall. The drawback is that if challenged by c2-c4, the black pawn on d5 can't be supported by another pawn. Therefore Black will be obliged to concede the centre. But never mind: the bishop on e6 will then have a rather nice square on d5.

10 e3

Anand's plan is also starting to unfold: ♘bd2, e2-e3, ♕e2 and then c2-c4, when he takes apart Black's centre in a very precise manner, without giving him the ghost of counterplay.

A counterattacking plan on the king-side with 10...h6 and 11...g5 would be too slow; therefore Nakamura decides to break things up on the queenside.

10...a5!

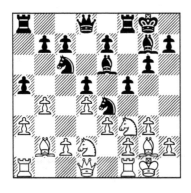

Finally White is obliged to advance

b4-b5. The drawback from Black's point of view is that he can no longer reply ...♘a5, the square being occupied by his own pawn.

11 b5 ♘a7 12 ♕e2

Anand decides he needs to bring his pieces into action on the queenside as quickly as possible: hence ♕e2 and ♖fc1. Instead he could have taken a time out for 12 a4, but Black has enough counterplay with 12...c6 13 bxc6 bxc6 when he can play or further prepare ...c6-c5 next move.

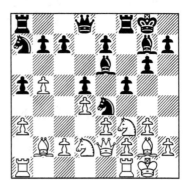

12...a4!

A very useful move. White is prevented from consolidating on the queenside with a3-a4 and then c2-c4 – therefore he can't claim a nice, neat positional advantage on the queenside. We shall consider further the value of 12...a4 once we have seen how the battle unfolds.

13 ♖fc1 c6!

So Black is able to support his pawn on d5 with another pawn after all, despite his ...♘c6 and ...♗e6 moves – see the comment at move nine.

14 bxc6 bxc6 15 c4 ♘c8!

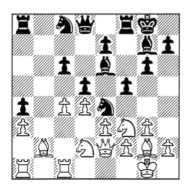

The knight is to be recentralized via d6. If White prevents it with 16 c5 then he has forfeited any pressure along the c-file.

16 ♗c3 ♘cd6 17 cxd5 ♘xc3!

An important lesson in the art of exchanging. Black exchanges before White can play ♗b4 when he has solid domination of the queenside. Furthermore, Nakamura wants the a5-square for his queen.

18 ♖xc3 ♗xd5!

The active choice. Besides, after 18...cxd5 the reply 19 ♘g5 is awkward. Having maintained the pawn on c6, where it obstructs any action by the white rooks along the c-file, Nakamura is ready to build up pressure of his own with moves like ...♕a5 and ...♖ab8, exploiting the b-file.

19 ♘e5!

Anand, however, has other ideas. He won't give Black the necessary time to build up a queenside initiative.

19...♗xg2 20 ♔xg2 ♗xe5 21 dxe5

It looks as if Black's game is about to collapse, but Nakamura is ready to counterattack.

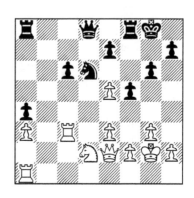

21...♕a5! 22 ♖ac1

Or 22 ♖xc6 ♕d5+ 23 ♕f3 ♘e4 24 ♖c2 ♕xe5 with equality.

22...♕xe5 23 ♖xc6 ♕b2

Black's kingside is slightly fragile due to the move 1...f5, but on the other hand, the black pieces are active and the a3-pawn is a target. Anand is obliged to simplify to a draw.

24 ♕d3 ♖fd8 25 ♖1c2 ♕b5 26 ♕xb5 ♘xb5 27 ♘b1 ♖d3 28 ♘c3 ♘xc3

Black's knight is trapped after 28...♘xa3? 29 ♖a2.

29 ♖2xc3

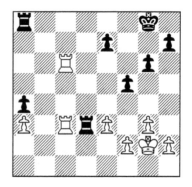

29...♖dd8!

If Nakamura's 17th move was a lesson in the art of exchanging, this move is a lesson in the art of *not* exchanging.

After 29...♖xc3 30 ♖xc3 the black rook can be tied to the defence of the a4-pawn with 31 ♖c4 and then the white king can edge forwards. So Nakamura keeps a pair of rooks on the board in order to gain counterplay with 30...♖db8 and 31...♖b3. Anand prevents this, but the a3-pawn then becomes a target.

30 ♖b6 ♔f7 31 ♖b4 ♖d2 32 ♖cc4 ♖d3 33 ♖xa4 ♖xa3 ½-½

Well, Black got a lot of exclamation marks in the game above, and he still had to play precisely to keep the balance. But then handling the black pieces against a player such as Anand is no easy task, and Nakamura achieved a draw without too much trouble. Note that if White had played less accurately, Black would have achieved winning chances.

Note too the excellence of the move 12...a4. It fixed the a3-pawn as a target and cleared the a5-square for the queen – both vital aspects of Black's queenside counterplay. It thus prevented White from consolidating with a3-a4, when the bishop on b2 could be activated with ♗a3. When Anand tried to bring the bishop into the game by the route ♗c3 and ♗b4, Black was able to lop it off with ...♘xc3.

A move such as 12...a4 easily passes

by an average player – but what an important move it is!

Scheme Two: 5 c4 0-0 6 b4 c6!

M.Dziuba-M.Bartel
Warsaw (rapid) 2009

1 d4 f5 2 g3 ♘f6 3 ♗g2 g6 4 ♘f3 ♗g7 5 c4 0-0 6 b4

White has already played c2-c4, so 6...♘c6? fails to 7 b5 ♘a5 8 ♕d3 when White keeps his queenside pawns ship-shape, because Black hasn't exerted control over c4. So a different plan is required:

6...c6!

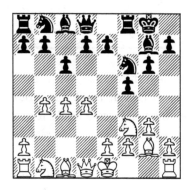

The rule is:

When White has played b2-b4, but delayed c2-c4 – Black plays ...♘c6. However, if White has played c2-c4 and then b2-b4 – Black plays ...c7-c6.

But in both cases, Black is intent on a light-square strategy. His general deployment of pieces and pawns is almost identical.

7 0-0 ♘e4

The knight jumps into the centre as a prelude to setting up the Stonewall centre.

8 ♗b2 d5 9 ♘bd2 ♗e6

A familiar square for the bishop.

10 ♕c2 a5!

As in the Nakamura game, Black's a-pawn is enlisted to undermine the white queenside pawns.

11 a3 ♘d7

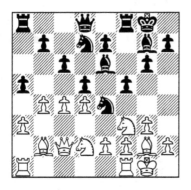

A key difference with the ...♘c6 variation is that Black can't put pressure on b4 to force a liquidation on the queenside.

12 e3 h6 13 c5

A committal move. White now intends 14 ♘b3 when after 14...axb4 15 axb4 he will profit the most from the opening of the a-file. Or 14...a4 15 ♘a5 and the a4-pawn is hanging.

13...a4!

And so Bartel prevents ♘b3 and blocks the queenside, temporarily at least. Now in view of the fixed pawn structure, the plan of advancing b4-b5 suggests itself for White, and ...e7-e5 suggests itself

for Black.

Don't forget the ...a5-a4 move in this type of pawn centre – it almost always comes in handy.

14 ♘e1 ♘xd2 15 ♕xd2 ♗f7 16 ♘d3 ♕b8 17 ♖ab1 ♖c8!

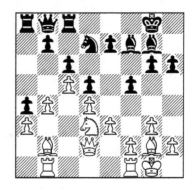

Bartel isn't attracted by 17...e5 as it leads to exchanges that would leave him weak on the dark squares. And so he overprotects his c6-pawn in preparation for his next move.

18 ♗a1 b5 19 cxb6

After 19 f4 ♗e6 (but not 19...♘f6 20 ♘e5 ♘e4 21 ♗xe4 fxe4 22 f5! when White has a breakthrough) the game would probably be a draw as it's so blocked up. But Dziuba is ambitious and a very sharp struggle ensues.

19...♘xb6

The black knight finally has its sights on the c4-square.

20 ♘e5 ♗xe5

In giving up the 'Indian' bishop, Bartel is putting absolute trust in his Stonewall structure to shield his dark-square weaknesses.

21 dxe5 ♘c4 22 ♕d4 ♗e6!

It is essential to prevent 23 e6.

23 ♕h4

White temporarily wins a pawn as both e7 and h6 are hanging.

23...♔f7 24 ♕xh6 ♖h8

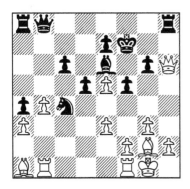

When calculating and assessing this position before playing 18...b5, Bartel would have had to convince himself that it is Black, not White, who profits from the opening of the h-file. The Dutch is truly a complex opening.

25 ♕f4 ♘xa3 26 ♖bc1 ♘c4 27 ♗c3

Black won't be able to queen the passed a-pawn as the a1-square is guarded three times by the white pieces. Meanwhile White is ready to break open the centre with 28 e4, when after 28...dxe4 29 ♗xe4 Black is collapsing along the c-file: not only is the c6-pawn directly hanging, but the knight on c4 can be targeted by retreating the bishop from c3.

27...♕g8!

Bartel therefore forgets about the queenside and looks for counterplay with threats against the white king and queen.

28 h4

Here 28 e4? runs into 28...g5! 29 ♕f3 ♕h7 30 h3 g4! exploiting the h-file to the maximum.

28...♕h7 29 e4

White is understandably keen to stay active, but this leads to disaster. He should play a waiting move with, say, 29 ♖fd1 and leave it to Black to start the next round of tactics.

29...dxe4 30 ♗xe4 g5!

31 ♕f3

Taking on g5 loses the bishop or the king, but now Black breaks through along the g-file.

31...gxh4 32 g4 ♖ag8 33 ♔h1 ♖xg4 34 ♗xc6 h3

Missing the elegant win 34...♖g3! Then 35 fxg3 hxg3+ followed by mate on h2, or 35 ♕f4 ♖hg8 36 ♔h2 ♖8g4, trapping the queen: 37 fxg3 hxg3+! Finally, 35 ♕e2 ♖h3+ 36 ♔g1 (36 ♔g2 f4! defends h3 followed by a killer check on the g-file) 36...♖g8+ 37 ♗g2 ♕g6 38 f3 ♕g3 and 39...♕h2+ topples g2.

35 ♖g1 ♖hg8 36 ♖g3 ♖xg3 37 fxg3 ♕h6

38 ♖e1 a3 39 ♔h2 ♕g5 40 b5 ♕g4 41 ♕f2 ♖d8 42 ♖e4 ♕g5 43 ♖f4 ♖d3 44 ♗a1 ♖d2

Winning the white queen. My score of the game gives the gobbledegook 45 ♗c3 ♖d3 and then **0-1**.

That was a really hard fight that shows the dynamic chances available to Black in the Dutch. White was a very highly-rated player, but he seemed a bit bemused by the uncompromising play of his opponent.

The conclusion is clear: the Stonewall gives Black excellent counterchances against White's b2-b4 system.

Part Two:
b2-b3 without c2-c4

First of all, after **1 d4 f5 2 g3 ♘f6 3 ♗g2 g6 4 ♘f3 ♗g7 5 0-0 0-0 6 c4 d6 7 b3** Black can equalize or more with **7...e5!** due to White's weakness along the a1-h8 diagonal.

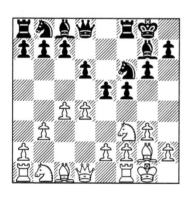

For example, 8 dxe5 (or 8 ♗b2 e4,

shutting in the bishop on g2) 8...dxe5 9 ♘xe5? ♘fd7 10 ♕d5+ ♔h8 loses material for White, as does 9 ♕xd8 ♖xd8 10 ♘xe5? ♘g4. Instead, after 9 ♗e3 ♕xd1 10 ♖xd1 ♖e8 11 ♘c3.e4 12 ♘d4 c6 Black had more space in M.Mielczarski-V.Malaniuk, Mielo 2005.

This means that White can't get an effective b2-b3 and ♗b2 formation with c2-c4 also played, unless he first enters the main line, say, with 7 ♘c3 c6 or 7...♘c6, and even then b2-b3 isn't very special for White. So if White wants to avoid the main line, but get in b2-b3 and ♗b2, he needs to delay c2-c4. (Lest there's any confusion, I'm talking about b2-b3 and ♗b2 ideas in the Leningrad structure after four or five moves, not sidelines such as 1 d4 f5 2 b3.)

The main position under consideration here is:

1 d4 f5 2 g3 ♘f6 3 ♗g2 g6 4 ♘f3 ♗g7 5 0-0 0-0 6 b3

If White had played c2-c4 I could direct you to the relevant coverage in our next two chapters. Here, however, the c-pawn stays resolutely at home. If now 6...d6 7 ♗b2 and we are in a dilemma, especially if we wanted to play the 7 c4 ♘c6 variation, as there's no pawn on c4 to attack.

Returning to the position after 6 b3, I have checked out all the ideas for Black that have been played here in international chess, including 6...d6 and the interesting move 6...c5!?. However, there's no escaping the fact that Black scores best when he adopts a Stonewall set-up:

6...♘e4 7 ♗b2

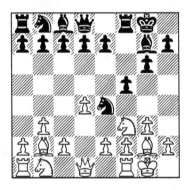

7...d5

Before we go any further, I think I will save you at least one nasty loss if I remind you that:

After White's b2-b3 you should never set up a Stonewall with ...d7-d5 and ...c7-c6 if White can still play his bishop to f4.

That means that when ...d7-d5 is played the white bishop must either already be on b2 or on c1 but obstructed from going to f4, as is the case if ♘bd2 has been played.

For example, imagine that the game has started as above with 1 d4 f5 2 g3 ♘f6 3 ♗g2 g6 4 ♘f3 ♗g7 5 0-0 0-0 6 b3. Now 6...♘e4! is the recommended move...

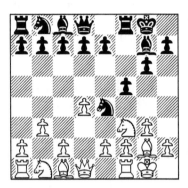

...so that 7 ♗b2 d5 sets up the Stonewall.

White could instead play 7 ♗f4?!, but it is a harmless and bad idea. Black could respond with 7...c5 trying to exploit White's looseness on the a1-h8 diagonal, or 7...d6 and then arrange ...e7-e5 to drive away the white bishop. What Black shouldn't do is play 7...d5? as the white bishop on f4 suddenly becomes securely placed and puts pressure on c7 and e5.

Here's an even worse scenario for Black. Imagine that after 6 b3 Black plays 6...d5? 7 c4 c6. All is well for him if White plays 8 ♗b2, but much stronger is 8 ♘c3 ♔h8 9 cxd5 cxd5 10 ♗f4! ♗e6 11 ♕d3 ♘bd7 12 ♘b5 and Black is under great pressure along the c-file, with 13 ♘c7 already looming.

Returning to the position after 6 b3 and Black's correct 6...♘e4, White can delay putting the bishop on b2 with 7 c4. In that case Black should play 7...c6. Then 8 ♗b2 d5 is fine, while 8 ♗f4 is still no good as Black has kept the option of renouncing the Stonewall with 8...d6, when the bishop on f4 is badly placed – a target for ...e7-e5 or even ...g6-g5 or ...♘h5.

A.Nechaev-N.Firman
Khmelnitsky 2008

1 d4 f5 2 g3 ♘f6 3 ♗g2 g6 4 ♘f3 ♗g7 5 0-0 0-0 6 b3 ♘e4 7 ♗b2

The bishop has gone to b2, which means no more ♗f4 and so...

7...d5

...we can safely set up the Stonewall. Both of White's bishops now find themselves on blocked diagonals.

8 c4 c6

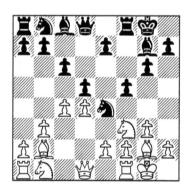

This game actually started 1 d4 f5 2 g3 ♘f6 3 ♗g2 g6 4 ♘f3 ♗g7 5 0-0 0-0 6 c4 c6!? which is a respectable move order for Black against 6 c4, assuming that he is happy to play the variation that normally arises after 6...d6 7 ♘c3 c6 as given in Chapter Six. Only here did White swerve from the mainline with 7 b3, giving us the Stonewall after 7...♘e4 8 ♗b2 d5. But I've changed the move order for the sake of our discussion of a delayed c2-c4 by White.

9 ♘bd2

Or 9 ♘c3 ♗e6 10 ♕c2 ♘d7 11 ♖ad1 a6!? 12 ♘xe4 fxe4 13 ♘e5 when 13...♕b6?! didn't have the intended effect as White was able to ignore the pressure on d4 and get some edge with 14 ♘xd7 ♗xd7 15 ♗a3! ♖f7 (15...♗xd4? 16 c5 wins) 16 ♗c5 ♕d8 17 f3 in R.Lubczynski-M.Bartel, Illes Medes 2006. Instead 13...♘xe5 14 dxe5 ♕a5!? looks at least equal for Black: 15 ♗c3 ♕c7, attacking e5, or 15 a3 ♖ac8.

9...♗e6

One of the good features of Black's structure is that the light-squared bishop finds a useful role in bolstering d5 and putting pressure on c4.

10 ♖c1

After 10 ♕c2 a5 11 ♖ad1 a4 12 ♘xe4 fxe4 13 ♘e5 ♘d7 14 ♘xd7 axb3 15 axb3 ♕xd7 16 c5 ♗h3 Black was striving for the win in L.Guidarelli-M.Bartel, Illes Medes 2006.

10...♘d7 11 e3

Upon 11 cxd5 the recapture 11...cxd5 hands the c-file over to the white rook, whereas 11...♗xd5! keeps it closed and activates the bishop.

11...h6

Probably better than 11...♔h8. Both moves neutralize ideas of White playing

♘xe4 followed by ♘g5 to harass the bishop on e6 (after 11...♔h8 because the retreat ...♗g8 is possible). But 11...h6 also gives Black the option of ...g6-g5 to generate kingside counterplay. And since he wants to put his queen on f7 in some lines it is good to have the g5-square actually guarded against ♘g5.

12 ♕e2

White's long-term plan is to advance in the centre with f2-f3 and e3-e4. For this purpose he puts his queen on e2 and manoeuvres his knight from f3 to d3. It is extremely difficult to carry out this strategic task without making a tactical or positional slip: Black's pieces are active and ready to pounce if White weakens any point or allows his pieces to become uncoordinated. For example, if 12 ♘e1, preparing f2-f3, Black has 12...♕a5!, hitting a2 and d2, when 13 ♘xe4 fxe4 is an unfavourable exchange for White.

One question is whether the white queen should go to e2 or c2, where she helps defend the queenside. After 12 ♕c2 play might go 12...a5 13 a4! (to rule out the pawn-ram 13...a4) 13...♕e8 (the queen heads for an active post on f7) 14 ♖fd1 ♖c8 (at first glance this might seem something of an irrelevance, as Black is in principle always going to answer c4xd5 with ...♗xd5, keeping the c-file closed; but as we shall see, the rook comes in handy on c8 to support ...c6-c5) 15 ♘e1 ♕f7 and now 16 f3?! ♘xd2 17 ♖xd2 c5! is a fine example of a favourable dissolution of the Stonewall pawn structure by Black. So White should play 16 ♘d3, when 16...g5! gives Black good kingside counterplay. I borrowed these moves from a similar position (11...♔h8 had been played instead of 11...h6) in the game A.Kharitonov-E.Bareev, Sochi 1987.

12...a5!

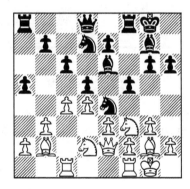

13 ♘e1?

Objectively speaking, White isn't necessarily worse after he lets Black open lines on the queenside. On the other hand, any smooth advantage he might have gained from preparing the f2-f3 and e3-e4 advance has vanished. Instead he has to act on the defensive.

Best was 13 a4 as in the above extract, when Black could have carried on with the plan of ...♕e8 and ...♕f7, or else tried to benefit from the absence of the white queen from c2 with 13...♕b6.

13...a4 14 ♘d3 axb3 15 axb3 ♕b6!

Here there is no doubt that the black queen belongs on b6, where she can combine her pressure with that of the rook along the a-file.

16 c5 ♕b5 17 b4 b6

Trying to whittle away the white pawns.

18 f3 ♖a2?

Black makes a blunder... and ends up winning the game. Objectively speaking he should make do with 18...♘xd2 19 ♕xd2, with approximate equality.

19 ♘b1?

To be successful in the Dutch you don't have to understand everything that's going on – you just have to be less confused than the opponent. Due to an inability to handle the tension of the situation, or a less-developed ca-

pacity to calculate variations, White comes off worse in the complications.

After 19 fxe4! the recapture 19...fxe4 is just good for White following 20 ♖xf8+ ♘xf8 21 ♘xe4, so Black should try the exchange sacrifice 19...♖xb2 20 ♖f2! ♖xd2 (otherwise d5 drops to ♘f4, etc) 21 ♕xd2 dxe4, but then 22 ♘f4 looks rather good for White.

19...bxc5

After the sequence 19...♖xb2 20 ♕xb2 ♕xd3 21 ♖fe1, the threat to trap the queen with 22 ♗f1 is awkward for Black.

20 fxe4

He might have tried to hold on with 20 ♕d1 cxb4 21 ♕b3.

20...dxe4 21 ♘c3 exd3 22 ♕f2 ♖xb2! 23 ♕xb2 ♕b8

Black's strong bishop-pair, queenside pressure and passed pawn are worth more than the exchange. White soon crumbles:

24 dxc5 ♘xc5 25 ♕a3 ♘b3! 26 ♖b1 ♘d2 27 ♘a4 ♘xb1 28 ♖xb1 ♕a7 0-1

Part Three: 4 c3 or 4 ♘d2

1 d4 f5 2 g3 ♘f6 3 ♗g2 g6 4 c3

As Black is going to fianchetto on g7, White hastens to reinforce the d4-pawn. His motto seems to be 'no weaknesses at all!' However, there springs to mind the contradictory motto about not being able to make an omelette without breaking any eggs. With his safety-first approach White forfeits, for at least the time being, the moves c2-c4 and ♘c3, which are regarded in most other systems as the best way to put pressure on the black centre.

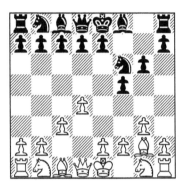

On the other hand, Black mustn't be complacent as after 4...♗g7 5 ♕b3 he has been prevented from castling. Once again I'm going to recommend the Stonewall approach. It secures the right to castle and takes a considerable amount of central space. And if our opponent decides after all to attack us with c3-c4, he will be a tempo down on most lines where White plays c2-c4 in one go. The drawback, of course, is the hole on e5, which will have to be carefully watched.

S.Bromberger-M.Bartel
Warsaw (rapid) 2007

1 d4 f5 2 g3 ♘f6 3 ♗g2 g6 4 c3 ♗g7 5 ♕b3

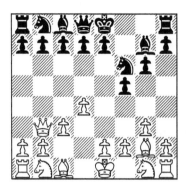

If White is going to justify his restrained play this is surely the moment. The queen prevents Black from castling and attacks the b7-pawn.

5...♘c6 6 ♘h3

The opportunities for the knight on b1 have been restricted by c2-c3, so White reserves the f3-square for it. This is a good decision, as in the Stonewall set-up the king's knight has the excellent f4-square.

6...d5 7 ♘f4

Attacking the d5-pawn for a third time.

7...e6 8 ♘d2 0-0 9 0-0 b6

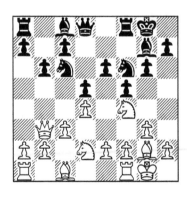

Black is deploying his pieces in methodical style. He only needs two or three more moves – 10...♕e8 to guard e6 and then 11...♗a6; or maybe 10...a5!? to begin with, to seize space, and then ...♕e8 and ...♗a6 – and he will have solved the eternal problem of how to effectively develop his queen's bishop.

If White plays 10 ♘f3, intending to exert his control over e5 with 11 ♘d3 and 12 ♗f4, Black could respond 10...♕e8, but as White intends 11 ♘d3 in any case, when the attack on e6 vanishes, Black might as well reply 10...♘e4! and after 11 ♘d3 go 11...♗a6.

10 ♕a4

White tries to throw a spanner in the works by attacking c6 and preventing ...♗a6. Nonetheless, he should have played 10 ♘f3 with ♘d3, ♗f4, etc.

10...♕e8

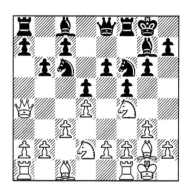

11 ♖e1 ♗d7 12 ♕c2 ♖c8!

Nimzowitsch would have loved this mysterious rook move. The black rook moves to a hopelessly-blocked file. The reason why soon becomes clear.

13 ♘f3 ♘e4

The black knight is usually bril-

liantly placed on e4 in this structure. It isn't technically speaking an outpost square, but arranging the move f2-f3 is difficult for White – or rather we should say White can't play f2-f3 without spending a lot of energy, both in time and in the reduced cohesion of his pawn structure.

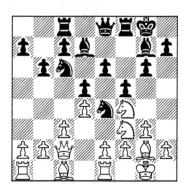

In contrast, the e5-square, which really is a hole in the black centre, is contested by the black bishop on g7, as well as the knight on c6; therefore it is currently a less stable outpost for a white knight than e4 is for the black knight.

14 b3??

This is completely against the spirit of the 'safety-first' 4 c3. White weakens himself along the c-file when Black has made it clear with ...♖c8 that he intends to arrange ...c7-c5. It still wasn't too late for 14 ♘d3.

14...♘a5! 15 ♘e5 c5 16 f3

So White achieves his aim of driving the black knight away from e4, but unfortunately for him it can go forwards as well as backwards...

16...♘xc3! 17 ♕xc3 cxd4 18 ♕xd4 ♘c6 19 ♘xc6 ♖xc6!

White would have one or two swindling chances after 19...♗xd4+ 20 ♘xd4 e5 21 ♘xf5 ♗xf5 22 ♘xd5 thanks to his dark-squared bishop.

20 ♕d3 ♗xa1 21 ♗a3 ♗g7

After this Bartel still has to fight to subdue his opponent, whereas immediately decisive was 21...♗c3! as 22 ♖c1 fails to 22...♕c8! 23 ♗xf8 ♗d4+ 24 ♕xd4 ♖xc1+ 25 ♔f2 ♕xf8.

22 ♗xf8 ♕xf8 23 e4 ♖c3 24 ♕d1 ♕c5+ 25 ♔h1 fxe4 26 fxe4 d4 27 e5 ♗c6 28 ♕g4 ♗xg2+ 29 ♔xg2 ♕c6+ 30 ♔h3 ♖c2 31 ♕xe6+ ♕xe6+ 32 ♘xe6 d3 33 ♘d4 ♖xa2 34 e6 ♔f8 35 ♖f1+ ♔e8 36 ♘b5 ♗e5!

The black pieces have stalemated the white knight.

37 ♖e1 d2 38 ♖xe5 d1♕ 39 ♘c7+ ♔e7 0-1

A closely-related approach to that employed by Bromberger is **1 d4 f5 2 g3 ♘f6 3 ♗g2 g6 4 ♘d2 ♗g7 5 c3**. Before we come on to that, we should note that here White can also play for an immediate advance in the centre with 5 e4. However, it is ineffective as long as Black is aware that he should gambit the d5-pawn for the initiative with 5...fxe4 6 ♘xe4 ♘xe4 7 ♗xe4 d5 8 ♗g2 ♘c6 9 c3 (instead 9 ♘e2 ♗g4 10 c3 e5 11 dxe5 ♘xe5 12 f4 ♘c6 transposes) 9...e5!

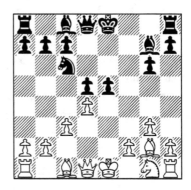

10 dxe5 ♘xe5 11 f4 ♗g4! 12 ♘e2 (too risky for White is 12 ♕xd5 ♕xd5 13 ♗xd5 ♘d3+ 14 ♔f1 0-0-0 or 12 ♕a4+ ♕d7 13 ♕xd7+ ♘xd7 14 ♗xd5 0-0-0; in both cases Black has huge activity for the pawn) 12...♘c6 13 h3 (still too dangerous for White is 13 ♕xd5 ♕xd5 14 ♗xd5 0-0-0 when the black rook come into the game far too quickly) 13...♗e6, intending 14...♕d7 and 15...0-0-0 with a full mobilization for Black.

I.Khenkin-M.Bartel
European Team
Championship, Novi Sad 2009

1 d4 f5 2 g3 ♘f6 3 ♗g2 g6 4 ♘d2 ♗g7 5 c3

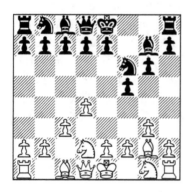

A more reliable choice than 5 e4.

5...♘c6 6 ♘h3

Instead 6 e4 fxe4 7 ♘xe4 ♘xe4 8 ♗xe4 d5 9 ♗g2 e5 transposes to our analysis, above, of 5 e4.

6...0-0

So White has avoided ♕b3 and let Black castle. Is he feeling generous? No, he is hoping to lure Black into a positional trap.

7 ♘f3

If Black merrily sets up a Stonewall pawn structure with 7...d5, White can respond vigorously with 8 ♘f4 ♘e4 9 h4 when there are ideas of 10 h5 to undermine g6 and begin an attack. It's not the end of the world, and some players would relish defending the black side; but I think most of us want to take the initiative ourselves when we play the Dutch.

The reason we play ...d7-d5 is to block out the white queen on b3 and secure the right to castle. It isn't automatically the best move in this pawn structure.

7...d6!

Bartel keeps things flexible: already he threatens to create a centre with 8...e5 and leave the knight on h3 in limbo by denying it the f4-square.

8 d5 ♘e5

9 ♘d4

White has stopped ...e7-e5 (or so he thinks) and imposed a grip on the centre. If Black plays passively, say with 9...♗d7, then 10 ♘f4 and 11 ♘fe6 follows. In that case White's strategy would be a complete triumph, and Black would have failed the first test in the Leningrad Dutch: don't let White post an unchallenged knight on e6.

9...c5!

This game features an intriguing battle between statics and dynamics. White is trying to impose solid control on the position with his schematic plan of exploiting the hole on e6, whereas Black is seeking to disrupt the pawn structure, even if it involves a sacrifice. You might recall Bartel's similar pawn sacrifice versus Elsness in the 2 ♘c3 chapter. Black is required to be adventurous in the Dutch.

10 dxc6 ♘xc6 11 ♘xc6 bxc6 12 ♗xc6 ♖b8 13 ♘f4

Khenkin gets the knight into the centre before it is shut out by 13...e5.

13...e5 14 ♘d5 f4!

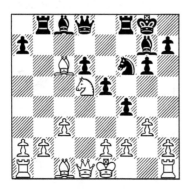

Our good friend, the Dutch pawn-ram. Black must continue to play vigorously, as otherwise White will consolidate his extra pawn.

15 ♘xf6+

Not surprisingly, Khenkin's priority is to get castled, and he avoids breaking up the residence with g3xf4. Taking on f6 first allows ...♗h3 to be answered by ♗g2, as occurs in the game.

Computers like to grab pawns, but 15 gxf4 ♘xd5 16 ♕xd5+ (or 16 ♗xd5+ ♔h8 17 fxe5 ♗xe5) 16...♔h8 gives Black good practical chances. If White allows ...e5xf4 then another pawn-ram appears, and besides he only has one extra pawn. Moreover, after 17 fxe5 ♗xe5 the f2-square is exposed and can be attacked further by ...♕h4. As well as his unsafe king, White is hampered by the pressure on b2 which prevents him developing his bishop from c1, which

means the rook on a1 also remains shut in.

15...♕xf6 16 0-0 ♗h3 17 ♗g2 ♗xg2 18 ♔xg2 ♕e6!

Seizing control of the light squares before White can play ♕d5. Black's mobile centre and active rooks give him full compensation or more for the pawn. In contrast, White's rooks are passive and his bishop remains confined to c1. Still, Black has to keep pressing forwards or Khenkin will unwind his position, when the extra pawn might have the last laugh.

19 f3 e4!

20 ♕c2

The bishop's control of f4 is illusory as 20 ♗xf4 ♖xb2 is bad for White, in view of 21...exf3+ exposing e2 to attack. If instead 20 gxf4 then 20...e3 keeps the bishop entombed on c1, after which Black can regain the pawn on f4.

20...fxg3 21 hxg3 ♖b5!!

An excellent way to add energy to the black attack, as after 22 ♕xe4 ♖e5! the e2-pawn drops. Secondly, the rook supports Black's next move which adds another pawn to the onslaught. And, finally, as we shall see in the critical variation at move 26, the chance to play ...♖h5 might have won for Black.

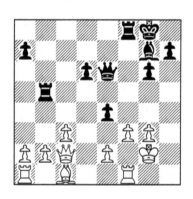

22 ♗f4 g5 23 a4 ♖a5 24 ♗d2 e3 25 ♗e1

The bishop is better here than on c1, as it defends g3, is out of the way of the rook on a1, and can be freed with c3-c4.

25...g4 26 fxg4?

A blunder, although even after 26 ♕e4 gxf3+ 27 exf3 ♖e5 Black has a strong passed pawn to add to his initiative.

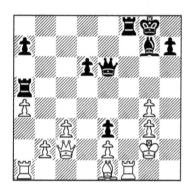

26...♖xf1?

On the ChessPublishing.com website Glenn Flear points out that 26...♖xg4! should be winning: for example, 27 ♖xf8+ (or 27 ♕b3+ ♔h8 28 ♖xf8+ ♗xf8 29 ♕b8 ♕xe2+ 30 ♔g1 ♖f5) 27...♗xf8 28 ♖d1 ♖h5 29 ♖d4 ♕h3+ 30 ♔f3 ♕h1+ and Black wins the bishop, as 31 ♔g4 ♖e5 intending 32...♕h5+ is mate in two.

After the text move White managed to escape, with the game concluding in perpetual check:

27 ♔xf1 h5 28 c4 ♖g5 29 ♕d3 ♕xg4 30 ♕xe3 h4 31 ♗c3 ♗xc3 32 bxc3 ♖e5 33 ♕d3 ♕h3+ 34 ♔e1 ♕h1+ 35 ♔d2 ♕xa1 36 ♕g6+ ♔f8 37 ♕xd6+ ♖e7 38 ♕d8+ ♔f7 39 ♕d5+ ♔f6 40 ♕d6+ ♖e6 41 ♕f8+ ♔g6 42 ♕g8+ ♔f6 ½-½

A fine example of how the dynamism of the Dutch can ruffle even the strongest players of White.

Part Four:
White Plays ♘h3

There are two main ideas in this section. Firstly, an aggressive approach with a quick ♘h3 and ♘f4 that does without an early c2-c4: 1 d4 f5 2 g3 ♘f6 3 ♗g2 g6 4 ♘h3 ♗g7 5 ♘f4.

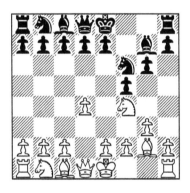

And, secondly, a positional approach in which White delays ♘h3 with a sequence such as 1 d4 f5 2 g3 ♘f6 3 ♗g2 g6 4 c4 ♗g7 5 ♘c3 0-0 6 ♘h3.

Before we examine those, here is a sharp line that may involve ♘h3: 1 d4 f5 2 g3 ♘f6 3 ♗g2 g6 4 h4. After 4...♗g7 5 h5 ♘xh5 6 e4 e6!

(see following diagram)

7 exf5? exf5 8 ♖xh5 ♕e7+ 9 ♗e3 gxh5 10 ♘c3 c6 11 ♕xh5+ ♕f7 White

had insufficient compensation for the exchange in N.Sulava-V.Malaniuk, Montecatini Terme 1994.

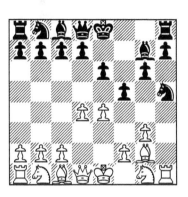

Instead White should try 7 e5! when Beim gives the variation 7...0-0 8 ♗f3 ♕e8 9 ♗xh5 gxh5 10 ♘h3 d6 11 ♘f4 dxe5 12 ♘xh5 ♕c6 as 'unclear'. In fact 13 d5 then looks awkward for Black, as there is the idea of ♘xg7 and ♗h6+. So maybe 12...♔h8!? should be preferred when 13 ♗h6 ♕c6 is indeed unclear, perhaps good for Black. This time after 14 d5 ♕xd5 the white rook won't get to h7 after the exchanges on d5 and f8. Or if 14 ♖h4 ♖d8 15 ♗g5 ♖xd4 and Black is doing well.

If after 4...♗g7 White settles for the solid 5 ♘h3, then 5...d6 6 c3 (after 6 ♘f4 e5 the h2-h4 move is looking irrelevant) 6...c6 7 ♘d2 (if 7 ♕b3 then 7...e5 followed by ...♕e7 and ...♗e6) 7...e5 8 ♘c4 ♗e6! 9 dxe5 ♗xc4 10 exf6 ♗xf6 with equality or more for Black in R.Knaak-A.Illner, German League 1993.

Finally, after the ultra-early 1 d4 f5 2 ♘h3 we can play as we do against 2 ♘f3 and 3 ♗g5, with 2...♘f6 3 ♗g5 e6.

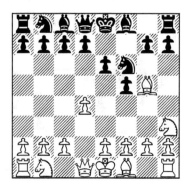

After 4 e3 h6!? 5 ♗xf6 ♕xf6 6 ♘f4 g5 7 ♘d3 ♗g7 8 h4 g4 9 g3 d6 10 ♗g2 e5 11 c3 c6 12 a4 ♗e6 13 b4 ♘d7 14 b5 ♖c8 Black had achieved a powerful centralization in V.Korchnoi-A.Muzychuk, Marianske Lazne 2009.

The aggressive approach: a quick ♘h3-f4

O.Rodriguez Vargas-G.Danner
Dresden 2010

1 d4 f5 2 g3 ♘f6 3 ♗g2 g6 4 ♘h3 ♗g7 5 ♘f4 ♘c6!

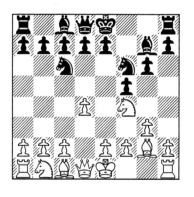

Answering ♘f4 with ...♘c6 has become an important motif in Black's handling of various lines with a quick ♘h3. Ideally he would like to drive the knight back from f4, but in the real world he has to accept the opportunity of getting his queen's knight to a square which is almost as good as f4. And this isn't so bad either: after all, Black often has difficulty developing his queenside pieces in the Dutch, so landing the knight on e5 is nothing to be sneezed at.

6 h4

White threatens 7 h5 to smash up the black kingside, when 7...g5 is answered by 8 h6!.

Instead 6 d5 ♘e5 7 ♘c3 takes some territory, but without the support of a pawn on c4 the white centre can be dissolved with 7...c6!: for example, 8 e4 d6 (note how Black takes action in the centre before castling) 9 0-0 0-0 10 exf5 ♗xf5 11 ♘ce2 ♕b6 12 ♘d4 ♗g4 13 f3 ♗d7 and the pawn couldn't be maintained on d5 in T.Vasilevich-V.Malaniuk, Odessa 2007.

Similarly after 6 d5 ♘e5 7 h4, the white centre can be removed at once with 7...c6! when 8 ♘c3 cxd5 9 ♘cxd5 ♘xd5 10 ♕xd5 e6 was already fully equal for Black in K.Stupak-M.Bartel, Warsaw 2008.

6...e5!

This is the idea: the black knight will now become well centralized and involved in the defence of g6.

7 dxe5 ♘xe5 8 h5 c6

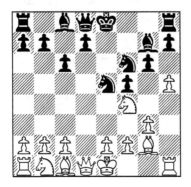

Calmly played. Black builds a big centre which will take control of the light squares, shutting out the white bishop on g2. Now White gains nothing from 9 hxg6 hxg6 10 罩xh8+ 盒xh8. His rook on a1 is just as far from the h-file as the black rook on a8. Also fruitless is 9 h6 as after 9...盒f8 the kingside is blocked and the pawn on h6 is a liability for White. We might say that in this type of position the pawn should only advance to h6 if having to retreat the bishop to f8 causes a significant problem to Black's development. Obviously that isn't the case here.

9 c4

The poisonous 9 ②d2 is examined in the next game.

9...0-0

Safer seems to be the alternative 9...d6 10 ②c3 (if 10 ②d2 豐e7 11 ②f3 ②fg4) 10...豐e7 11 h6 盒f8 12 b3 盒d7, albeit still with quite double-edged play. But the Austrian Georg Danner is a real fighter.

10 hxg6 hxg6 11 ②c3 豐e7 12 盒e3 g5 13 ②h5 ②xh5 14 罩xh5 f4

Black achieves his famous pawn-ram. On the other hand, his kingside is full of holes. A real Dutch mêlée is in progress.

15 gxf4 gxf4

16 ②d5?

We've seen it all before: White buckles under the pressure of playing against the Dutch. He fails to tread the narrow path between being too aggressive and too passive, which the complications of the opening obscure from him.

The position remains absolutely unclear after, say, 16 盒d4 f3 17 盒h1 fxe2 18 豐c2 (or 18 豐xe2 d6 19 盒xe5 盒xe5 20 盒e4 豐g7 21 盒h7+ 含f7) 18...②f3+ 19 盒xf3 盒xd4, etc.

16...豐e8!

After this calm retreat White has a knight, bishop and rook all hanging. The wild fight continues, but Black is playing with an extra piece.

17 罩h1 fxe3 18 豐c2 exf2+ 19 含d2 cxd5 20 豐h7+ 含f7 21 盒xd5+ 含e7 22 豐xg7+ 含d8 23 c5 豐e7 24 豐g3 d6 25 罩af1 盒d7 26 罩h5 罩c8 27 b4 豐f6 28 e3 0-1

A.Vaisser-M.Bartel
European Championship,
Istanbul 2003

1 d4 f5 2 g3 ♘f6 3 ♗g2 g6 4 ♘h3 ♗g7 5 ♘f4 ♘c6 6 h4 e5 7 dxe5 ♘xe5 8 h5 c6 9 ♘d2!?

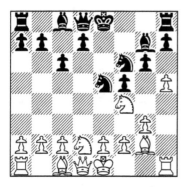

White begins a plan of development which has caused Black a lot of problems. We have said that Black intends to fortify his light squares with ...d7-d5. White's knight move aims to put pressure on the dark squares with ♘f3, ♗e3 and ♗d4. If he succeeds in exchanging off the bishop on g7, Black's position will be full of holes.

9...d5 10 ♘f3

Challenging the guardian of the g6-pawn. Black has to reinforce it with the other knight.

10...♘fg4 11 ♘xe5 ♘xe5 12 ♗e3! ♗f6?!

He should play 12...♕d6! – see below.

13 hxg6 hxg6 14 ♖xh8+ ♗xh8 15 ♗d4!

The pin on f6 is very annoying. Black

also has to reckon with ♗xe5 and ♘xg6 at some point

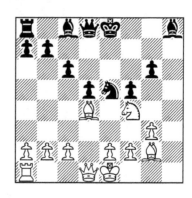

15...♕a5+??

A horrible check – the queen moves away from the defence of the kingside and centre.

16 c3 ♔f7 17 ♕b3 b6 18 0-0-0 ♗e6 19 ♖h1 ♗g7 20 ♖h7 1-0

White's plan of seizing the dark squares has been a complete triumph. One of e6, e5 or g7 is going to drop off.

Having seen this game, with the two question marks appended to 15...♕a5, you have probably made the mental note that 'the one thing Black must never, ever do in this variation is give a check with the queen on a5'. Incidentally, that is how our intuition about what is a good or bad move or idea in an opening line or a pawn structure develops. A valuable asset, but sometimes intuition becomes prejudice – when it makes us reject a good move just because it doesn't look right.

Some months after Bartel's debacle

in the game above, Black's play was strengthened by the centralizing **12...♕d6** (rather than 12...♗f6). Play went 13 ♗d4 ♗f6 (the immediate 13...g5? 14 h6! ♗f6 15 ♘h5 would be bad for Black, but putting the bishop on f6 threatens 14...g5, driving away the white knight, as the riposte h5-h6 is no longer available; the upshot is that White is obliged to take on g6, which eases the pressure on the black kingside) 14 hxg6 hxg6

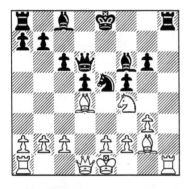

15 ♖xh8+ ♗xh8 16 c3 (Black looks to be okay too after 16 ♕d2 ♘c4 17 ♕c3 ♗xd4 18 ♕xd4 ♕e5 19 0-0-0 ♕xd4 20 ♖xd4 ♘e5) 16...♗d7 and Black held the draw in G.Murawski-M.Kuziola, Krakow 2003.

The positional ♘h3 method with c2-c4

If White delays the ♘h3 move by playing c2-c4, it probably indicates that he isn't looking for a quick attack on the kingside or a violent fight in the centre. Instead he wants to establish the familiar cramping pawn centre with d4-d5.

A.Karpov-V.Malaniuk
Tallinn (rapid) 2005

1 d4 f5 2 g3 ♘f6 3 ♗g2 g6 4 c4 ♗g7 5 ♘c3 0-0

Black makes all the normal Leningrad Dutch moves. He doesn't commit himself to ...d7-d6 until White reveals more about his intended opening scheme.

6 ♘h3

This is why we have waited for White to reveal his cards. If 6 ♘f3 we would have continued 6...d6, but now we respond with our anti-♘h3 move.

6...♘c6! 7 0-0 d6

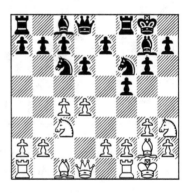

The move ...d7-d6 is part of Black's standard plan of development, but it does allow the white knight control over the hole on e6.

8 d5 ♘e5 9 b3 c5

Black grabs some space on the queenside. Objectively White is perhaps a bit better, but I find this variation quite attractive for Black. It feels good to know what you are doing, and here Black has a clear plan of preparing the ...b7-b5 pawn break.

10 ♘f4 ♘e8!?

The knight heads for c7 where it protects the e6-square and adds its weight to a ...b7-b5 advance. White also has to watch out for a 11...♘xc4 cheapo.

11 ♕c2 ♘c7 12 ♗d2 a6 13 a4

Now it wouldn't be a good idea to let the positional maestro obtain a clamp on the b6-square with 14 a5 and so:

13...b6!

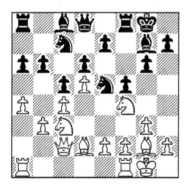

Now there is nothing to stop Black achieving the ...b6-b5 pawn break. Therefore Karpov gives up on preventive chess and focuses on his own pawn advance in the centre.

14 ♘d3

Clearing the way for f2-f4 and also planning to eliminate the knight on e5 before the pressure on the c4-pawn is increased by ...b6-b5.

14...♖b8 15 ♖ae1 b5 16 ♘xe5 ♗xe5 17 f4 ♗g7 18 e4 bxc4 19 bxc4

Black has the open b-file and the c4-pawn has been undermined. On the other hand, immediate measures have to be taken before White steam rollers through the centre with 19 e5.

19...e5!

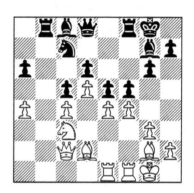

A great defensive but also counter-attacking move. If now 20 dxe6 ♘xe6 and the black knight heads for d4.

**20 a5 ♗d7 21 fxe5 ♗xe5 22 ♔h1 ♘e8!
½-½**

Mission accomplished on the queenside, the knight heads back to f6 where it is involved in the struggle for the e4-square. Black is at least equal here but chose to call it a draw.

A rather short game, but it reveals the ideas available to both players in the positional ♘h3 system.

S.Klimov-E.Berg
Maastricht 2009

1 d4 f5 2 g3 ♘f6 3 ♗g2 g6 4 ♘h3 ♗g7 5 ♘f4 ♘c6

The game begins with the moves of

the aggressive ♘h3 system...

6 c4

...but then White shows his willingness to enter into the positional line. What should Black do?

6...d6!

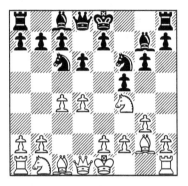

An important moment as Berg had to choose which pawn structure to adopt in the middlegame. Incidentally it shows the danger of a 'one size fits all' approach to opening strategy. As Black plays 5...♘c6 and then 6...e5! versus 6 h4, and gets awarded with an exclamation mark, it's easy to simplify matters to 'Black always plays ...♘c6 and ...e7-e5 against ♘h3 and ♘f4'. The human brain likes to find rules and precepts, and they come in very handy in chess. But we shouldn't rely on them so much that we become blind to the needs of the specific position in front of us.

After 6 h4 Black is threatened with 7 h5, so 6...e5 makes sense. It negates the potential attack on g6 and brings the knight to an active square. On the other hand, Black has weakened his pawn structure – but we are a tempo

ahead in the central battle because White has played 6 h4. In contrast, after 6 c4 White hasn't 'wasted' a move putting the pawn on h4. And if there is no threat of h4-h5, why should Black still insist on 6...e5, compromising his pawns?

Hence the strongest players tend to prefer 6...d6.

7 d5 ♘e5 8 ♕c2

White is going to avoid ♘c3 in favour of ♘d2. Also, in contrast to the Karpov game, he puts his bishop on b2 where it has more central scope but less influence over events on the queenside.

8...c5 9 ♘d2 ♕a5

The black queen takes an immediate interest in the queenside action. Already White has to reckon with 10...b5, so he covers the b5-square a second time.

10 a4 0-0 11 0-0 ♖b8 12 ♖a3 ♕c7

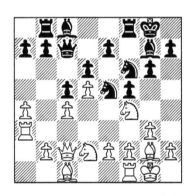

And now the lady retreats, happy to have persuaded the white rook to go to a bad square.

13 b3 b6 14 ♗b2 a6 15 ♘f3

White is willing to compromise his pawns in order to open the e-file and increase his pressure on e6.

15...♞xf3+ 16 exf3 b5 17 cxb5 axb5 18 axb5 ♜xb5 19 ♜e1 ♜b7 20 ♝f1

Shut in on g2, the bishop seeks a post on c4 where it at least defends a couple of important pawns.

20...♜a7 21 ♜xa7 ♛xa7 22 ♝c4

If Black does nothing then White can gradually improve his position with moves like 23 ♚g2 and 24 h4, followed by a well prepared h4-h5. Meanwhile Black can't move his bishop from c8 without dropping the e7-pawn. So doing nothing isn't in Black's interest. Berg found a way to cajole White into exchanging off his knight for the passive black bishop on c8.

22...♝h6!

Threatening to triple the white pawns.

23 ♞e6 ♝xe6 24 ♜xe6 ♝g7

The bishop returns, having helped to reduce White's pressure.

25 ♛e2 ♜f7

Klimov's attack has come to a halt as he doesn't have enough power to conquer e7. He looks around for a way to strengthen his attack and comes up with a weakening move:

26 g4?

Either White played this because he was feeling overly optimistic: 'I have Black tied up, it's time to attack with my pawns!' or overly pessimistic: 'If I just sit tight then I'm going to be gradually outplayed!'

Overaggressive actions are often a sign of an inherent lack of confidence. In fact there was no good reason why White should lose if he just sits tight. For example, after 26 ♚g2 Black could offer another favourable exchange: 26...♞h5 27 ♝xg7 ♞xg7 when after 28 ♜e3 f4 29 ♜e4 fxg3 30 hxg3 ♞f5 the black knight aims for the excellent d4-outpost square. However, even here after 31 f4 Black is far from having a 'real advantage'.

26...♛a2 27 ♝xf6 ♛xe2 28 ♜xe2 ♝xf6 29 ♚g2 ♝e5 30 ♜a2 ♚g7 31 ♜a8 ♝d4 32 g5 ♝e5 33 h4 h6 34 gxh6+ ♚xh6 35 ♝b5 g5 36 ♚h3?

White should survive without too many difficulties after 36 hxg5+ ♚xg5 37 ♜g8+ ♚f4 38 ♝d7, but psychologically it feels like he is losing ground in letting the black king come to f4.

36...♝d4 37 ♜g8 gxh4 38 ♜g2 ♝f6 39 ♝e8 ♜f8 40 ♜g6+ ♚h7 0-1

Chapter Six

The Main Line Leningrad: 7 ♘c3 c6

Here we shall examine the key variation **1 d4 f5 2 g3 ♘f6 3 ♗g2 g6 4 ♘f3
♗g7 5 c4 0-0 6 0-0 d6 7 ♘c3 c6.**

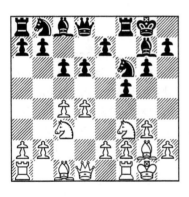

This move is very flexible. As we see,
it enables Black to use his queen on the
a5-, b6- and c7-squares, which are options unavailable to him after the
popular alternative 7...♕e8. It also rules
out any ♘d5 systems by White.

Against 7...c6 White can either seize
space with 8 d5 or play the less committal 8 b3. The difference in the pawn
structure that results is enormous, and
the two moves have unique plans.

Part One: White Plays ♘bd2 not ♘c3

First of all, we'll take a step backwards and look at lines in which White
avoids ♘c3 in favour of ♘bd2. This im-
plies that White won't be advancing
d4-d5 to gain space, as the knight
would be poorly placed on d2 to support a big centre. Therefore Black's
fundamental plan is to arrange the
moves ...d7-d6 and ...e7-e5 to mobilize
his own centre pawns.

S.Feller-H.Nakamura
Cap d'Agde (rapid) 2008

1 d4 f5 2 g3 g6 3 ♗g2 ♘f6 4 b3 ♗g7 5

♗b2 0-0 6 ♘f3 d6

Against this move order a Stonewall approach was recommended in Chapter Five with 6...♘e4, and if 7 c4 then 7...c6 and 8...d5. However, if like Nakamura you are happy to play ...c7-c6 systems, then the text is fine as well.

7 c4 c6 8 0-0 ♛a5!

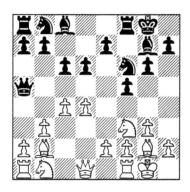

No messing around: Nakamura prepares ...e7-e5 in direct fashion.

9 ♘bd2 ♖e8 10 ♛c2 e5 11 dxe5 dxe5 12 e4 ♘a6 13 a3

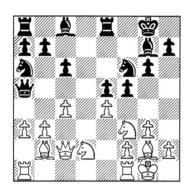

13...fxe4

Here I think Black missed a good chance with 13...♘c5! as the b3-b4 fork isn't to be feared: 14 b4? ♛a4 when

after 15 ♛xa4 ♘xa4 16 ♗xe5? fxe4 White drops material, so he has to grovel with 15 ♛d1 ♛xd1 16 ♖axd1 ♘d3 which looks excellent for Black.

Black also has strong dynamic chances after 14 ♗xe5 fxe4 15 ♗c3 ♛d8 or 14 ♘xe5 fxe4.

14 b4 ♛d8

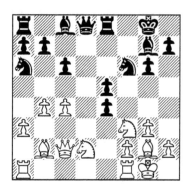

15 ♘xe4

White could have kept the edge with 15 ♘fg5, intending 15...♛d3 16 ♗xe4!, so here Nakamura might have tried the following sharp line: 15...e3 16 ♘de4!? exf2+ 17 ♛xf2 ♗f5 18 ♖ad1 ♛e7 19 ♘d6 ♘g4 20 ♛d2 and White has a lot of pressure for the pawn, but Black remains alive with tactical chances of his own.

15...♘xe4 16 ♛xe4 ♗f5 17 ♛e3 ♛d3!

A very fine move. The exchange of queens allows Black to advance ...e5-e4 without exposing his king to tactical threats, or allowing White to consolidate his hold on the d4-square as would be the case after 17...e4 18 ♘d4 ♛d7 19 ♖ad1. It might sound paradoxical, but the energy of the black position is increased by the exchange of queens – or it might be said that the exchange of queens diminishes the cohesion of the white position.

18 ♖fe1

White might have tried 18 ♖ad1 ♕xe3 (if 18...♕xc4 19 ♘xe5) 19 fxe3 so that after 19...e4 20 ♘d4 his knight is well fortified on d4 – compare this with the game.

18...♕xe3

Not 18...♕xc4 19 ♘xe5 when the white knight finds a stable central square where it can be further bolstered by 20 f4.

19 ♖xe3 e4! 20 ♘d4 ♖ad8 21 ♘xf5 ♗xb2 22 ♖b1 ♗xa3 23 ♖xa3 gxf5 24 ♗f1 c5!

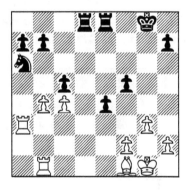

An important move. In the long run Black would have to give back the extra pawn, so he returns it at once to fix the white pawn on c4. This ensures that the white bishop remains shut in on f1.

25 bxc5

After 25 b5 ♘b4 26 ♖xa7 ♖e7 the black knight isn't quite as well placed as in the game, but on the other hand

the black b-pawn can't be subjected to frontal pressure by the rook on b1.

25...♘xc5

The knight finds an ideal post on a blockade square.

26 ♖xa7 ♖d6 27 ♖a5 b6 28 ♖ab5 ♖ee6 29 ♖5b2 ♔g7 30 ♖a2 ♔g6

One of the advantages of the Dutch kingside structure for Black is that his king usually finds it easier to amble up the board in an endgame. The carapace of pawns on f2, g3 and h2 might give the white king added protection in the middlegame, but in the endgame it becomes a straight-jacket.

31 ♖a8?

Feller loses patience. If White had waited with 31 ♖ab2, Nakamura might have increased the pressure: 31...♖f6 32 ♖a2 f4 33 gxf4 ♔f5! and 34...♔xf4.

31...♖d2!

Nakamura doesn't miss the chance to seize the seventh rank.

32 ♖g8+ ♔f7 33 ♖h8 ♔g7 34 ♖b8 ♘d7!

Refuting White's try for counterplay. The b6-pawn is defended and the knight is ready to leap to e5 and f3.

35 ♖b7?

He should slow down Black's attack with 35 ♖d8!.

35...♔f6 36 ♖a7 h5 37 ♖a8 ♘e5 38 ♖ba1 ♘f3+ 39 ♔g2 e3 40 ♖8a2 ♘e1+ 0-1

P.Harikrishna-J.Ehlvest
Merida 2008

1 d4 d6 2 c4 f5 3 ♘f3 ♘f6 4 g3 g6 5 ♗g2 ♗g7 6 0-0 0-0 7 ♘bd2

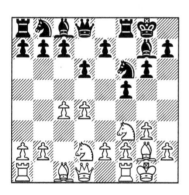

Nimzowitsch described such moves as 'decentralizing' even though formally speaking the knight is moved to a central square. The point is that by avoiding its natural post on c3, the knight has lost its chance to exert influence over the crucial d5-square, or indeed support a pawn on that square. Perhaps Harikrishna wanted to avoid the 7 ♘c3 ♘c6 line, as after 7 ♘bd2 going 7...♘c6 8 d5 ♘a5 is much less attractive for Black with the c4-pawn defended.

However, it is hardly upsetting for Ehlvest to be deprived of 7...♘c6 when he has the chance to expand with a rapid ...e7-e5.

7...♕e8 8 b3

Instead 8 d5 c6!? would give Black a pleasant variant of the 7...c6 main line – after all, White is going to have to reroute the knight with ♘b3 at some point, which amounts to a lost tempo as it is no better placed there than after 7 ♘c3.

However, perhaps the best response to 8 d5 is 8...e5! 9 dxe6 ♘c6! (there's no need to hurry to recapture on e6, so let's block a possible attack on b7 first), and then 10...♗xe6 when Black has a good version of the 7 ♘c3 ♘c6 line.

8...e5 9 dxe5 dxe5

Now Black has the typical mobile centre that is ready to spring forwards.

10 e4 ♘c6 11 ♗a3 ♖f7 12 ♖e1 f4!

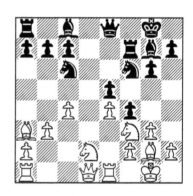

Our characteristic move. Of course Black has to be careful now as his centre and queenside are shaky. But in how many other openings does Black get good development, a space advantage and an attack after only 12 moves?

13 b4 a6 14 ♗b2 fxg3 15 hxg3

In this type of centre White often faces a dilemma when recapturing the pawn on g3. Capturing 'away from the centre' is in principle wrong and, indeed, 15 fxg3 would weaken his dark squares along the a7-g1 diagonal, in particular e3. On the other hand, after the text...

15...♘g4!

...the absence of an h-pawn to kick back the black knight with h2-h3 is keenly felt. Even if White achieves a great position in the centre or on the queenside, he can never feel completely comfortable with the enemy horse rearing itself at his king.

In similar situations, Black might pin the f3-knight with ...♗g4, again profiting from the fact that there is no h2-h3 to drive it away. In this instance, however, the knight move is undoubtedly stronger.

16 b5 ♘d4 17 a4 c5!

A fine move that obliges White to break up his queenside pawn phalanx.

18 bxc6

Of course it's bad enough with one black knight on g4; White can't tolerate the other one permanently fixed on d4.

18...♘xc6

Observe how the positional maestro Jaan Ehlvest has managed to restore his knight to the excellent c6 post from which it can never again be driven by a b4-b5 advance.

19 ♖f1 h6!

The first move in Black's long-term goal of getting his queen to the h5-square, where in partnership with the knight on g4 she can create threats against the white king.

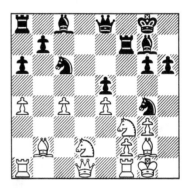

20 c5

With the positional threat of 21 ♘c4 followed by 22 ♘d6 when suddenly it is the white knight that is star of the show.

20...♗f8!

Ehlvest knows there's more to Black's strategy in the Dutch than attacking crazily in the hope that a mate appears before the queenside caves in. Though many other players (including, I have to admit, your author) sometimes forget this. The retreat of the bishop not only prevents the immediate 21 ♘c4 as 21...♗xc5 follows, but it also makes the knight manoeuvre hard to arrange in the long term: even after a preparatory move like ♕c2 or ♖c1, White still can't play ♘c4 as it would cut off the defence of c5.

Harikrishna therefore gives up a pawn to achieve counterplay:

21 ♘c4 ♗xc5 22 ♕d5 b6 23 ♘d6

Instead 23 ♘cxe5 ♘xe5 24 ♘xe5 ♗e6! leaves White in great trouble as f2 is attacked three times.

23...♗xd6 24 ♕xd6 ♖f6 25 ♕d2

White hopes to take possession of the open d- and c-files, and then, aided by his dark-squared bishop which has no rival, subject Black to long-term pressure.

25...g5!

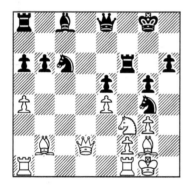

At last everything is ready for the black queen to go to h5 (it took the moves ...h6, ...g5 and ...♖f6 to prepare the way).

26 ♖ac1 ♗b7 27 ♖fd1 ♕h5 28 ♕e2 ♖af8 29 ♖d3

The position is now very tense.

The black pieces crowded on the kingside are wonderfully placed for an attack, but horribly misplaced when it comes to defending against an invasion of the white pieces along the open central files. Therefore, if Ehlvest's build-up proves merely symbolic, because no breakthrough is possible, he faces defeat.

Power needs to be added to the black onslaught – how can this be done?

29...a5!!

A brilliant move. Most players get myopic once they start an attack, and can't see beyond combinations in the vicinity of the king. In contrast, Ehlvest has seen a way to get his queenside minor pieces involved in the attack. The threat is 30...♗a6: once the bishop is aiming at f1 there will be no escape square for the white king.

30 ♖b3 ♘b4! 31 ♖bc3

White flounders around for a decent defence, but there is none available.

31...♗a6

If now 32 ♕d1 ♖xf3 when recapturing on f3 allows 33...♕h2 mate.

32 ♖c4

32...♘h2

Quite sufficient to win as the pin on f3 costs White a piece. However, more elegant was 32...♘d3! after which all the black pieces would be directly involved in the attack – a model of harmony. After 33 ♕xd3 ♖xf3 White is mated on f2 if he takes the rook, while the threat is 34...♕h2+ then 35...♖xf2+. He can only give some delaying checks with 34 ♕d5+ ♖8f7 35 ♖c8+ ♔h7.

33 ♘d4

If 33 ♗xe5 then 33...♘xf3+ 34 ♘xf3 ♕xf3 wins a piece for Black.

33...♕xe2 34 ♘xe2 ♗xc4 35 ♖xc4 ♖xf2 0-1

Part Two: 7 ♘c3 c6 without 8 d5

1 d4 f5 2 g3 ♘f6 3 ♗g2 g6 4 ♘f3 ♗g7 5 c4 0-0 6 0-0 d6 7 ♘c3 c6

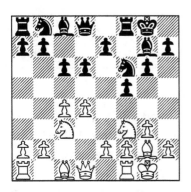

Here, before we turn our attention to White's main move, 8 d5, the alternatives 8 ♕c2, 8 ♖e1, 8 ♖b1 and 8 b3 ♕a5 followed by 9 ♗b2 or 9 ♗d2 will be examined.

As in the examples above, White's avoidance of d4-d5 enables Black in many cases to prepare the freeing ...e7-e5 advance. The Kozul-Volokitin game, below, is also a useful warning about the dangers of being too carried away by the chance to attack in the Dutch.

Z.Kozul-A.Volokitin
European Team
Championship, Novi Sad 2009

1 d4 f5 2 g3 ♘f6 3 ♗g2 g6 4 ♘f3 ♗g7 5 0-0 0-0 6 c4 d6 7 ♘c3 c6 8 ♕c2

After 8 ♖e1 ♘a6 9 e4 (or 9 b3 ♕c7 with a familiar plan after 10 ♗b2 of taking space with 10...e5 11 dxe5 dxe5) 9...fxe4 10 ♘xe4 ♘xe4 11 ♖xe4 e5 12 dxe5 dxe5 13 ♕xd8 ♖xd8 14 ♗g5 ♖e8, intending ...♗f5 or ...♘c5, Black has more than enough dynamic play to offset the weakness on e5.

An important alternative is 8 ♖b1 which Kramnik used to beat Nakamura in a game at Wijk aan Zee 2010, that went 8...♘e4 9 ♕c2 ♘xc3 10 bxc3!. This game was far from clear, but I prefer a different treatment for Black, namely 8...♔h8.

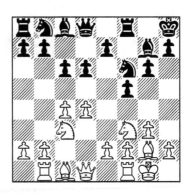

If now 9 b3 Black can try 9...♗e6!? 10 ♗b2 ♘bd7, as the bishop can if necessary retreat to g8. If given the chance, such as by 11 ♖e1 or 11 ♕c2, planning 12 e4, Black can switch to a Stonewall next move with 11...d5! with equal space and a safe game. So that means that 11 d5 is the critical move. After 11...cxd5 12 ♘xd5 (the pawn on d5 could become a target after 12 cxd5 ♗g8) 12..♘xd5 13 cxd5 ♗g8 14 ♗xg7+ ♔xg7 Black can play moves like ...♕b6 and ...♘f6 when he is solid on the dark squares.

Instead 9 b4 continues in 'Kramnik' style, when 9...♘bd7 plans to put pressure on the c4-pawn with ...♘b6 and ...♗e6. In V.Tarasova-V.Cmilyte, Rijeka 2010, Black was soon better after 10 ♘g5?! ♘b6 11 c5 (or 11 b5 ♗d7) 11...♘bd5.

The knight was well placed on d5 and giving up the light-squared bishop with 12 ♘xd5 ♘xd5 13 ♗xd5 cxd5 didn't help White at all.

Perhaps the immediate 10 c5 is best, when 10...e5!? is an intriguing reply, since after 11 b5 e4 12 ♘g5 ♘b8! the white centre is breaking up, or if 11 cxd6 e4 12 ♘g5 ♘b6 and Black regains

the pawn with control of the d5-square as 13 ♗f4? ♘fd5 is bad for White.

8...♘a6 9 a3

After 9 ♗g5 ♕e8 10 ♖fe1 Black can set up his mobile pawn centre with 10...e5: for example, 11 dxe5 dxe5 12 e4 ♘c5 13 exf5 ♗xf5 with great activity to compensate for the isolated queen's pawn.

9...♕e8

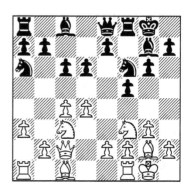

10 b4

Instead 10 d5 ♗d7 brings us into 8 d5 territory where I don't think the queen is well placed on c2.

Or if 10 e4 fxe4 11 ♘xe4 ♗f5 12 ♘xf6+ and here Beim analyses 12...exf6!? 13 ♕b3 ♕f7 14 ♗f4 (the simple 14 ♖e1 should be preferred) 14...♖ad8 15 ♖fe1 g5 16 ♗e3 h6 with an edge to Black.

10...e5 11 dxe5 dxe5

White's slow play on the queenside has allowed Volokitin to seize space in the centre. He has achieved the 'King's Indian' pawn centre, e5 and f5, without any resistance.

12 e4 f4

Everything has gone so swimmingly for Black that he feels justified in beginning an onslaught on the kingside with his pawns.

13 ♗b2 ♗g4 14 c5 ♘c7 15 ♘b1!

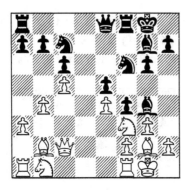

Another slow move, but with the excellent idea of manoeuvring the knight to c4 via d2, where it attacks e5 and can invade on d6 in some cases.

15...♗xf3 16 ♗xf3

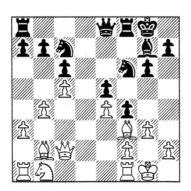

16...g5?

Volokitin begins a plan of decentralization. If there is a mate, it's fine: the game is over. But if there isn't a mate, then Black has over-committed himself. With hindsight it turns out

that the correct plan was 16...♘e6! aiming at the outpost square on d4. Then 17 ♗xe5? is a blunder as 17...♘g5! leaves two white bishops hanging, while after 17 ♘d2 ♘d4 18 ♗xd4 exd4 19 ♘c4 ♘d7! (stabilizing his control of the e5-square) 20 ♘d6 ♕e6 Black has a strong position, and 21 ♘xb7 ♘e5 would be very bad for White.

17 ♘d2 g4 18 ♗e2 f3

Contrary to what it says in books on tactics, having a pawn on f3 doesn't always mean that a combination will appear. In fact the pawn might well block a favourable tactical operation by its pieces.

19 ♗c4+ ♔h8 20 ♖fe1 ♕h5 21 ♗f1 ♘e6 22 ♘c4

22...♘g5

The lure of the h3-square proves too strong for the knight. It wasn't too late to revert to a centralizing strategy with 22...♘d4 23 ♗xd4 exd4 24 ♘d6?! (this knight is probably in too much of a hurry) 24...♘e8! 25 ♘xb7 d3 26 ♕xd3 ♗xa1 27 ♖xa1 ♕e5 28 ♖d1 ♘f6 with a defensible position for Black.

23 ♗xe5 ♞h3+ 24 ♔h1

Black has a very aggressive set up – but where is the mate?

24...♖ac8 25 ♗xf6 ♖xf6 26 ♖ad1 ♖h6 27 ♞d6

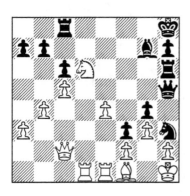

27...♞g5

He could have tried for a last swindle with 27...♗f6 28 ♞xc8?? ♞f4 29 h4 ♗xh4!, but 28 ♗c4! ♖f8 29 ♞f5 would prevent a breakthrough on the kingside and win easily. Equally if 27...♞f4 28 h4 ♗f6 29 ♞f5 wins for White.

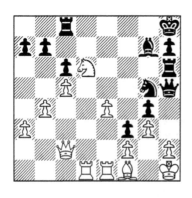

28 h4! 1-0

After 28...gxh3 the rook on c8 can be taken. A game that shows that even the strongest players can become intoxicated by the attacking options offered by the Dutch. The moral is: if you don't see a mate, remember to keep your pieces centralized and flexible.

Let's turn after **1 d4 f5 2 g3 ♞f6 3 ♗g2 g6 4 ♞f3 ♗g7 5 c4 0-0 6 0-0 d6 7 ♞c3 c6** to **8 b3** when after **8...♕a5**...

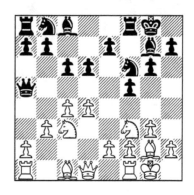

...White can reply 9 ♗b2 or 9 ♗d2.

T.Kaliszewski-T.Warakomski
Warsaw (rapid) 2009

1 d4 g6 2 ♞f3 ♗g7 3 g3 d6 4 ♗g2 f5 5 0-0 ♞f6 6 c4 0-0 7 ♞c3 c6 8 b3 ♕a5

Our basic idea: the queen jumps to a5 where she attacks the white knight and wins time for ...e7-e5. We wouldn't have this option after 7...♕e8 8 b3.

9 ♗b2 e5 10 dxe5

We examined the inferior 10 ♕c2? in the Introduction – see the game Buehl-Reifurth.

10...dxe5 11 ♕c2?

This is still a poor idea. The usual

move is 11 e4, preventing Black's next move, for which see the next game.

11...e4!

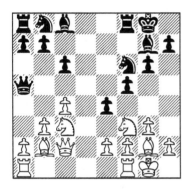

If there is no immediate punishment, Black will always be at least equal whenever he carries out this type of pawn advance. He seizes space in the centre, dislodges the white knight from f3 and shuts in the white bishop on g2.

12 ♘d4

Well, perhaps Kaliszewski was happy hereabouts: after all, it isn't obvious how Black is to complete his development. If 12...♘bd7? then 13 ♘e6 will deprive him of the vital bishop on g7. And 12...c5 would be a positional blunder as after 13 ♘db5 the white knight is poised to invade on d6. As a matter of fact Black has a simple move that confounds White's strategy:

12...a6!

Denying the white knight the b5-square and actually threatening to trap it mid-board with 13...c5!.

13 ♕c1

A feeble reply. He should stand his

ground in the centre with 11 a3!, although after 13...c5 14 b4 ♕d8 Black is at least equal.

13...c5 14 ♘c2 ♗e6 15 f3

White needs some space – he can't just wait for something like ...♘c6, ...♖ad8 and ...♘d4 to happen.

15...exf3 16 exf3 ♘c6 17 ♖e1 ♗f7 18 a3 ♕c7

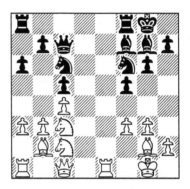

Black's potentially weak square on d5 is guarded by a bishop and a knight, whereas White's hole on d3 has no protection – and imagine what chaos would be caused if a black knight landed there, hitting the white queen, rook on e1 and bishop on b2. Furthermore, the black pawn on c5 supports a possible knight invasion on d4.

Kaliszewski tries to bolster the defence of the vulnerable d3- and d4-squares whilst also solving the strategic problem of his queen blocking in the rook on a1. Unfortunately for him, Black's f-pawn is waiting in ambush:

19 ♕e3 f4! 20 ♕xc5?

Instead 20 gxf4 ♘h5 is good for Black as getting the knight to a formidable post on f4 is worth more than a pawn. For example, 21 ♕xc5 b6 22 ♕f2 ♘xf4 23 ♖ad1 ♖ad8 24 ♗f1 (to stop 24...♘d3) 24...♘a5 and Black will regain his pawn with a strong initiative. Nonetheless, that is how White should have played, as his kingside now disintegrates.

20...fxg3 21 ♘d5

After 21 hxg3 ♕xg3 22 ♕f2 Black can simply exchange queens and go after White's weak queenside pawns with 22...♕xf2+ 23 ♔xf2 ♘a5! when there is no good way to hold on to both b3 and c4.

It's all too easy to become obsessed with an attack on the enemy king and try to maintain the tension with a move like 22...♕g5 rather than exchange queens. You should remember that it's not all crash-bang-wallop in the Dutch – sometimes it is the simple positional solution that is best.

21...♗xd5 22 cxd5 gxh2+ 23 ♔h1 ♘d7!

Refuting White's bid for counterplay as both his queen and bishop on b2 are hanging. The rest isn't too hard

for Warakomski.

24 ♕c4 ♘b6 25 ♕c5 ♗xb2 26 ♖ab1 ♖f5 27 ♘e3 ♗d4 28 ♕c2 ♗xe3 29 dxc6 ♗f4 30 ♗h3 ♖f6 31 ♗e6+ ♔g7 32 ♕b2 bxc6 33 ♖e4 ♖af8 34 ♖be1 ♔h6 35 ♕g2 ♖e8 36 a4 a5 37 ♕h3+ ♔g7 38 ♗g8 ♖xe4 39 ♖xe4 ♔xg8 40 ♖e8+ ♔g7 0-1

D.Jakovenko-M.Gurevich
Odessa (rapid) 2010

1 d4 f5 2 g3 d6 3 ♘f3 ♘f6 4 ♗g2 g6 5 0-0 ♗g7 6 c4 0-0 7 ♘c3 c6 8 b3 ♕a5 9 ♗b2 e5 10 dxe5 dxe5 11 e4

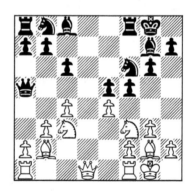

Blocking the ...e5-e4 advance that proved so strong in the previous game.

11...f4!

A critical moment. Does Black's position contain enough energy to support the pawn-ram? After all, his queenside pieces are still asleep and the central situation isn't stable. So won't the e5-square fall into White's hands?

Let's see how Dutch maestro Mikhail Gurevich answers these questions.

12 gxf4 ♘h5!

Vitality at all costs. Instead after 12...exf4? Black's attack on the kingside is stymied, and White can conquer space with 13 e5! ♘g4 14 ♖e1. If then 14...♘xe5 White's attack will arrive first thanks to the following combinative sequence: 15 ♘xe5 ♗xe5 16 ♗d5+! cxd5 17 ♖xe5 (the exchange of his dark-squared bishop is fatal for Black) 17...♘c6 18 ♖xd5 ♕c7 (or 18...♕b4 19 ♖d6, intending 20 ♕d5+) 19 ♘b5 ♕e7 20 ♕d2, intending 21 ♖e1 then 22 ♕c3, etc, with decisive pressure.

13 ♘e2

If 13 fxe5 ♗g4 14 h3 ♗xf3 15 ♗xf3 ♘f4 with excellent pressure for the pawns.

13...♗g4

14 h3

Now according to my database Black played 14...♘xf4?? and White replied 15 ♘xf4?? which is a strange double blunder as 15 hxg4 is a safe win of a piece. So the game no doubt actually went:

14...♗xf3 15 ♗xf3 ♘xf4?!

Here Black missed the interesting alternative 15...exf4!. In contrast to the situation after 12...exf4, above, White can't do anything sharp and tactical in the centre. I think Black might even have the edge after 16 ♗xg7 ♔xg7. He can exert control over the dark squares, in particular e5, which could become a strong base for a knight (contrast this with White's 13 e5! breakthrough after 12...exf4).

16 ♘xf4 ♖xf4 17 ♗g4!

The bishop finds an active post.

17...♘a6 18 ♕d6 ♖af8?

Here I believe Black lost his chance to equalize with 18...♘c5! bringing his knight into the battle.

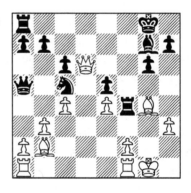

Then a sharp tactical sequence leads to perpetual check: 19 ♗xe5 ♖xe4 20 f4 (Black can play for the advantage after 20 ♗xg7 ♔xg7; a typical turnaround in the assessment of a Dutch position) 20...♗xe5 21 fxe5 ♕c3 22 ♕xc5 ♕g3+ 23 ♔h1 ♖xg4 24 hxg4 ♕h3+ 25 ♔g1 ♕g3+ with a draw.

19 ♖ad1

Now White's kingside is secure and

he went on to grind out a win due to his bishop-pair and pressure on the queenside. The remaining moves were: **19...♔h8 20 a3 ♕c5 21 b4 ♕xd6 22 ♖xd6 ♘c7 23 ♖d7 ♖4f7 24 ♖fd1 h5 25 ♖xf7 ♖xf7 26 ♗c8 ♘a6 27 ♖d7 ♖xd7 28 ♗xd7 ♘c7 29 c5 ♔g8 30 ♗c8 b6 31 cxb6 axb6 32 a4 ♔f7 33 a5 bxa5 34 bxa5 ♔e7 35 a6 ♘b5 36 ♗a3+ ♔d8 37 ♗e6 ♔c7 38 ♗c5 g5 39 ♗f7 h4 40 ♔g2 ♘d4 41 ♗xd4 exd4 42 ♗c4 ♗f8 43 ♔f3 ♗c5 44 ♔g4 d3 45 ♗xd3 ♗xf2 46 ♔xg5 ♔d6 47 ♔f5 ♗d4 48 e5+ ♔e7 49 ♗e4 ♔d7 50 ♔f6 ♔c7 51 ♔e6 ♗c3 52 ♔f5 ♗d4 53 ♔f6 ♔d7 54 ♗f3 ♔c7 55 ♔f5 ♔d7 56 ♔e4 ♗b6 57 ♗e2 ♗c5 58 ♗c4 ♗b6 59 ♔f5 ♗d4 60 ♔g5 ♔c7 61 e6 ♗f2 62 ♔f6 1-0**

I don't wish to claim that the hole on e6 that often appears in Black's pawn structure is a virtue rather than a defect of the 1...f5 move. Such marvellously twisted logic is beyond me. On the other hand, the Dutch is about provocation – White is cajoled into pushing his pieces and pawns forwards, and what could be better bait than waving the e6 outpost for a knight before his eyes? Who knows, he might forget all about the dark squares, as in the following game.

R.Damaso-K.Spraggett
Andorra 2007

1 g3 g6 2 ♗g2 ♗g7 3 c4 f5 4 d4 ♘f6 5 ♘f3 0-0 6 0-0 d6 7 ♘c3 c6 8 b3 ♕a5 9 ♗d2

Rather than 9 ♗b2, as in the previous games.

9...♕c7

The black queen retreats from the line of the bishop's fire and is ready to support 11...e5, but White clamps down upon the d5-square.

10 d5 ♘a6

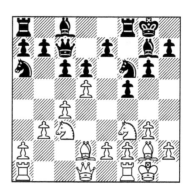

The knight heads for the c5-square that has been weakened by White's last move.

11 ♖c1 ♘c5

After 12 ♗e3 the black knight continues its onward journey: 12...♘ce4 13 ♘xe4 ♘xe4 14 ♗d4 e5 (breaking White's grip on the centre, though compared to the games above Black doesn't get a solid structure) 15 dxe6 ♗xe6 16 ♗xg7 ♕xg7 17 ♘d4 ♖ae8 18 ♘xe6 ♖xe6 19 ♗xe4 fxe4 and ½-½ was O.Cvitan-E.Agrest, Oberwart 1994. There's still plenty of play in the position, though, and I rather like Black's space advantage.

Instead Damaso was too eager to get his hands on the e6-square:

12 b4?!

Entirely unnecessary. White isn't properly organized to punch through the queenside with a subsequent b4-b5 or c4-c5, nor is he restricting the black knight – it simply hops into the e4-square. (Things would be different, though, if the black knight were back on a6, and White had played ♖b1 and b2-b4, stopping it going to c5.)

All that is achieved by the game move is a loosening of White's own queenside pawns, for which he will pay dearly.

12...♘ce4 13 ♘xe4 ♘xe4

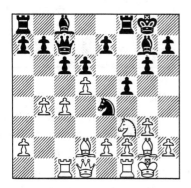

14 ♘g5?!

He could save his bishop from exchange with 14 ♗e3, though 14...c5 is an annoying reply. However, Damaso has his attention focused on the hole on e6.

14...♘xd2!

The right exchange. After 14...♘xg5 15 ♗xg5 White is in charge again as he can press forwards on the queenside.

15 ♕xd2 c5!

White is prevented from breaking open lines with 16 c5 or 16 dxc6 bxc6 17 b5. The situation therefore stabilizes in the centre, with Black well entrenched on the dark squares, and White trying to prove something on the light squares.

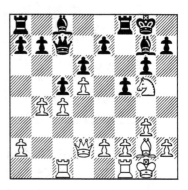

16 bxc5?!

It was better to block lines with 16 b5. Then 16...a6 17 a4 axb5 18 axb5 leaves Black in control of the a-file (see how convenient it is that the bishop on g7 controls the a1-square). Still, the white pawn on c4 wouldn't be subject to frontal attack by the black rooks and queen, as occurs in the game. Furthermore, White could answer 16...a6 with 17 ♖b1!? when 17...axb5 18 ♖xb5 leaves him with a weak pawn on a2, but b7 is also weak.

So it seems that White's position could withstand the imprecisions 12 b4 and 14 ♘g5 and still be okay – they turned a slight edge into a slightly worse position. However, after the third mistake, 16 bxc5?!, things start to become very awkward for him.

16...♕xc5 17 e3 b6 18 ♖c2 ♗f6 19 ♘e6

♗xe6 20 dxe6 ♖ac8 21 ♖b1 ♕a3 22 ♖b3 ♕a4 23 ♕d3 ♖c7 24 ♗d5 ♖fc8 25 h4 ♔g7

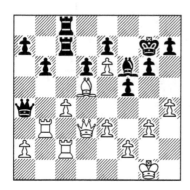

White does his best to drum up counterplay on the kingside. Nonetheless, the black monarch is very secure. His pawns and bishop fortify the light and dark squares respectively without getting in each other's way, whereas White's pawn on e6 shuts out his own bishop from the attack.

26 h5 ♖c5 27 ♖e2 b5 28 ♖xb5 ♖xb5 29 cxb5 ♖c3 30 ♕d2 ♕xb5

Threatening 31...♖d3. Under pressure Damaso now miscalculates:

31 h6+? ♔xh6 32 e4+ ♔g7 33 ♔g2

Perhaps when he played 31 h6+ Damaso missed that after 33 e5, cutting off the defence of the rook on c3, Black can simply play 33...dxe5, as if 34 ♕xc3 ♕xe2. Therefore he remains a pawn down.

33...♖d3 34 ♕c2 fxe4 35 ♗xe4 ♖c3 36 ♕d1 ♕c4 37 ♗f3 a5 38 ♕d5 ♕xd5 39 ♗xd5 ♖d3 40 ♗f3 ♗d4 41 ♗e4 ♖d1 42 ♗c2 ♖c1 43 ♗b3 ♖c3 44 ♖e4 ♗f6 45 ♖c4 ♖d3 46 ♔f1 ♖d2 47 ♔e1 ♖b2 48

♖c2 ♖b1+ 49 ♔e2 h5 50 f4 ♖g1 51 ♔f3 ♖d1 52 ♔e4 a4 0-1

Part Three:
7 ♘c3 c6 8 d5

1 d4 f5 2 g3 ♘f6 3 ♗g2 g6 4 ♘f3 ♗g7 5 0-0 0-0 6 c4 d6 7 ♘c3 c6 8 d5

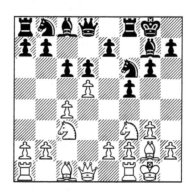

In the ultimate main line of the 7...c6 Leningrad with d4-d5 White establishes a space advantage in the centre. He begins with the 'trademark' white pawns on c4 and d5, and tries to edge up the b-pawn as well.

An imposing pawn structure isn't normally a killer in itself – only rarely does it succeed in suffocating the enemy army. Paradoxically, an advanced pawn phalanx becomes a fearsome weapon at the point of its death – it *collapses* and so opens up lines of power for the pieces waiting behind it. Of course, that is the ideal for the attacker; but if the pieces haven't been positioned on good squares in anticipation of this dissolution, they will lack energy. In such a scenario it will be the opponent's pieces that profit from the opening of lines. The fragments of the broken centre will be weaknesses, and avenues of counterattack will emerge for the hitherto pent-up pieces of the defender.

The above may sound abstract, but again and again in Leningrad Dutch games we see the white centre dissolving, whereupon the crucial question is: will the white pieces be able to batter the black centre now that it is open to attack? Or will they be able to force forwards a passed pawn on b5 that has emerged from the exploding white centre? Or are the white pieces too meek, too powerless, and will have to simply watch as a black counterattack streams through the open lines?

H.Zoebisch-D.Semcesen
Schwarzach 2008

1 d4 f5 2 g3 ♘f6 3 ♗g2 g6 4 ♘f3 ♗g7 5 c4 0-0 6 0-0 d6 7 ♘c3

If 7 d5 at once, 7...c6 should transpose to our main game after 8 ♘c3 ♗d7. However, players who intend to play the 7 ♘c3 ♘c6 variation should also examine what follows.

7...c6 8 d5 ♗d7

Black develops his bishop, overprotects the c6-square as a prelude to playing ...♘a6, and for the moment keeps the option of the queen going to a square on the d8-a5 diagonal.

9 ♖b1

The moves 9 ♘d4, 9 e4 and some others are discussed in later games.

9...♘a6 10 b3

The alternative 10 b4 is the subject of the next game.

10...♕e8

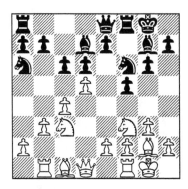

Finally Black commits the queen to a kingside deployment. She heads for f7 to put pressure on d5 and bolster the black defences.

11 ♗b2 h6

A useful move. Black wants to play ...♕f7 without being bothered by ♘g5 and also prepares ...g6-g5 to utilize his kingside pawns – see his 14th move.

12 ♘d2

White's last three moves have been rather passive: he has quietly developed his pieces without any thought of putting pressure on the black queenside.

12...♕f7

One of the fruits of 1...f5: the black queen has found an excellent niche in her pawn structure.

13 a3 ♖ac8 14 e3 g5 15 f4

After 15 b4 the 'safe' move would be 15...♘c7, but the aggressive 15...f4! looks promising, even though it gives away the e4-square. Black can then attack with 16...♘g4, etc.

After the game move, it appears that White has stymied any attempt by Black to attack on the kingside. But Semcesen finds a way to add some dynamism to his set-up:

15...♘g4!

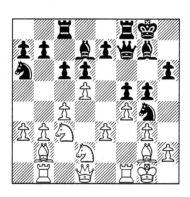

16 ♕e2 e5!

Now all four of Black's kingside pawns are working. The immediate threat is 17...exf4 and, after either pawn recapture on f4, 18...♖ce8 will exert strong pressure along the e-file. White can't allow this rearrangement of the pawn structure.

17 h3

After 17 dxe6 ♕xe6! the e3-pawn is a target and can be attacked further with 18...♖ce8.

17...♘f6 18 fxe5 dxe5 19 e4?

A colossal mistake that removes a vital restraining force from the f4-square. Black is now able to advance

...f5-f4 without the drawback of handing over the e4-square to the white pieces.

The position remains tense after 19 dxc6 bxc6 (19...♗xc6 leaves f5 hanging) 20 ♘f3. Now 20...♖ce8 is the gradual build-up approach, but Black can go all in with 20...♘h5 21 ♔h2 f4!.

19...♘h5!

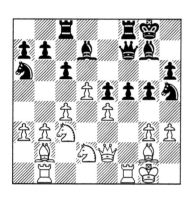

A key move to add vital power to the kingside attack.

20 ♖f3 f4 21 g4

Or 21 ♘f1 g4! and the pawns keep rolling.

21...♘g3 22 ♕f2 h5!

Relentless pressure from the kingside pawns.

23 ♖xg3 fxg3 24 ♕xg3 hxg4 25 hxg4 ♕f4 26 ♕xf4 ♖xf4 27 ♘e2 ♖xg4 28 ♘f1 ♘c5 29 ♘e3 ♖h4 30 ♘g3 ♖e8 31 ♗c3 ♘d3 32 ♖d1 ♘f4 33 ♗e1 ♖f8 34 ♘gf5 ♘xg2 0-1

That was a very nice game by Black, but let's not forget that White gave him a helping hand with his passive middlegame moves, in particular 12

♘d2. Most of the time in this variation Black has to make do with consolidating moves such as ...♘c7. Or if he does attack, it is more of a touch and go thing as to whether he has enough power to carry it out to a finish.

U.Andersson-A.Beliavsky
Bazna 2008

1 d4 f5 2 g3 ♘f6 3 ♗g2 g6 4 ♘f3 ♗g7 5 c4 0-0 6 0-0 d6 7 ♘c3 c6 8 d5 ♗d7 9 ♖b1 ♘a6 10 b4

Sharper than 10 b3: White plans an immediate pawn advance on the queenside.

10...♕e8

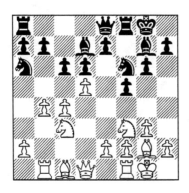

11 a3

White stabilizes his queenside pawns. He could play more sharply with 11 dxc6 bxc6 12 b5 cxb5 13 cxb5 when he has a mobile queenside pawn majority. The usual response is 13...♘c5, but I quite like 13...♘c7 as played in T.Rahman-M.Dzhumaev, Dhaka 2003, which went 14 a4 (after

14 ♗b2!? ♖b8 – we might even contemplate the risky-looking 14...♘xb5 as White has nothing clear in reply – 15 a4 a6 16 ♘d4 axb5 17 ♘cxb5 ♘xb5 18 ♘xb5 ♕f7, intending ...♗e6 or ...♘e4, and Black has enough counterplay to offset the passed pawn) 14...♘e4 15 ♘xe4 fxe4 16 ♘h4 d5 17 ♗e3.

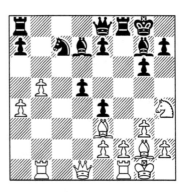

The game continued 17...♗e6 when Black was struggling, but because it is the Dutch you won't be surprised to learn that he won after bamboozling White in the tactics: 18 ♖c1 ♕d7 19 ♗xe4 ♘xb5 20 ♗xd5 ♗xd5 21 axb5 e6 22 ♗d4 ♗h6 23 ♖a1 ♖f7 24 ♕d3 g5 25 ♘g2? (25 ♗e3! avoids losing a piece) 25...♗xg2 26 ♔xg2 ♖d8! (pinning and winning) 27 ♖a4 (alternatively, 28 ♗e2 ♕b7+ or 28 e3 e5) 27...♕b7+ 28 ♔h3 e5 29 ♖xa7 g4+ (he prefers to finish in style rather than grab a rook with 29...♕c8+ and 30...♖xa7) 30 ♔h4 ♕g2 31 ♔xg4 ♖f4+ 0-1. It's mate next move.

Here 17...♕d8!? looks like an improvement. Then White can't do anything fast because of the latent threat of ...g6-g5 winning his knight if the bishop leaves e3. For example, 18 b6 (intending to pin the knight on c7) 18...axb6 19 ♗xb6 ♖xa4 20 ♖c1 ♗e5! 21 ♗xc7 ♗xc7 22 ♕xd5+ e6 23 ♕d2 ♗a5 when Black is very dynamic and White has to watch out for ...g6-g5. Alternatively, if 18 ♖c1 e6 19 b6 (or 19 ♕d2 ♘e8 20 ♖fd1 a6) 19...♘e8 when 20 bxa7 again allows 20...g5.

11...♘c7 12 ♗b2 ♖c8 13 ♕d2

Andersson discourages the idea of ...e7-e5, as after 13 ♘d4 e5 14 dxe6 ♘xe6 15 ♘b3 ♕e7 16 ♕d2 ♖fd8 17 ♖bd1 ♗e8 Black was solidly placed in M.Konopka-V.Beim, Aschach 2001. Upon 18 ♖fe1 ♕f7 White decided to rule out a space-gaining ...g6-g5 move with 19 f4? but this left a hole on e4. Black was able to break out from his cramped position with 19...d5! 20 cxd5 cxd5.

The tactical justification is that White loses two pieces for a rook and pawn after 21 ♘xd5 ♘xd5 22 ♗xd5 ♖xd5 23 ♕xd5 ♗xb2. In the game White tried 21 h3, but after 21...♘e4 22 ♘xe4 dxe4 moving the queen to safety

allows 23...♘xf4!, winning a pawn due to a discovered attack on b3. Instead after 23 ♘d4 the white centre soon crumbled away: 23...♘xd4 24 ♗xd4 ♗xd4 25 exd4 ♗a4 26 ♖c1 ♕d5 27 ♗f1 ♖c6 28 ♔f2 ♕xd4+ 29 ♕xd4 ♖xd4 30 ♖xc6 bxc6 31 ♔e3 ♖d7 32 ♗e2 ♔f7 33 ♖c1 ♔e6 34 ♖c5 ♗b5 35 ♗xb5 cxb5 36 ♔e2 a6 37 g4 fxg4 38 ♔e3 ♖d5 39 ♖c8 ♖h5 40 ♖c6+ ♔d5 41 ♖c5+ ♔d6 42 ♖c2 ♖h3+ 43 ♔xe4 ♖xa3 44 ♖d2+ ♔e6 0-1.

13...♘a8!

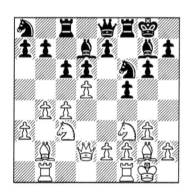

An unusual and pretty move. The knight makes use of the corner square to reach b6, where it will attack the c4-pawn. Moreover, the white queen looks misplaced on d2, as it is a knight's move away from c4.

14 dxc6!

Andersson finds the best solution.

14...♗xc6

He takes back with the bishop to keep up the pressure on c4.

15 ♘d5

After 15 b5 there is a long forcing variation that proves Black is okay: 15...♗e4! 16 ♘xe4 ♘xe4 17 ♕d5+ e6 18

♕xb7 ♗xb2 19 ♖xb2 ♖f7 20 ♕a6 ♘b6 21 ♖c2 ♖xc4 22 ♖xc4 ♘xc4.

15...♘e4!?

Alas, there is a problem with the simple 15...♗xd5 16 cxd5 (forced) 16...♘b6, as the white knight can aim at the hole on e6 with 17 ♘d4!.

16 ♕d3 ♗xb2 17 ♖xb2 e6 18 ♘e3 b5!

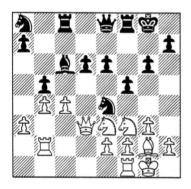

Breaking up the white queenside before White can gain control with 19 ♘d4.

19 ♖c2 bxc4 20 ♖xc4 ♘b6 21 ♖c2 ♗a4

The position is now about equal and ended as a draw after a hard fight:

22 ♖xc8 ♕xc8 23 ♘d2 d5 24 ♘xe4 dxe4 25 ♕d2 ♖d8 26 ♕b2 ♕d7 27 ♕f6 ♖c8 28 f3 exf3 29 ♗xf3 ♕f7 30 ♕e5 ♘d7 31 ♕a5 ♘b6 32 ♕e5 ♕d7 33 g4 ♗b3 34 ♖b1 ♘c4 35 ♘xc4 ♗xc4 36 gxf5 exf5 37 ♖c1 ♗f7 38 ♖xc8+ ♕xc8 39 a4 ♕d7 40 a5 ♗c4 41 ♕c5 ♗b5 42 ♗d5+ ♔g7 ½-½

T.Kantans-D.Semcesen
Stockholm 2008/09

1 ♘f3 f5 2 g3 ♘f6 3 ♗g2 g6 4 0-0 ♗g7 5

c4 0-0 6 ♘c3 d6 7 d4 c6 8 d5 ♗d7 9 ♘d4

White is now exerting pressure against the c6-pawn with the knight on d4, bishop on g2 and pawn on d5. This means that the move Black wants to play, the developing 9...♘a6??, simply drops the pawn to 10 dxc6 bxc6 11 ♘xc6. A natural way to overprotect the c6-pawn as a preliminary to ...♘a6 is 9...♕e8?!, but then 10 ♕b3! is an awkward reply. The b7-pawn has to be defended, and after 10...♕c8, to defend b7, White has the strong breakthrough 11 c5!.

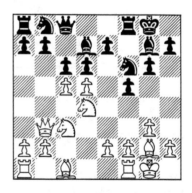

The threat is 12 dxc6+ winning a piece by a discovered attack. Now after 11...♔h8 12 cxd6 exd6 13 ♖d1 c5 (it's better to submit to a weak pawn on d6 after 13...♘a6 14 dxc6 bxc6) 14 ♘e6 Black's strategy has clearly suffered a fiasco.

Black has a much better way to defend against White's idea of 10 ♕b3:

9...♕b6!

An excellent post for the black queen. Now in some lines White has to reckon with a discovered attack on the knight on d4 with ...♘xd5, and he can't develop the bishop from c1 without dropping the b2-pawn. Furthermore, the black queen can expand her power on the queenside by attacking the c4-pawn – perhaps with the restraining ...a7-a5 combined with ...♕a6, or the more direct ...♕b4 as in the game.

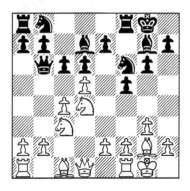

Note that the natural reply 10 b3? would be met by 10...♘e4! when the pressure along the long diagonal costs White a piece.

10 dxc6 bxc6 11 ♘b3

Now routine play would do Black no good at all, as White is threatening the pawn-ram 12 c5! dxc5 13 ♗e3 followed by 14 ♘a4 if necessary to win the c5-pawn, when Black is left with weak pawns on the queenside. And 11...♘a6 doesn't stop the threat, as 12 c5! follows anyway – 12...♘xc5 13 ♗e3, and then ♘xc5 and ♘a4 will regain the pawn as above.

Black must never forget about the ramming potential of the move c4-c5 in the Dutch.

11...♕b4!

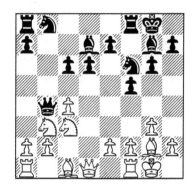

Note that Black's aggressive moves with his queen, 9...♕b6 and 11...♕b4, also had a defensive function, namely they dealt with the positional threats 10 ♕b3 and 12 c5. That is one of the hallmarks of the Dutch – defence through counterattack.

12 ♕d3

The pawn-ram misses the mark thanks to the tactical sequence 12 c5 d5 (Black wants to keep his pawns compact in the centre) 13 ♘xd5? cxd5 14 ♗xd5+ ♘xd5 15 ♕xd5+ ♔h8 16 ♕xa8 ♘c6 and the white queen is trapped.

12...♘a6

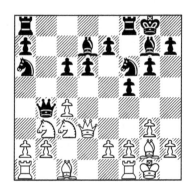

Only now does Black develop his knight.

13 ♗d2 ♛b7

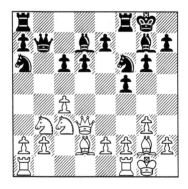

14 ♗f4

Semcesen has successfully neutralized the threat of c4-c5. White therefore switches to the plan of preparing an exchange of dark-squared bishops with ♛d2 and ♗h6. This cannot hurt Black.

We might conclude that if White exchanges with d5xc6, conceding a broad centre to Black, he needs one of the following as compensation:

1. A strong tactical blow available along the h1-a8 diagonal and/or a2-g8 diagonal – see the comment to his 9th move, above.

2. A pawn-ram against the black centre with c4-c5 (or more rarely an e4-e5 advance) at a moment when Black can't keep his pawns intact with ...d6-d5.

3. The opportunity to create a passed pawn on the queenside with a rapid b4-b5 advance.

If White can carry out none of these

plans, then the exchange d5xc6 can be adjudged a positional concession to Black.

14...♖ad8 15 ♖fd1

The weakness on f2 created with this move will be exploited to the maximum. Instead 15 ♖ad1 is more solid, but Black already has a good game.

15...♘c7

The knight heads for a fine centre post on e6 where it will attack the white bishop.

16 ♛d2 ♘e6 17 ♗h6 ♗xh6 18 ♛xh6 ♛b4!

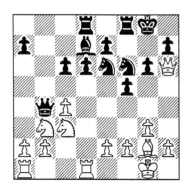

Back again, and this time the attack on c4 is awkward to meet.

19 ♛e3 f4!

Our familiar Dutch pawn-ram. If now 20 gxf4 ♛xc4 and f4 is hanging.

20 ♛d3 ♘g4 21 ♛e4

Rather desperately trying to stop the attack by pinning the f4-pawn.

21...♛b6 22 e3 ♘f6 23 ♛f3 fxe3 24 ♛xe3 ♛xe3 25 fxe3

It might seem that White has escaped the worst through exchanging queens, but the black rooks and knights combine to produce a rapid attack along the undefended f-file.

25...♘g4 26 ♖e1 ♘g5 27 ♘d2 ♖f2 28 ♖ad1 ♖df8 29 b3

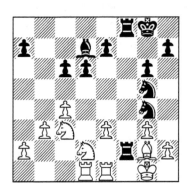

29...♖xg2+! 0-1

A sudden finish. White doesn't wish to see 30 ♔xg2 ♖f2+ 31 ♔h1 (or 31 ♔g1 ♘h3+ and mate on h2) 31...♖xh2+ 32 ♔g1 ♘h3+ 33 ♔f1 ♖f2 mate.

Z.Kozul-M.Grunberg
Bizovac 2006

1 d4 f5 2 g3 ♘f6 3 ♗g2 g6 4 ♘f3 ♗g7 5 0-0 0-0 6 c4 c6 7 ♘c3 d6 8 d5 ♗d7 9 e4!?

A vigorous attempt to seize the initiative in the centre. The opening of the e-file will expose the e6-square to frontal attack by a white rook from e1.

Other alternatives not already looked at are 9 ♗e3 and 9 ♕b3:

a) If 9 ♗e3 ♘a6 10 ♕d2, with ideas of 11 ♗h6, then 10...♘g4! 11 ♗f4 ♘c5 looks comfortable for Black, while 11 ♗d4? is a mistake after 11...♗h6! when 12 e3? c5 loses the bishop.

b) After 9 ♕b3 I wish that 9...♘a6? were possible, but it seems that White can get away with 10 ♕xb7 ♘c5 11 ♕b4. However, shielding b7 with 9...♕b6! is perfectly okay for Black.

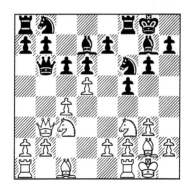

For example:

b1) 10 ♗e3 ♕xb3 11 axb3 cxd5 12 ♘g5 (or 12 cxd5 ♘a6) 12...h6 13 ♘h3 g5 14 cxd5 ♘a6 15 ♗d4 ♖fc8 and Black had the more active pieces in B.Tiller-R.Akesson, Oslo 1981, as the white knight on h3 and bishop on g2 were both out of the game.

b2) 10 ♕xb6 axb6 11 ♗e3 cxd5 12 cxd5 b5 13 a3 ♘a6 14 ♖fd1 b4 15 axb4 ♘xb4 and in P.Stigar-C.Niklasson, Copenhagen 1983, having exchanged off his doubled pawn, Black had the better of it – again the white bishop on g2 was passively placed.

b3) 10 ♘g5 (the knight is tempted by the hole on e6, but the white pawn that results on e6 is weak) 10...h6! 11 ♘e6 ♗xe6 12 dxe6 ♘a6 13 ♕c2 ♘c5 14 e4 (White has to rush through this centre advance before e6 drops) 14...fxe4 (instead 14...♘xe6 15 ♗e3 ♘d4 16 ♗xd4 ♕xd4 17 exf5 gxf5 18 ♘e2 ♕e5 19 ♘f4, eyeing the e6- and g6-squares, gives White sufficient play on the light squares for the pawn) 15 ♗e3 ♘g4 16 ♗xc5 ♕xc5 and ½-½ was I.Farago-S.Kindermann, Austrian League 1996. After 18 h3 ♘f6 19 ♖ae1 the white knight gets to e6 upon 19...♕xe6? 20 ♘c5 ♕f7 21 ♘e6, so Black would prefer a solid alternative like 19...♖ae8, with equality.

9...fxe4 10 ♘g5 ♘a6!

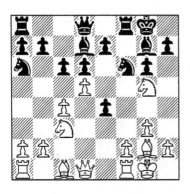

The black knight heads for c7 in order to cover the hole on e6 and put pressure on the d5-pawn.

11 ♘cxe4 ♘xe4 12 ♘xe4

If 12 ♗xe4 the black knight can go to c5: 12...♘c5 13 ♗g2 a5 or 13...♕b6, and Black has a queenside initiative.

12...♘c7 13 ♖e1 cxd5 14 cxd5 ♗f5!

Black frees d7 for his queen.

15 ♕b3 ♕d7!

'The best answer to a threat is to ignore it.' Black refuses to be side-tracked from his methodical centralization by the attack on the b7-pawn.

16 ♘g5

After 16 ♕xb7 ♖fb8 17 ♕c6 ♕xc6 18 dxc6 ♗xb2 19 ♖b1 ♗xc1 20 ♖exc1 ♖b6! Black would try to prove that the pawn on c6 is a weakness.

16...♘b5 17 ♘e6 ♘d4 18 ♘xd4 ♗xd4 19 ♗e3 ♗f6!

It's important to avoid exchanging bishops as after 19...♗xe3 20 ♕xe3 Black has no queenside pressure to offset the structural weakness on e7.

20 ♗f1 ♖fc8 21 ♗b5 ♕d8 22 ♗d3

Instead the position looks fairly equal after, say, 22 ♖ac1. The attempt by White to breakthrough along the b-file leads to him overpressing – a common danger for both players in the Dutch. In his game above with Volokitin, Kozul was the beneficiary, whereas here he becomes the victim of this psychological malaise.

Here are the remaining moves, with the black pieces gradually taking control:

22...♗xd3 23 ♕xd3 ♗xb2 24 ♖ab1 ♗c3 25 ♖ec1 ♗f6 26 ♖xb7 ♖xc1+ 27 ♗xc1 ♕c8 28 ♕b1 ♕c4 29 ♗e3 a5 30 ♖b5 a4 31 a3 ♔f7 32 h4 h5 33 ♔g2 ♖c8 34 ♔h2 ♕e2 35 ♖b4 ♖c4 36 ♖b8 ♖c2 37 ♖a8 ♗b2 38 ♖xa4 ♕d3 39 ♖f4+ ♔g7 40 ♔h3 ♕xd5 41 ♕e1 ♖e2 42 ♕f1 ♗c3 43 ♔h2 ♖a2

Here the game score finishes in my database with the laconic '**0-1**'. White is under pressure, but he can fight on with 44 a4 as 44...♖a1 45 ♕g2 is nothing special for Black. Instead Black could keep up the pressure with, for example, 44...♗e5.

Chapter Seven

The Main Line Leningrad: 7 ♘c3 ♘c6

1 d4 f5 2 g3 ♘f6 3 ♗g2 g6 4 ♘f3 ♗g7 5 0-0 0-0 6 c4 d6 7 ♘c3 ♘c6

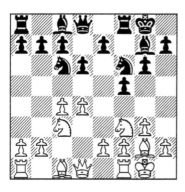

Black develops his knight to its best square and intends to grab space with 8...e5. Then he will have active pieces supporting a mobile centre – and what more can we ask from an opening?

For this reason the usual reply is 8 d5, to cripple the black pawns before 8...e5 can be played. After 8...♘a5 the black knight is offside and vulnerable to attack. So White claims to have two

advantages: more space and a badly-placed enemy piece.

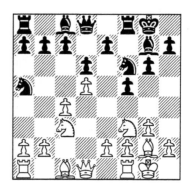

Black has a different version of the tale. He feels he has provoked White into loosening his pawn centre with 8 d5, and that after 8...♘a5! the knight is by no means isolated and badly placed on a5: it is at the forefront of Black's strategy of undermining the c4-pawn, which is a vital supporting pillar of the white centre.

Both White and Black are to some

extent right in their assessment of 8 d5 ♘a5. It is this tension between ideas that leads to a double-edged and exciting struggle.

Note that after 1 d4 f5 2 g3 ♘f6 3 ♗g2 g6 4 ♘f3 ♗g7 5 0-0 0-0 6 c4 d6 the immediate 7 d5 is comparatively rare. However, it is slightly annoying that we can be deprived of our ...♘c6 move in this cavalier fashion. I recommend that you play 7...c6, transposing to the main line in Chapter Six after 8 ♘c3 ♗d7. I'm not sure how happy that makes a 7...♘c6 player feel, but at least it's only one line of the 7...c6 variation you have to have ready!

Part One: White Avoids 8 d5

One of the good things about 7...♘c6 is that White is more or less compelled to play 8 d5 if he wants to try for an advantage, in contrast to 7...c6 and 7...♕e8 against which White has the choice of some interesting sidelines. So choosing 7...♘c6 simplifies the amount of preparation you need to do. The lack of a decent alternative also makes things rather unpleasant for a player of White who dislikes in general the pawn structure after the advance d4-d5.

There are various alternatives to 8 d5 to consider after 1 d4 f5 2 c4 ♘f6 3 ♘c3 d6 4 ♘f3 g6 5 g3 ♗g7 6 ♗g2 0-0 7 0-0 ♘c6. However, only really 8 ♕c2!?

and 8 b3, the move featured in the Radjabov-Ivanchuk game, below, deserve much attention.

If 8 ♖b1 Black can get a promising King's Indian style scenario with 8...e5 9 d5 ♘e7.

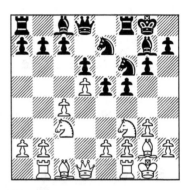

He will follow up with moves like ...h7-h6, ...g6-g5 and ...♘g6, aiming for a direct attack within the pawns.

Against most other moves Black can play ...♘e4 to put pressure on the d4-pawn and clear the way for the space gaining ...e7-e5. For example:

a) 8 ♗f4 ♘e4, intending ...e7-e5.

b) 8 ♕b3 ♘e4, intending 9...♘xc3 and then 10...e5.

c) 8 ♘d5 ♘e4, intending to evict the white knight with 9...e6.

d) 8 ♗g5 ♘e4 9 ♘xe4 fxe4 10 ♘d2 ♘xd4 11 ♘xe4 ♗f5 with equality.

e) 8 ♖e1 ♘e4, blocking the e2-e4 advance.

This brings us to White's trickiest alternative, **8 ♕c2!?**, which prevents 8...♘e4 and clears the way for ♖d1 to exploit the opening of the d-file:

8...e5 9 dxe5 dxe5 10 ♖d1

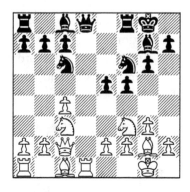

Some strong players have tried 10...♕e8?! here, but after 11 ♘d5 White has the edge.

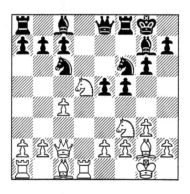

That's because the only active move, 11...e4, seems inadequate after 12 ♘xc7 ♕f7 13 ♘xa8 exf3 14 ♗xf3 ♗e6 15 b3 and now 15...♖xa8 leaves White with a rook and two pawns for two minor pieces. I assume this gives him the advantage after 16 ♗b2 – not that it is an easy position to play. Instead Black speculated in V.Prokopisin-L.Seres, Hungarian League 1996, with 15...♘b4 16 ♕d2 ♘e4 17 ♕xb4 ♗xa1 and got a good game after 18 ♗h6? ♗g7 19 ♗xg7 ♔xg7, but White missed a posi-

tional queen sacrifice with 18 ♗a3! ♗g7 19 ♕xf8+! ♗xf8 20 ♖d8 ♔g7 21 ♗xf8+ ♔f6 22 ♗a3 when Black faces a very unpleasant defence indeed.

So returning to 10 ♖d1, I think we should prefer **10...♗d7!** and then **11 ♗e3 e4**.

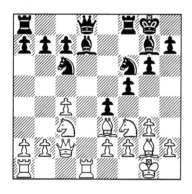

Now there are two interesting knight moves:

a) After 12 ♘d4 ♘g4! Black has excellent play in the case of the queen sacrifice 13 ♘e6 ♘xe3 14 fxe3 ♗xe6! 15 ♖xd8 ♖axd8. He has a solid structure and a great bishop on g7, whereas White's own bishop on g2 is entombed and the e3-pawn is horribly weak. So White should prefer 13 ♘xc6 ♘xe3 14 ♕c1 (to avoid the doubled pawns) 14...♕e8 15 ♕xe3 ♗xc6, although again Black has a promising game due to his kingside space and powerful dark-squared bishop.

b) More challenging is 12 ♘g5. Now in R.Kempinski-A.Hnydiuk, Krynica 1995, Black dealt with the threat of 13 ♘e6, winning the exchange, with 12...♕e8? only to lose the exchange instead to 13 ♗c5!. However, 12...♕c8!? 13 ♘d5 ♖e8 looks safe enough for Black, as 14 ♕d2 can be met by 14...♘e5, defending d7 again and planning 15...c6 to oust the white knight.

Finally there is 8 b3, which was tried in a game between two Super Grandmasters.

T.Radjabov-V.Ivanchuk
Odessa (rapid) 2008

1 d4 f5 2 c4 ♘f6 3 ♘c3 d6 4 ♘f3 g6 5 g3 ♗g7 6 ♗g2 0-0 7 0-0 ♘c6 8 b3

This was a rapidplay game and, perhaps surprised by an opening variation he had never studied in detail, Radjabov decides to play solidly. This is a common-sense approach, but unfortunately for him, it is when White tries to avoid a fight that the Dutch most often shows its teeth.

8...e5

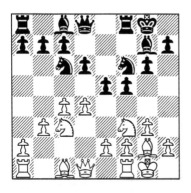

Already Black is striving for the initiative by seizing space in the centre.

9 dxe5 dxe5 10 ♗a3 ♖e8

With the plan of 11...e4.

11 e4

Black has no problems after the simplifying 11 ♕xd8 ♖xd8 12 ♖ad1 ♖xd1 13 ♖xd1 e4, as in A.Mirzoev-K.Movsziszian, Balaguer 2005. Still, perhaps White should have used this as an escape route from an awkward position.

11...♘d4

Making full use of the outpost square.

12 ♖e1 c6!

A scenario well known to King's Indian players. White's knight won't enjoy an outpost on d5 to balance the black knight's possession of d4.

13 exf5 ♗xf5!

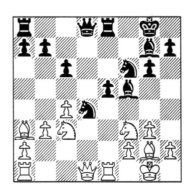

The correct recapture. Black's minor pieces are now excellently placed.

14 ♘h4?

This is a serious mistake that should lose at once, and failing that is going to lose in the long term as the knight will get trapped on h4. But White was already in a bad way, since, for example, exchanging on d4 leads to disaster: 14 ♘xd4 exd4 15 ♖xe8+ ♕xe8 16 ♘e2

(or 16 ♕xd4 ♘e4) 16...♘e4! when 17 ♘xd4 loses a piece to 17...♘c3 18 ♕d2 ♗xd4 because of the fork on e2, and 17 g4 allows Black a decisive attack with 17...♘xf2! 18 ♔xf2 ♕e3+ 19 ♔e1 d3 20 gxf5 ♖e8 21 ♖c1 dxe2 when his threats include 22...♕g1+.

14...♗c2?

He could win the exchange with 14...♘c2 15 ♘xf5 ♕d1! 16 ♖axd1 gxf5 when White can't save both the rook on e1 and the bishop on a3.

15 ♕c1 e4 16 ♗b2 ♗d3 17 ♖d1 ♕a5 18 ♕d2 ♖ad8

Ivanchuk has achieved a superb centralization of his pieces.

19 ♖ac1 ♕h5

It turns out that despite the missed opportunity on move 14 Black is winning anyway because the knight on h4 can't escape.

20 ♔h1

Instead the hari-kari line 20 ♗h1 g5 21 ♘g2 ♘f3 mate would be highly amusing for everyone apart from Rad-jabov.

20...g5

Trapping the knight. Because it is a rapidplay game, White permits himself to play on a long time in the hope of a swindle.

21 ♘d5 ♘xd5 22 cxd5 gxh4 23 h3 hxg3 24 fxg3 ♖xd5 25 g4 ♕g6 26 ♖e1 ♖ed8 27 ♕f2 ♖f8 28 ♕d2 ♗h6 29 ♕b4 ♗xc1 30 ♗xd4 ♗d2 31 ♕xd2 ♖xd4 32 ♕e3 ♖d7 33 ♕xa7 ♖df7 34 ♕e3 ♕f6 35 b4 ♕f4 36 ♕c5 ♖g7 37 a4 ♕f2 38 ♖e3 ♗f1 39 ♗xe4 ♔h8 40 a5 ♗c4 41 ♗g2 ♗g8 42 ♕c3 ♕f6 43 ♕e1 ♗d5 44 ♗xd5 cxd5 45 ♔g1 ♖gf7 0-1

In how many openings would a player rated 2735 be so summarily beaten as White because he played a bit too passively? That's the great thing about the Leningrad Dutch. It forces White into taking on the commitment of defending an extended pawn structure in the centre, whether this type of chess appeals to him or not.

Part Two:
8 d5 ♘a5 9 ♕d3

1 d4 f5 2 g3 ♘f6 3 ♗g2 g6 4 ♘f3 ♗g7 5 0-0 0-0 6 c4 d6 7 ♘c3 ♘c6 8 d5 ♘a5 9 ♕d3 *(see following diagram)*

White threatens to trap the black knight with 10 b4, so the usual reply is 9...c5, but Black might prefer to get maximum value out of the pawn on f5 with 9...e5!?.

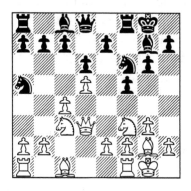

V.Babula-M.Bartel
Prievidza 2009

1 d4 f5 2 g3 ♘f6 3 ♗g2 g6 4 ♘f3 ♗g7 5 0-0 0-0 6 c4 d6 7 ♘c3 ♘c6 8 d5 ♘a5 9 ♕d3 e5!?

There is the immediate threat of a fork on e4. If now 10 e4 fxe4 11 ♘xe4 ♘xe4 12 ♕xe4 ♗f5 13 ♕e2 (to defend c4) 13...♗g4 (threatening 14...♕f6) 14 ♕e4 ♗xf3 (we could repeat with 14...♗f5 which shows the whole line isn't ideal for White) 15 ♗xf3 ♘xc4 16 ♗g4 ♘b6 and White doesn't have enough for the pawn.

10 dxe6 ♗xe6 11 b3 ♘c6

This is by no means an ignominious retreat. Bartel's efforts have restored the knight to an excellent post from which it can't easily be driven again by a white pawn. It's no small matter to have all the black minor pieces well centralized.

On the other hand, we might have wished to strike a telling blow against the white queenside when we played 8...♘a5, with our pawns getting involved in the battle. That hasn't happened, and the black queenside pawns are static. Furthermore, although the cramping white pawn has gone from d5, White still has control of this key square, and given time he can try to establish a knight there.

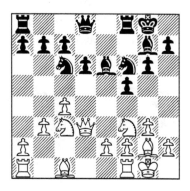

As this is the Dutch, Black should look to the pawn on f5 to spearhead some kingside counterplay. But first some patient manoeuvring is needed.

12 ♖b1

Instead 12 ♗b2 ♘e4! is an awkward pin: for example, 13 ♖ab1 ♘b4 when White has nothing better than to agree to a repetition with 14 ♕e3 ♘c2 15 ♕d3 ♘b4, etc; or 13 ♘xe4 ♗xb2 14 ♘eg5 ♗c8 15 ♖ad1 ♗f6 when Black consolidates and then enjoys the bishop-pair.

12...h6

Black prevents ♘g5, not only to maintain the bishop on e6 but also as preparation for putting his queen on f7.

13 ♗a3

The solid move was 13 ♗b2, but Babula is dreaming of a crushing onslaught against the black queenside involving moves like c4-c5.

13...♕e8 14 e3 ♕f7 15 ♘d4

White continues with his plan of putting pressure on the queenside, but he has forgotten about the unique power of Black's advancing f-pawn in the Dutch. More circumspect was 15 ♖bd1 when the f4-square remains defended by the e3-pawn.

15...♘xd4 16 exd4 f4!

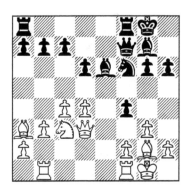

Bartel seizes his chance to carry out the traditional Dutch pawn-ram. The way is cleared for ...♗f5 to skewer the white queen against the rook on b1, but Babula underestimates this.

17 ♗xb7

This is the culmination of White's strategy: he wins a queenside pawn. Unfortunately for Babula, he has misjudged the power of Black's initiative.

17...♖ab8 18 ♕f3

Alternatively, 18 ♗g2 ♗f5 19 ♘e4 ♖be8 20 ♖be1 ♘xe4 21 ♗xe4 ♗xe4 22 ♖xe4 ♕f5! is awkward for White, as the black queen takes over the pin: 23 f3 (if 23 ♖fe1 fxg3 24 fxg3 ♕f2+ 25 ♔h1 ♖xe4 26 ♕xe4 ♕xa2 27 ♗c1 ♕xb3 and Black is a pawn up) 23...fxg3 24 hxg3 ♖xe4 25 ♕xe4 ♕xe4 26 fxe4 ♗xd4+ 27 ♔g2 ♖xf1 28 ♔xf1 ♔f7, and White has a difficult endgame due to the weak e4-pawn and Black's kingside pawn majority.

18...♘h7

The knight uncovers an attack on d4 and prepares to spring forwards to g5.

19 ♗d5

Instead 19 ♖ad1 ♘g5 20 ♕c6 ♗h3 puts the white king in terrible danger, so Babula returns the pawn to try to organize his pieces.

19...♗xd4 20 ♕e4 ♗xd5

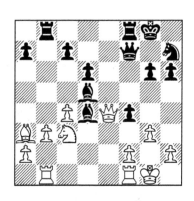

21 ♕xd4

He would prefer to eliminate the other bishop, but 21 ♘xd5 ♘g5! 22 ♕d3 fxg3 23 hxg3 ♕e6!, intending ...♕h3 and ...♘f3+ is lethal.

21...♗c6 22 h4 ♕f5 23 ♗b2 ♘f6 24 ♖be1 ♕h3 0-1

White is mated on g2 after 25 ♘d5 ♗xd5 26 cxd5 f3.

Your wins in the Dutch won't always be as dramatic as that!

Part Three:
8 d5 ♘a5 9 ♕a4

D.Izquierdo-L.Tristan
Mar del Plata 2009

1 d4 d6 2 ♘f3 f5 3 g3 ♘f6 4 ♗g2 g6 5 0-0 ♗g7 6 c4 0-0 7 ♘c3 ♘c6 8 d5 ♘a5 9 ♕a4

A modern idea. By attacking the knight White wants to force Black to compromise his pawn structure.

9...c5 10 dxc6 ♘xc6

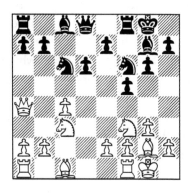

The best recapture. Experience has shown that Black has a hard time of it after 10...bxc6 11 c5!.

11 ♖d1

White's persists with the idea of giving Black a pawn weakness on d6 with 12 c5.

11...♘e4!?

This is the move Black wants to play

– he responds to White's decentralizing queen move with a counterattack in the centre that gets full value out of 1...f5. However, we can't always play the moves we want, even in the Dutch – so can Black get away with it?

The question is whether the resulting dynamism will compensate for the weak pawn that appears on e4 and Black's generally reduced control of the light squares.

12 ♘xe4

In the next game the radical 12 ♘g5!? is examined.

12...fxe4 13 ♘g5 ♘d4

Now the other black knight jumps into the centre. The e2-pawn is hanging and White really has little choice but to put his rook on d2 or e1 to defend it, crucially vacating the square on d1 for his queen. For example, 14 ♗f1? ♗d7 and White will lose at least the exchange after 15 ♕b4 or 15 ♕a3 to a fork on c2.

14 ♖d2 ♗g4

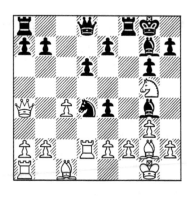

And now the bishop joins in the attack.

15 ♕d1 ♕b6 16 ♘xe4

A good time to recapture the pawn as the knight now rules out possible combinations from the black queen and rook on f8 against f2. For example, if 16 h3? then 16...♖xf2!? is already on the cards, intending 17 ♔xf2? ♘xe2+ 18 ♔e1 ♕g1+ 19 ♗f1 ♕xg3 mate, or 17 hxg4 ♘xe2+ 18 ♖xe2 (if 18 ♔h2 ♕e3, attacking g3, when 19 ♘xe4? ♕h6 is mate!) 18...♖xe2+ 19 ♔h2 ♕f2 and luckily for White he can bail out with 20 ♕d5+ ♔h8 21 ♘f7+ ♔g8 22 ♘h6+ ♔h8, etc, with perpetual check.

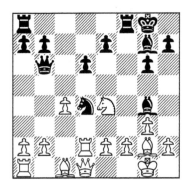

16...♖ac8

All the black pieces are superbly active, and White won't be able to hold on to the c4-pawn. So Black regains his pawn with a good game, right? Well, things aren't that easy. Black has light-square weaknesses along the a2-g8 diagonal, especially on d5. Moreover, the black bishop on g4 and the knight can be driven back with the moves h2-h3 and then e2-e3. So if White manages to solve his strategic problems, the blocked-in bishop on c1 and the

passive rook on a1, he may yet emerge with the better game. That is why accuracy is required of Black.

17 h3

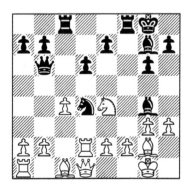

17...♗e6!

Covering d5. Instead after 17...♗f5? 18 ♘c3! in J.Parker-T.Rendle, British League 2008, the threat of 19 ♘d5 obliged Black to waste a move with 18...♗e6 when 19 e3 ♘c6 20 ♘d5 was horrible for him. In a position where one player is trying to unravel his game, and the other to preserve the dynamism of his pieces, the loss of a single tempo often changes the assessment.

18 e3

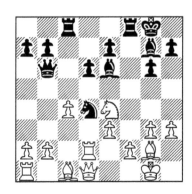

18...♘f5?

The knight should go to the queen-side with 18...♘c6! when the b7-pawn is shielded. After 19 c5 (White can't hold on to his pawn, so he gives it up to weaken the black centre) 19...dxc5 20 ♘g5 ♗c4! 21 ♕a4 ♕b4! Black has rather the better of it due to his queen-side pressure.

19 c5 dxc5 20 ♘g5 ♔h8 21 ♘xe6 ♕xe6 22 ♖c2?

White is understandably reluctant to grab a pawn with 22 ♗xb7! as it looks like Black might sacrifice a knight on e3 or g3. In fact both 22...♘xe3 23 ♗xc8 and 22..♘xg3 23 ♗xc8 ♕xc8 24 fxg3 ♕xh3 25 ♖g2 are entirely hopeless for Black, so he would have to remain a pawn down after 22...♖b8 23 ♗d5.

22...♘d6

Now Black is okay again and even gets some chances before a draw is eventually agreed.

23 ♗d2 ♘e4 24 ♗e1 h5 25 ♖ac1 b6 26 ♕d3 ♘g5 27 h4 ♘f3+ 28 ♗xf3 ♖xf3 29 b4 ♖f5 30 ♕a3 ♖c7 31 ♕a6 ♕e4 32 a3 ♔h7 33 ♕c4 ♕f3 34 ♖d2 g5 35 hxg5

♖xg5 36 ♕d3+ ♖g6 37 ♕d5 ♕g4 38 ♖c4 ♕h3 39 ♕g2 ♕e6 40 ♖d5 ♗h6 41 bxc5 bxc5 42 ♖cxc5 ♖xc5 43 ♖xc5 h4 44 ♕d5 hxg3 45 ♕xe6 ½-½

In the following game White introduced a sharp improvement on move 12.

E.Gasanov-M.Zelic
European Championship,
Rijeka 2010

1 ♘f3 f5 2 g3 ♘f6 3 ♗g2 d6 4 d4 g6 5 0-0 ♗g7 6 c4 0-0 7 ♘c3 ♘c6 8 d5 ♘a5 9 ♕a4 c5 10 dxc6 ♘xc6 11 ♖d1 ♘e4 12 ♘g5!?

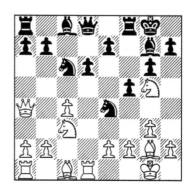

Rather than 12 ♘xe4, White offers a gambit...

12...♘xc3?

...and Black takes the bait. He wins a pawn, but ends up in an unpleasant bind.

More in the spirit of the Dutch is 12...♘c5! 13 ♕c2 (13 ♕a3 ♘d4 threatens a fork on c2) 13...h6 14 ♗e3 (otherwise, 14 ♘h3 g5! shuts out the knight, while 14 ♘f3 ♗b4 – or even 14...g5!? – 15 ♕d2 ♕b6! gives Black splendid chances; the immediate threat is 16...♘e4 to exploit a potential attack on f2 by the black queen) 14...hxg5 (14...♕a5!? also looks fine) 15 ♗xc5 ♗e6 and Black is at least okay thanks to his activity.

13 bxc3 ♗xc3 14 ♖b1 ♕a5 15 ♗d5+ ♔g7 16 ♗xc6 bxc6 17 ♕xc6 f4

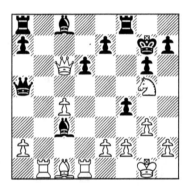

The only way to defend the cornered rook on a8 is by playing 17...♗a6, but then the white knight jumps into e6. Zelic therefore tries to mix things up with an exchange sacrifice, but his position soon falls apart in any case:

18 ♕xa8 ♕xg5 19 ♗xf4 ♖xf4 20 ♕xc8 ♗d4 21 ♖f1 ♖e4 22 ♖b8 ♔h6 23 ♕h3+ ♔g7 24 ♕c8 ♔h6 25 e3 ♖xe3 26 ♕h3+

Refuting the desperate rook offer. If instead 26 fxe3?? ♕xe3+ 27 ♔g2 ♕e2+ 28 ♔h3 ♕xf1+ and only Black can win.

26...♔g7 27 fxe3 ♕xe3+ 28 ♔h1 1-0

Novelties such as 12 ♘g5!? often do well when they are first introduced, but

the move shouldn't trouble a well-prepared Dutch player.

Part Four:
8 d5 ♘a5 9 ♘d2

1 d4 f5 2 g3 ♘f6 3 ♗g2 g6 4 ♘f3 ♗g7 5 0-0 0-0 6 c4 d6 7 ♘c3 ♘c6 8 d5 ♘a5 9 ♘d2

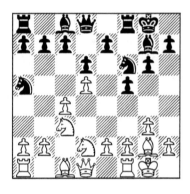

This is the traditional way for White to counter the threat to the c4-pawn. Indeed, over the years it has amassed a fair bit of theory which is summarized below.

Note that the move order 9 ♕c2 c5 (instead 9...♘xc4 runs into 10 ♘b5 which is slightly awkward) 10 ♘d2 e5 11 dxe6 ♗xe6 allows Black to reach the 9 ♘d2 c5 10 ♕c2 e5 11 dxe6 ♗xe6 lines given below, which seem favourable for him.

An important alternative is 9 b3!?. This looks like a blunder, but in fact things are by no means easy for Black after 9...♘e4 10 ♘xe4 ♗xa1 11 ♘eg5 c5 (definitely bad is 11...♗g7? 12 ♘d4 when Black has the ghastly choice of letting a knight into e6 or giving up his dark-squared bishop with 12...♗xd4) 12 e4 ♗g7 13 ♘h4 with an enduring initiative for White and no counterplay for Black – the knight on a5 looks awful when it isn't the centre of attention, and here all the action is on the kingside.

Instead after 9 b3, 9...c5 tries to take play into familiar territory, but 10 ♗d2!? is tricky. The slow 10...♔h8 turned out badly in I.Lutsko-D.Trifonov, Minsk 2005, after 11 e4 fxe4 12 ♘g5. Because the g5-square is so important for the white knight on its journey towards the hole on e6, perhaps 10...h6!? should be played to keep it out.

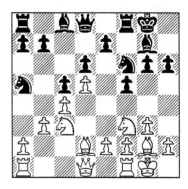

The move 10 ♗d2 prevents the natural ♘d2 to support an e2-e4 breakthrough, so the knight on f3 is quite hemmed in – a bit like the knight on a5, in fact. After 10...h6 play might continue 11 ♕c2 g5 (directed against White's plan of 12 ♘h4 and 13 e4) 12 e4 fxe4 13 ♘xe4 ♗f5 14 ♘xf6+ ♖xf6 15 ♕c3 b6 with unclear play. The open f-

file and advanced pawns give Black some dynamic compensation for having the knight still out of play on a5.

9...c5

Now we shall look at 10 a3 in the Quenallata-Rodriguez game that follows.

I think that is a better way for White to play than 10 ♕c2 which encourages Black to begin counterplay in the centre with 10...e5!.

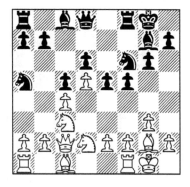

Then:

a) If White settles for 11 a3 then after 11...b6 12 b4 ♘b7 Black has a compact pawn centre and a solid queenside. Now the game E.Brondum-M.Gurevich, Copenhagen 2001, was highly curious: 13 ♖b1 ♗d7 14 ♘b5? (White begins an extraordinary manoeuvre of the knight to a6) 14...♕e7 15 ♘c7 ♖ac8 16 ♘a6 e4 (Black seizes more space and then prepares a kingside attack) 17 ♕b3 ♘g4 18 e3 h5! 19 bxc5 dxc5 (White has no way through on the queenside; his knight is a truly pathetic piece on a6) 20 ♗b2 ♗xb2 21 ♕xb2 h4 22 ♖fd1 hxg3 23 hxg3 ♗a4 24

♖e1 ♕h7 25 ♘f1 ♘d6 26 ♕a2 ♗e8 0-1. The game ends abruptly as 26...♕b7 will pick up the ridiculous knight.

b) 11 dxe6 ♗xe6 and now:

b1) 12 b3 d5! 13 cxd5 ♘xd5 14 ♗b2 ♘b4 15 ♕c1 ♖c8 gives Black a free position.

b2) However, 12 ♖d1 is worse, allowing Black to build up a decisive attack in surprisingly quick fashion: 12...♕e7! (defending b7 so that c4 is now hanging)

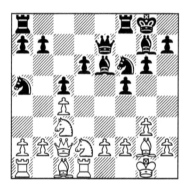

13 b3 ♘c6 14 ♗b2 (White doesn't have time for 14 e3, as then 14...♘b4 15 ♕b1 f4! gives Black a tremendous initiative: for example, 16 gxf4 ♗f5 17 e4 ♘h5 18 exf5 ♗xc3 with ideas of ...♗xa1 and ...♘xf4) 14...♘d4 15 ♕d3 f4! 16 gxf4 ♗f5 17 e4 ♗e6. Now the f4-pawn is going to drop and White's position soon fell apart in D.Berkovich-B.Annakov, Ufa 1993: 18 ♗f3 ♘d7 19 e5 ♖xf4 20 exd6 ♕g5+ 21 ♗g2 ♘e5 22 ♕f1 ♖af8 23 ♘ce4 ♖xe4 24 ♘xe4 ♘ef3+ 25 ♔h1 ♕h4 26 h3 ♕xe4 0-1.

Finally, 10 ♖b1 e5 11 dxe6 ♗xe6 12 ♘d5 ♘xd5 13 cxd5 ♗d7 14 b4 cxb4 15 ♖xb4 b5 turned out well for Black in A.Truskavetsky-S.Kovalov, Sevastopol 2000, as he managed to utilize his queenside pawn majority after 16 ♗b2 ♗xb2 17 ♖xb2 ♕f6 18 ♖b1 ♖ac8 19 ♘b3 ♘xb3 20 axb3 a5, etc.

L.Quenallata-A.Rodriguez Vila
Buenos Aires 2009

1 d4 f5 2 g3 ♘f6 3 ♗g2 g6 4 ♘f3 ♗g7 5 0-0 0-0 6 c4 d6 7 ♘c3 ♘c6 8 d5 ♘a5 9 ♘d2 c5 10 a3 ♗d7!

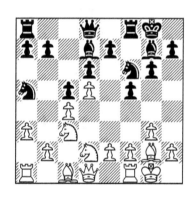

Black can afford to ignore the 'threat' of 11 b4? as he regains the piece with advantage after 11...cxb4 12 axb4 ♘xc4! 13 ♘xc4 ♕c7 14 ♕b3 ♖fc8 etc. On the other hand, Black has been prevented from playing a line with the pawn advance ...e7-e5: he must concentrate for the time being on the narrow front of the queenside.

11 ♕c2 ♕c7

Once again indirectly meeting the threat of 12 b4, which would again permit 12...cxb4 13 axb4 ♘xc4.

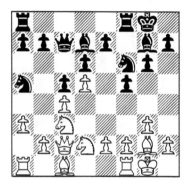

12 b3 a6

Beginning a pawn advance to put more pressure on c4.

13 ♗b2 b5 14 e4

Ambitious. After the regrouping 14 ♘d1 b5 15 ♗c3, as played by the great Botvinnik versus Matulovic at Belgrade 1970, Black gets sufficient counterplay with 15...bxc4 16 bxc4 ♖b7! (better than Matulovic's 16...♘g4). For example, 17 ♖b1 ♖fb8 18 ♖xb7 ♖xb7 19 ♘b2 ♕b8 20 e3 ♘b3 21 ♘f3 ♘e4 22 ♗xg7 ♔xg7 23 ♘d3, as in E.Magerramov-Mi.Tseitlin, Balatonbereny 1989, and here Tseitlin has recommended 23...a5.

14...♖ab8 15 ♖ab1 bxc4 16 bxc4 ♘g4

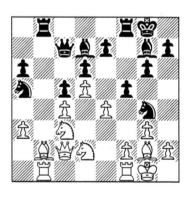

Rodriguez plans to advance ...f5-f4 and turn the e5-square into a strong central post for his knight.

17 ♘d1 ♗xb2?!

Instead 17...♗d4!? was an interesting possibility. Then 18 ♗xd4 cxd4 would expose the c4-pawn to attack, but otherwise Black is poised to advance with 18...f4.

18 ♖xb2 f4 19 ♖xb8 ♕xb8 20 ♕c3 ♕d8 21 f3 ♘e5 22 ♘f2

Black stands well on the kingside, but the knight on a5 is a liability.

22...e6?

Now White is able to break the blockade on f4. I would suggest 22...♕c7 23 ♖b1 g5 to reinforce the dark squares and ensure that the knight gets to stay on e5.

23 gxf4 ♖xf4 24 ♘h3! ♖f8 25 f4

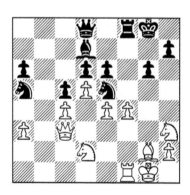

The knight is driven back and the white centre starts to roll forwards.

25...♘g4 26 e5 dxe5 27 fxe5

Positionally Rodriguez is busted, but let's not forget this is the Dutch. There are always going to be tactical resources for Black, and similarly plenty of opportunities for White to make a tactical oversight.

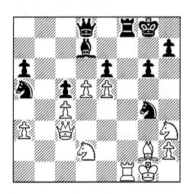

27...Ξxf1+ 28 ♗xf1 exd5 29 cxd5 c4 30 ♘xc4?

Here it is – the Dutch has done its job and confused White. Correct was 30 e6! when after 30...♗b5 31 ♘e4 or 30...♕b6+ 31 ♔h1 Black is in deep peril.

30...♘xc4

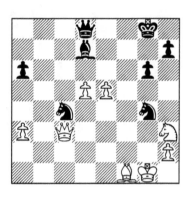

31 ♗xc4?

He had to try 31 ♕xc4, though Black is better after 31...♕b6+ and 32...♘xe5. **31...♕b6+ 32 ♔h1 ♕b1+ 33 ♔g2 ♕e4+ 34 ♔g3 ♘e3 35 e6 ♕g4+ 0-1**

The white queen is lost to a fork on d1.

Chapter Eight

The Dutch versus 1 ♘f3 and 1 c4

In this chapter we'll examine a series of variations in which White avoids an early d2-d4, or at least delays it for a long time. Chiefly we'll be looking at lines after 1 ♘f3 f5 and 1 c4 f5, although 1 b3 f5 also gets a mention at the end.

Part One: 1 ♘f3 f5

After **1 ♘f3 f5** White doesn't have to advance with d2-d4 or c2-c4, but might prefer a rapid e2-e4; a dangerous advance which Black must be prepared for.

The Lisitsyn Gambit

1 ♘f3 f5 2 e4 fxe4 3 ♘g5

This is the Lisitsyn Gambit. White hopes for an early attack against the black king.

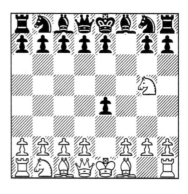

3...e5!

The simplest reply. Interesting is 3...d5 4 d3 ♕d6, but the following variation discourages me from giving it a go: 5 ♘c3 exd3 6 ♗xd3 ♘f6 7 ♘b5 ♕b6 8 ♗f4 ♘a6 9 ♕e2 ♗g4 10 f3 ♗d7 11 0-0-0 and White had a massive initiative for the pawn in M.Kazhgaleyev-P.Nikolic, Kemer 2007. Black actually won this game – the final move was 43...♕a1 mate – but it looks too risky even for the Dutch.

4 d3 e3!

Black gives up the pawn on e3 so that White is unable to develop an initiative after 4...exd3 5 ♗xd3 when 5...♘f6? 6 ♗xh7! ♘xh7?! 7 ♕h5+ is already a decisive attack.

5 ♗xe3 ♘c6!?

Or 5...♗e7 at once, but Black doesn't need to do the knight on g5 the favour of driving it back to f3. Indeed, if now 6 ♘f3 anyway Black can come up with a more useful move like 6...♘f6, and reserve the chance to play ...♗b4 or some other active bishop move. White's options don't seem as good as after 5...♗e7 6 ♘f3 ♘c6 7 d4. The fianchetto on g2 he now chooses is far from inspiring.

6 g3 ♗e7 7 ♗g2 ♘f6 8 ♘e4 d5 9 ♘xf6+ ♗xf6

Annoyingly for White, he can't centralize his knight as after 10 ♘c3 d4 or 10 ♘d2 d4 he loses a piece.

10 c3 d4 11 ♗d2 dxc3 12 ♗xc3 0-0 13 0-0 ♗e6 14 ♗e4 ♕d7 15 ♘a3 ♖ad8 16 ♘c2 ♗h3

Black had a good game and went on

to grind out the win on move 50 in O.Husser-V.Bronznik, Bad Wörishofen 2008.

The Delayed Lisitsyn: 2 d3!?

1 ♘f3 f5 2 d3!?

In recent years White has devised a two-part plan to refute the Dutch. First of all, he prepares the pawn thrust e2-e4, in order to liquidate Black's bastion on f5. Thereafter he will follow up with d3-d4, to free the bishop on f1 and gain the initiative in the centre. This system is surprisingly poisonous.

The main line is 2...d6 3 e4 e5 4 ♘c3 when White will exchange on f5 and break with d3-d4, but I prefer **2...g6!?**.

If we can get away with this then we keep the position in the style of the Leningrad Dutch.

Note that the statistics on 2...g6 on your database may well be rather misleading. They certainly are on mine, where the players of Black have been over a hundred Elo points on average weaker. Taking that into account,

Black's results have been pretty good.

We'll look at three alternatives for White after the critical line 1 ♘f3 f5 2 d3 g6 3 e4 d6 4 exf5 ♗xf5 5 d4 ♗g7: 6 ♗d3, 6 c3 and 6 ♘c3.

But first of all let's check out 1 ♘f3 f5 2 d3 g6 3 h4. It would be strange if this sharp gambit line were good for White when his bishop is shut in by the pawn on d3. After 3...♘f6 4 e4 e6!? Black is solid enough, or 4 h5 ♘xh5 5 ♖xh5 (5 e4 e6) 5...gxh5 6 e4 e6 7 exf5 ♕f6 and White doesn't have enough for the exchange. So my advice is: if White pushes the pawn to h5, take it with the knight. Onwards now to the main line!

L.Schandorff-M.Bartel
European Team
Championship, Novi Sad 2009

1 ♘f3 f5 2 d3 g6 3 e4 d6

This is played rather than 3...♗g7 in order to recapture on f5 with the bishop.

4 exf5 ♗xf5 5 d4

To free his bishop and take some space in the centre. The position is similar to Balogh's Defence: 1 d4 d6 2 e4 f5. That isn't especially highly regarded, but crucially in the Dutch version Black has achieved the 2...g6 move 'for free' as White played d4 in two goes.

5...♗g7 6 ♗d3!

The exchange of light-squared bishops increases the weakness of Black's

e6-square. Of course Leningrad players are used to enduring a hole in the pawn structure on e6, but here it is pronounced as White has already opened the e-file. That makes the e7-pawn a backward pawn on an open file. On the other hand, Black achieves a freer and faster development of his pieces than in the main line Leningrad. In the present game, Bartel has every single piece centralized and ready for action by move twelve. How often are Black's rooks so easily developed?

And we shouldn't forget that Black also has the half-open f-file for potential counterplay. Furthermore, the black queen finds an active post on f5.

6...♕d7!

A good move: the black queen will reach an active square and a defender is added to e6. In contrast, 6...♗xd3 7 ♕xd3 would activate the white queen, when already ideas of ♘g5, heading for e6, combined with ♕b3 or ♕e2 would be in the air.

7 0-0 ♘f6 8 ♗xf5 ♕xf5 9 c4

If 9 ♘c3 then 9...♘d5 10 ♘xd5 ♕xd5

looks okay for Black.

Instead 9 ♖e1 looks critical. After 9...♘c6 10 ♘c3 the 10...♘d5 idea again looks fine after 11 ♘xd5 ♕xd5 12 c3 0-0, so White should play 10 c4, when Black might block the d4-d5 advance with 10...d5.

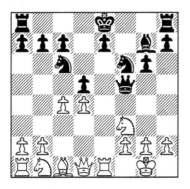

I think Black is again okay here. For example:

a) 11 ♘c3 dxc4 12 d5?! ♖d8 is good for Black.

b) 11 ♘e5 0-0 12 ♘xc6 bxc6 when the greedy 13 ♖xe7? could lose in spectacular style to 13...♘g4 14 f3 ♖ae8! 15 ♖xe8 ♖xe8 16 fxg4 ♗xd4+! 17 ♔h1 (or 17 ♕xd4 ♖e1 mate) 17...♕f2 18 ♗d2 ♖e2, and there's no good way to prevent mate on g2. So White should make do with 13 ♘a3 ♖ae8 or 13 ♘c3 when safe is 13...♖ae8, but I rather like 13...dxc4!? for Black. His pawns are a wreck, but he has an extra one and d4 is also a target. So the conclusion seems to be that Black has enough dynamic play after 9 ♖e1.

9...0-0 10 ♘c3 ♘bd7 11 ♗e3 c6 12 ♕e2 ♖ae8 13 ♖ad1 d5!

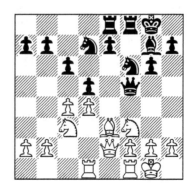

Stopping White from advancing with 14 d5. As in his game with Gerber below, Bartel gets a grip on the light squares in the centre by advancing ...d6-d5 and then ...e7-e6.

14 h3 dxc4 15 ♕xc4+ ♘d5 16 ♕b3 ♘7b6 17 a4 ♔h8!

Black now has a good and active position thanks to his well-entrenched central pieces. White's attempt to cause problems on the queenside will backfire.

18 ♖fe1

Black is better after 18 a5 ♘xc3 19 bxc3 ♕xa5 20 ♖a1 ♕d5!

18...e6 19 a5?

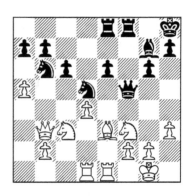

He should have given up on this idea.

19...♘xe3 20 ♖xe3

After 20 fxe3 ♕xa5 21 ♖a1 ♕h5 22 ♖xa7 ♖xf3! Black gets a dangerous attack for the exchange.

20...♕xa5 21 ♖xe6 ♖xe6 22 ♕xe6 ♕f5!

White's pawn structure has deteriorated even further. He could exchange queens and try to defend a bad endgame. Instead he tries for activity, comes under an attack and finally has to play an endgame after all a pawn down. The remaining moves were:

23 ♕e7 ♕f7 24 ♖e1 ♔g8 25 ♕e2 ♘d5 26 ♘g5 ♕f5 27 ♘f3 ♘f4 28 ♕c4+ ♔h8 29 ♖e3 ♗h6 30 ♖e5 ♘xh3+ 31 ♔f1 ♕c2 32 ♕e2 ♕c1+ 33 ♕e1 ♕xe1+ 34 ♖xe1 ♘g5 35 ♘e5 ♗g7 36 d5 cxd5 37 ♘xd5 ♖f5 38 f4 ♗xe5 39 g4 ♖xf4+ 40 ♘xf4 ♗xf4 41 ♖e7 ♗d6 42 ♖xb7 ♗c5 43 ♔g2 h6 44 ♖c7 ♗b6 45 ♖d7 ♔g8 46 ♖e7 ♔f8 47 ♖b7 ♘f7 48 ♔g3 ♔g7 49 ♔f4 ♔f6 50 ♖d7 ♔e6 51 ♖d1 ♗c7+ 52 ♔e4 ♘g5+ 53 ♔e3 ♔e5 54 ♖h1 ♗b6+ 55 ♔e2 ♘f7 56 ♖f1 ♔e6 57 ♖h1 ♔f6 58 ♖f1+ ♔g7 59 ♖f4 ♘e5 60 ♔d2 g5 61 ♖e4 ♔f6 62 ♔e2 ♔e6 63 ♖a4 ♔d5 0-1

B.Jacobsen-B.Christensen
Danish Championship,
Silkeborg 2009

1 ♘f3 f5 2 d3 g6 3 e4 d6 4 exf5 ♗xf5 5 d4 ♗g7 6 c3

White avoids exchanging bishops with 6 ♗d3. It leads to a sharp fight as Black's natural developing moves require him to offer a pawn sacrifice.

6...♘f6 7 ♘bd2 0-0! 8 ♕b3+

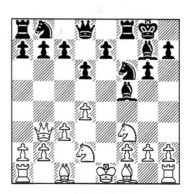

Winning the b7-pawn.

8...♔h8 9 ♕xb7 ♘bd7 10 ♗e2 e5

Black has plenty of compensation – the white queen is on an awkward square and the knight on f3 is going to be pushed back by ...e5-e4.

11 0-0

Or 11 dxe5 ♘c5 12 ♕b5 (not 12 ♕c6? ♗d7, trapping the queen) 12...a6 13 ♕c4 ♘g4! 14 exd6 ♕xd6 15 0-0 ♖ae8. White is two pawns up, but his position is very shaky. The black queen is poised to deliver mate on h2 if the knight can be removed from f3. If now 16 h3 ♘e5 17 ♘xe5 ♕xe5, the bishop on e2 is in trouble because of 18 ♗f3 ♗d3.

In fact there are so many attacking moves available to Black – ...♘e4, ...♗e6, and even ...♗d7 with ideas of ...♗b5 – that it is difficult to see how White can escape.

11...e4 12 ♘e1 ♘b6 13 ♕a6 ♘fd5

Threatening 14...♘f4.

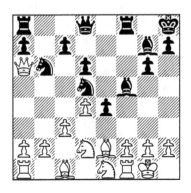

14 ♘c4 c5

Alternatively Black could try for a kingside attack with 14...♕h4. But Christensen adopts a positional approach – increasing his pressure on the white centre. In his confusion Jacobsen lets his queen be trapped.

15 ♘c2 cxd4 16 ♘xd4 ♗xd4 17 cxd4 ♘b4 18 ♕b7 ♔g8 19 ♗d2? ♖f7 20 ♕xf7+ ♔xf7 21 ♗xb4 ♘xc4 22 ♗xc4+ ♗e6 23 d5 ♗f5 24 ♗d2 h5 25 ♗e3 ♕f6 26 b3 g5 27 ♖ac1 ♔g6 28 ♖c2 a5 29 ♗b5 h4 30 h3 g4 31 hxg4 ♗xg4 0-1

R.Gerber-M.Bartel
Illes Medes 2007

---

1 ♘f3 f5 2 d3 d6 3 e4 g6 4 exf5 ♗xf5 5 d4 ♗g7 6 ♘c3 ♘f6 7 ♗g5 0-0 8 ♗c4+?

White has played a lot of active-looking moves, but in reality they don't do anything to harm the black position. On the contrary, Bartel is delighted that with 8 ♗c4+ White is positively encouraging him to transfer his pawns to e6 and d5.

8...e6 9 ♕d2 d5!

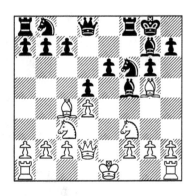

Having the pawns on d5 and e6 means that Black has more space behind them for his pieces. Furthermore, his c6-knight and g7-bishop are more adept at covering the hole on e5 than a hole on e6. This means that the freeing move ...e6-e5 is more likely to occur.

10 ♗d3 ♗xd3 11 ♕xd3 ♘c6 12 0-0-0 ♕d7 13 ♖he1 ♖ae8

Once again it can be observed how fluent Black's development is in the 2...g6 variation. Both his rooks are already well centralized.

14 ♕b5?

The same faulty strategy as at move eight. This time White uses his queen to cajole the black pawns to advance – which is exactly what suits Black's strategy.

14...♕c8 15 ♔b1 a6 16 ♕e2 b5 17 a3 ♘d7

It seems like the knight is heading for an attacking square on c4. However, Bartel doesn't want a battle between wing attacks. First of all he is going to keep the knight on b6 to support the d5-pawn so that the central break ...e6-e5 becomes possible. Only then will the knight consider going to the c4-square.

18 h4 ♘b6 19 ♗e3 e5!

Finally it is time for the central breakthrough.

20 ♘xe5 ♘xe5 21 dxe5 ♖xe5 22 f4 ♖ee8 23 ♕d2 c5!

Now Black comes steamrollering through the centre, as 24 ♘xd5 ♘c4 25 ♕f2 ♘xb2 is horrible for White.

24 ♗f2 d4 25 ♘e4 ♕c6 26 ♘g5 ♘c4

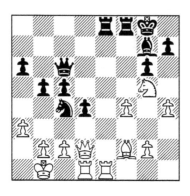

Finally the knight reaches c4.

27 ♕d3 ♕xg2 28 ♖e2 ♘xb2! 0-1

Too nasty to contemplate is 29 ♔xb2 ♖xe2 30 ♕xe2?! d3+.

Part Two: The Anglo-Dutch

1 c4 f5

If you decide to play the Dutch against everything, you will face the English quite often. If White wishes to push his d-pawn no further than d3, he usually fianchettoes on the kingside and then sets up with e2-e4 and ♘ge2, e2-e3 and ♘ge2, or just ♘f3. Before we come to those sensible approaches, we must consider an unusual gambit:

2 ♘c3 ♘f6 3 e4

Note that another route to this position is 2 e4 fxe4 3 ♘c3 ♘f6.

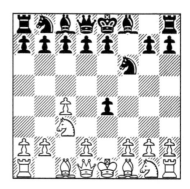

Here White can try 4 d3, but the simple 4...e5 seems fine for Black. For example, 5 g4 h6 (to stop the knight being driven from f6) 6 g5 hxg5 7 ♗xg5 ♗b4 8 ♗g2 0-0 9 ♗xe4 ♕e8 10 ♗g2 c6 11 ♘ge2 d6 12 ♘g3 ♗g4 13 ♕d2 ♘bd7 14 0-0 ♘h5 and Black was better due to his more compact pawn structure in A.Danilovic-V.Podinic, Belgrade 2008.

However, this is only half the story. If White plays 4 g4!? then the move 4...h6 is less attractive as White can play 5 ♗g2.

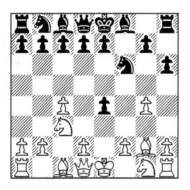

Here is a gamelet that shows the danger of this variation if Black is careless: 5...e5 6 h4 ♗e7? (essential was 6...d5!, involving the bishop on c8 in the game so that 7...hxg5 8 hxg5 ♘g4 becomes a possible answer to White's next move) 7 g5 hxg5 8 hxg5 ♖xh1 9 ♗xh1 ♘g8 10 ♕h5+ ♔f8 11 ♗xe4 c6 12 ♕f3+ 1-0 J.Mellado Trivino-F.Vallejo Pons, Oropesa del Mar 1996.

So against 4 g4 I would recommend 4...g6.

For example, 5 h4 d5 6 g5 ♘h5 7 cxd5 ♗g7 8 ♕a4+ c6 9 ♗g2 0-0 when White's game was something of a mess in J.Mellado Trivino-S.Del Rio Angelis, Zamora 1996. Or 5 d3 d5! 6 g5 d4 7 gxf6 dxc3 8 f7+ ♔xf7 9 bxc3 exd3 10 ♗xd3 ♗g7 with a clear advantage to Black.

The Botvinnik System

D.Laylo-F.Nijboer
Turin Olympiad 2006

1 c4 f5 2 ♘c3 ♘f6 3 g3 g6 4 ♗g2 ♗g7 5 d3

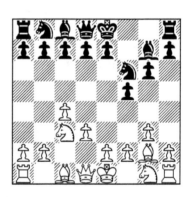

The features of the Botvinnik System begin to take shape. White aims to establish a pawn on e4. He has delayed developing the knight from g1 as he wants to put it on e2 rather than f3.

Black is allowed to develop all his pieces and get a foothold on the centre himself. Nonetheless, I can't say I enjoy playing against this rock-solid opening system all that much. Probably it is because Black needs to show more patience and restraint than in the usual Dutch variations. There are no ready targets for the black pieces, although of course there are no targets for White either.

5...0-0 6 e4 fxe4

This move is considered to be premature, but Black also has a particular opening scheme in mind. He wants to stabilize the centre at once so that he can put a triangle of pawns on d6, e5 and c5. I like this method as it gives Black a clear guiding path against a rather confusing opening scheme.

7 dxe4 d6 8 ♘ge2 c5

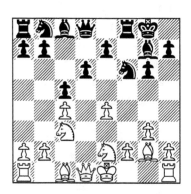

Black has delayed developing the knight on b8 until he could make this pawn move.

9 0-0 ♘c6 10 h3

A restraining move typical of the line as a whole. Instead 10 f4 ♗e6 11 b3 ♕d7 followed by 12...♗h3 allows Black to carry out a favourable exchange of bishops.

10...e5

This creates a hole on the d5-square

– but I guess we aren't too worried, as Black usually has at least one glaring structural weakness in the Dutch. And for once there is also a hole in the white pawn structure. The twin pillars of Black's pawn structure create a fine outpost on d4 for the black knight.

Of course, a brilliant strategic player such as World Champion Botvinnik would have noticed if Black could get a great position simply by plonking a knight on d4. Then the opening system would certainly never have been adopted by him and bear his name.

11 f4!

White needs the help of his pawns to make a dent on the black position. After 11 ♗g5 Black can develop with 11...♗e6, 12...♕d7, and play ...♘d4 whenever he pleases.

11...♗e6!

A very instructive moment, which shows that the natural move is not always the best one.

After 11...♘d4 White can make an excellent pawn sacrifice with 12 f5! gxf5 (otherwise 13 g4, etc, is position-

ally crushing) 13 exf5 ♘xf5 14 ♕d3!
♘d4 15 ♗g5 ♗e6 16 ♘e4 ♖c8 17 ♘2c3
and Black was in a terrible bind due to
the pin on f6 in B.Damljanovic-
S.Kindermann, Halkidiki 2002. It is
White who is getting by far the most
benefit from the central situation as
his knight on e4 supports the action
along the f-file.

The black knight looks pretty on d4,
but what exactly is it doing? The f4-f5
move has also opened up the diagonal
for White's bishop on g2, which Black
was careful to block in the opening
with 6...fxe4. In other words, Black's
opening strategy has ended in fiasco.

That is why 11...♗e6! should be
played. The pawn on c4 is hanging, so
Black wins time to take measures
against the f4-f5 advance.

12 b3 ♕d7!

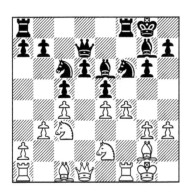

Continuing the fight against f4-f5.
The pawn on h3 is now hanging. Now
after 13 ♔h2 Black could either play
13...♘d4, as the sting has been take out
of the f4-f5 advance, or spend one
move on preparation with 13...♖ae8.

White therefore tries another plan.

13 g4 exf4!

It is essential not to allow White a
pawn wedge with 14 f5.

14 ♗xf4 ♘e5

So after all the talk about ...♘d4 the
knight ends up on the e5-square. But
let's not forget that the e5-square only
became accessible to the knight because White wanted to take some action before ...♘d4 was played. Black's
strategy has won his knight a fine central post.

15 ♗xe5

Alas the knight didn't enjoy itself on
e5 for long. Still, the fact that White
couldn't find anything better than to
give up the important dark-squared
bishop shows that Black has at least
equalized.

**15...dxe5 16 ♕xd7 ♘xd7 17 ♖ad1
♖xf1+ 18 ♗xf1 ♖c8**

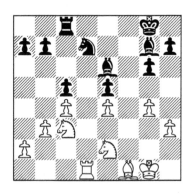

The most active square for the rook,
whence it may be able to attack the
white queenside after ...♖c6. It is also
available for the defence of the second
rank.

19 ♗g2 ♗f6

Next the bishop is brought around to d8, a more active post than g7 as it can then take part in the queenside action.

20 ♘d5 ♗d8 21 ♘ec3 a6

Keeping the white knight out of b5. White is now confronted with a problem that was discussed in Chapter Four – he has two knights, but only one great square for them on d5.

22 ♗f1 ♔g7 23 ♔g2 ♘f8

As the next step in improving the layout of the black pieces, the knight is brought to e6, where it is in contact with the celebrated outpost on d4.

24 a3 ♗f7 25 b4 ♘e6 26 ♖b1 ♗e8 27 ♔g3 h5

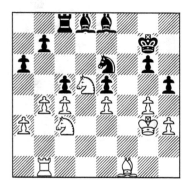

Finally some aggressive action begins. Nijboer has got exactly what he was hoping for: a strong but considerably lower-rated player has played a solid opening as White, and he has managed to make it into a double-edged fight.

He eventually manages to grind down his opponent – but the game

lasts until move 114! For those of you with stamina, here is the remainder: **28 gxh5 gxh5 29 b5 ♘d4 30 h4 axb5 31 cxb5 ♖a8 32 a4 ♗a5 33 ♖b2 ♗g6 34 ♖f2 ♘e6 35 ♖f3 ♘f4 36 ♘e7 ♗f7 37 ♘f5+ ♔f6 38 ♘d6 b6 39 ♘xf7 ♔xc3 40 ♖xc3 ♔xf7 41 ♖a3 ♔e7 42 ♗c4 ♔d6 43 ♖a2 ♔c7 44 ♔f3 ♖d8 45 a5 bxa5 46 ♖xa5 ♖d4 47 ♗f1 ♖d1 48 ♔f2 ♖d4 49 ♖a6 ♖xe4 50 ♖c6+ ♔d7 51 ♖xc5 ♔d6 52 ♖c6+ ♔d5 53 ♖c1 ♖b4 54 ♖d1+ ♔e6 55 ♖d2 ♔f5 56 ♖d8 ♔e4 57 ♖d2 ♖b3 58 ♗c4 ♖b4 59 ♗f1 ♔f5 60 ♖d8 e4 61 ♖g8 ♔e5 62 ♖d8 ♖b2+ 63 ♔g3 ♖b3+ 64 ♔h2 e3 65 ♗c4 ♖b4 66 ♖c8 e2 67 ♖e8+ ♔f5 68 ♗xe2 ♖b2 69 ♖f8+ ♔e5 70 ♖e8+ ♘e6 71 ♔g3 ♖xe2 72 b6 ♖e3+ 73 ♔f2 ♖b3 74 ♖h8 ♘f4 75 ♖b8 ♖b2+ 76 ♔g3 ♘e2+ 77 ♔f3 ♘d4+ 78 ♔e3 ♖b3+ 79 ♔d2 ♔d6 80 b7 ♘c6 81 ♖h8 ♖b5 82 ♖h7 ♘b8 83 ♔c3 ♔c6 84 ♔c4 ♖a5 85 ♔b4 ♖f5 86 ♔c3 ♔b6 87 ♔d3 ♖e5 88 ♔d4 ♘c6+ 89 ♔d3 ♔a7 90 ♖c7 ♘d8 91 ♖g7 ♘xb7 92 ♖g6 ♔b8 93 ♔d4 ♖a5 94 ♔e3 ♔c7 95 ♔f4 ♘d8 96 ♖f6 ♔d7 97 ♖f5 ♘e6+ 98 ♔e4 ♖a4+ 99 ♔d5 ♘d8 100 ♔e5 ♔e7 101 ♖f1 ♖a5+ 102 ♔e4 ♘f7 103 ♖b1 ♘d6+ 104 ♔f4 ♖f5+ 105 ♔e3 ♔f6 106 ♖c1 ♖a5 107 ♖c6 ♔e5 108 ♔f2 ♘f5 109 ♖g6 ♖a4 110 ♖g8 ♖f4+ 111 ♔e2 ♖xh4 112 ♖h8 ♔f4 113 ♔f2 ♘e7 114 ♖f8+ ♔e5 0-1**

After this marathon I don't suppose I need to remind you that the watchword for Black in the Botvinnik System is *patience*. White is hoping that you will become careless or reckless, when he can pick you off.

Classical English Development with ♘f3

1 c4 f5 2 ♘c3 ♘f6 3 g3 g6 4 ♗g2 ♗g7 5 ♘f3 0-0 6 0-0 d6

An alternative move order to reach this position is 1 ♘f3 f5 2 g3 ♘f6 3 ♗g2 g6 4 0-0 ♗g7 5 c4 d6 6 ♘c3 0-0.

7 d3

Finally deciding against 7 d4 and a main line Leningrad.

7...♘c6 8 ♖b1 a5

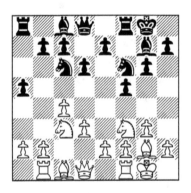

This might seem strange as it only temporarily prevents b2-b4 and leads to the opening of the a-file, which in Wunder-Buchal below falls into

White's hands. However, the exchange on b4 somewhat lessens the force of White's pawn-storm and avoids being left with a potential target on a7.

9 a3 e5

Note that Black delayed ...e7-e5 until here. He gave priority to ...♘c6 so that he was ready to meet White's ♖b1 with ...a7-a5.

10 b4 axb4 11 axb4

We have reached a standard English versus Dutch opening scenario. White hopes to keep things quiet in the centre, ward off any attack Black tries on the kingside, and gradually advance his queenside pawns.

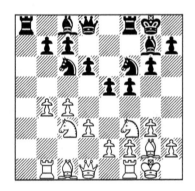

11...h6

A useful move. It rules out lines with 12 ♗g5 in which White plays ♗xf6 to increase his control over d5. It also prepares under some circumstances to expand with ...g6-g5, to begin a kingside pawn-roller. And finally it means that after ...♗e6 the bishop won't be hit by ♘g5.

Moreover, hesitant or passive play will be punished. Indeed, in

An.Timofeev-I.Kosov, Peterhof 2008, White invited an attack with a common English manoeuvre which proved badly misguided here:

12 ♘e1? g5 13 e3?! f4!

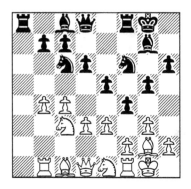

14 ♘d5

Black also has a rampant initiative after 14 exf4 gxf4 15 gxf4 exf4 16 ♗xf4 ♘g4, hitting both c3 and f4.

14...♘xd5 15 ♗xd5+

Safer was 15 cxd5, but Black can still attack after 15...♘e7.

15...♔h8 16 exf4 exf4 17 ♗b2 ♗xb2 18 ♖xb2 ♕f6 19 ♕h5

Stopping 19...♗h3, but losing the exchange.

19...♗g4 20 ♕xg4 ♕xb2 and Black was winning.

S.Wunder-S.Buchal
Bad Wiessee 2006

1 c4 f5 2 ♘c3 ♘f6 3 g3 g6 4 ♗g2 ♗g7 5 ♘f3 0-0 6 0-0 d6 7 d3 ♘c6 8 ♖b1 a5 9 a3 e5 10 b4 axb4 11 axb4 h6 12 b5

A much more sensible approach than the knight retreat to e1.

12...♘e7 13 ♗b2

The next game features the sharper 13 c5.

13...♗e6 14 ♖a1

White decides to seize control of the a-file. Black's aim is to keep body and soul together long enough on the queenside and in the centre so that his attack on the kingside can gain pace.

14...♖b8 15 ♘e1 g5 16 ♖a7 ♕c8 17 ♕b3 f4 18 ♗a3 ♘f5 19 ♘c2 ♖f7 20 b6 c6 21 ♘e4 c5

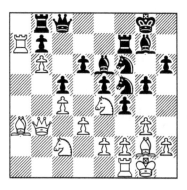

A major concession as now there is a hole on d5 and the white bishop can attack the b7-pawn. On the other hand, the pawn blocks the attack on d6, the linchpin of the black centre. The position is now very exciting – will the black kingside attack be in time, or will White smash through the queenside?

22 ♘c3 ♘d4 23 ♘xd4 exd4 24 ♘b5 ♘e8 25 ♗c1 ♗e5 26 ♗d2 ♘f6 27 ♖fa1

White has brilliant control of the a-file, but this means that his rooks, knight and queen are all a long way from the defence of their king.

27...♗h3

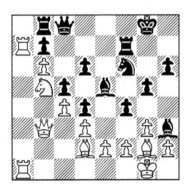

Offering to exchange off one of the few pieces defending the white king and clearing f5 for the black queen.

28 ♘c7 ♕f5 29 ♖a8 ♖xa8 30 ♖xa8+ ♔g7 31 ♗xb7

Now White is totally winning on the queenside and totally lost on the kingside. The king is the most important piece, of course.

31...fxg3

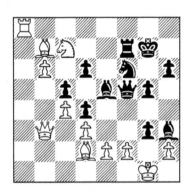

32 ♗f3

There is a pretty mate after 32 hxg3 ♕xf2+! 33 ♔xf2 ♘g4+ and 34...♖f1 mate.

32...gxf2+ 33 ♔xf2 g4 34 ♕d1

White is just too late with the passed pawn.

34...gxf3 35 ♘e8+ ♘xe8 36 ♕g1+ ♔h7 37 ♖xe8 fxe2+ 38 ♔xe2 ♕f3+ 39 ♔e1 ♗g4 0-1

E.Yanayt-H.Nakamura
Las Vegas 2006

1 c4 f5 2 ♘c3 ♘f6 3 g3 g6 4 ♗g2 ♗g7 5 ♘f3 0-0 6 0-0 d6 7 d3 ♘c6 8 ♖b1 a5 9 a3 e5 10 b4 axb4 11 axb4 h6 12 b5 ♘e7 13 c5

In contrast to the previous game, White seeks an immediate tactical slugfest – not necessarily a good idea against Nakamura.

13...♗e6!

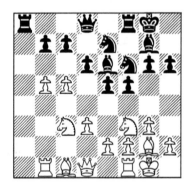

Black completes his development and prevents White playing the attacking move ♕b3.

14 b6

Ramming the centre structure on both d6 and c7. It becomes fragmented, but on the other hand the black pieces become very active.

14...dxc5 15 bxc7 ♕xc7 16 ♘b5 ♕d8!?

After 16...♕b8 White has the surprising tactic 17 ♘xe5! with the idea that 17...♕xe5? 18 ♗f4 wins the black queen. However, the position remains unclear after, say, 17...g5 or 17...♗a2. Instead Nakamura decides to give up the pawn straightaway.

17 ♘xe5

Black's centre has crumbled, but his bishops will exert enormous pressure on the white queenside.

17...♗a2! 18 ♖a1 ♘fd5 19 ♗a3

I also rather like Black's position after 19 ♕c2 ♗b3!? 20 ♕xb3 ♖xa1 21 ♘xg6 ♘xg6 22 ♗xd5+ ♔h7.

19...♖a5!

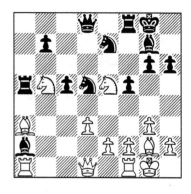

Black has to counterattack against b5 as 19...♗xe5 20 ♖xa2 is just pleasant for White.

20 ♖xa2 ♖xb5

Threatening both 21...♗xe5 and the fork 21...♘c3.

21 d4?

The unlikely move 21 ♕a1! would keep White alive, though Black has the initiative after 21...♘b4.

21...♘c3 22 ♕d3 ♕xd4! 23 ♕xd4 cxd4 24 ♗xe7 ♖e8

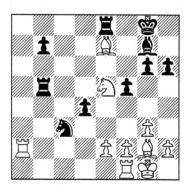

White is temporarily a piece for a pawn up, but with a knight, bishop and rook all hanging there is no way even to escape to equality.

25 ♖d2 ♖xe5 26 ♗d6 ♖5e6 27 ♗b4 ♘xe2+ 28 ♔h1 ♖b6 29 ♗a3 ♖b5 30 h4 g5 31 ♔h2 gxh4 32 ♖e1 hxg3+ 33 fxg3 ♖be5 34 ♗d6 ♖e3 35 ♗xb7 ♘xg3 36 ♖g1 ♘e2 37 ♖g2 ♔h7 38 ♗a6 ♘c3 39 ♗f4 ♖f3 40 ♗g3 ♘e4 0-1

White plays e2-e3 and ♘ge2

Just like the Botvinnik System, this requires a more distinct move order from White, as he has to avoid ♘f3 and first clear the way for the knight to go to e2.

P.Brodowski-H.Danielsen
Mysliborz 2008

1 c4 f5 2 g3 g6 3 ♗g2 ♗g7 4 ♘c3 d6 5 e3 ♘f6 6 ♘ge2 0-0 7 0-0

Putting the knight on e2 rather than f3 means that White is better prepared to meet a kingside pawn-storm by Black. He has more control of the f4-square and might even block things with f2-f4 if it looks like Black is threatening ...f5-f4.

7...a5!?

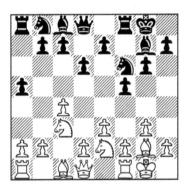

Black begins by restraining a possible b2-b4 by White. He plans a system of development with moves like ...c6, ...e5 and ...♗e6, with ...♘a6 usually preferred to ...♘bd7 if the knight is in no danger of being run down by a b4-b5 pawn advance.

8 ♖b1

After 8 d4 c6 9 b3 ♘a6 Black obtains an attractive Leningrad-style set-up: 10 ♗b2 ♗d7 11 ♕d2 ♖b8 12 ♖fd1 ♘c7 (if White now 'passes', then Black can expand on the queenside with 13...b5) 13 d5 ♘a6 (back again, now that the c5-square has appeared for the knight) 14 dxc6 bxc6 15 ♘f4 ♘c5 and Black was at least equal in P.Degembe-A.De Santis, Saint Vincent 2001.

8...c6 9 d4

Slightly inconsistent after putting the rook on b1. Instead White could

play for b2-b4, but 9 d3 e5 10 a3 ♗e6 11 b4 axb4 12 axb4 ♘bd7 13 b5 ♕c7 looks comfortable for Black. In time he can aim to expand with ...d6-d5.

Instead if White omitted d2-d3 and played the immediate 9 a3 e5 10 b4 axb4 11 axb4 then Black might continue 11...♗e6, but 11...e4 is interesting to shut in the bishop on g2 and target c4 with ...♗e6.

9...e5 10 dxe5 dxe5 11 b3 ♗e6

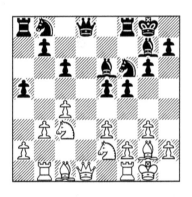

Already Black feels a bit better due to his space advantage and the fact that the bishop on g2 is passive.

12 e4

Evidently White didn't want to allow 12...e4, but he will pay a heavy price for weakening the d4- and f4-squares. Perhaps he should have simplified with 12 ♗a3 ♖e8 13 ♕xd8 ♖xd8.

12...♘a6 13 ♕xd8 ♖fxd8 14 ♗e3 ♘b4 15 ♗b6 ♖d2 16 ♖fd1

White hopes to evict the rook and emerge with a good game due to the pressure on the a5-pawn.

16...♖c2 17 a3 ♘a2 18 ♘xa2 ♖xe2 19 ♘c3 ♖c2 20 ♖dc1 ♖xc1+ 21 ♖xc1 ♘d7

22 ♗e3 f4!

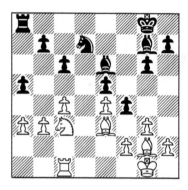

The Dutch pawn-ram strikes. It activates the bishop and wins the c5-square for the knight, after which the white queenside is on the point of collapse.

23 gxf4 exf4 24 ♗xf4 ♘c5

Now both captures 24...♘d3 and 24...♘xb3 are threatened. Brodowski tries to escape with a sacrifice, but it is inadequate.

25 ♘d5 cxd5 26 exd5 ♗f5 27 d6 ♘d3 28 ♗e3 ♘xc1 29 ♗xc1 ♗d4 30 ♗g5 ♖b8 31 b4 axb4 32 axb4 ♔g7 33 c5 ♗d7 34 ♗f4 h6 35 h4 ♗c3 36 b5 ♗xb5 37 d7 ♖d8 38 ♗xb7 ♗xd7 39 c6 ♗c8 40 ♔g2 ♖e8 41 ♔f3 ♗d4 0-1

Part Three: 1 b3

1 b3

The Nimzowitsch-Larsen Attack. Now 1...f5 2 ♗b2 ♘f6 3 ♗xf6 exf6 isn't very appealing for Black. So I'm going to recommend a non-Dutch approach:

1...e5 2 ♗b2 d6.

Then we can fianchetto in King's Indian-style and think about ...f7-f5 later on. For example:

a) 3 c4 g6 4 d4 ♗g7 5 dxe5 ♘d7! (a typical delayed recapture on e5) 6 ♕d2 dxe5 7 ♘f3 c6 8 ♘c3 ♘gf6 9 ♘g5 (White begins a manoeuvre that lets us play our Dutch move) 9...0-0 10 ♘ge4 ♘xe4 11 ♘xe4 f5 12 ♘d6 ♘c5 13 ♖d1 ♕e7 and Black had dynamic chances due to White's backward kingside development and rather vulnerable knight on d6 in S.Cicak-Cu.Hansen, Reykjavik 1998.

b) 3 e3 g6 and now 4 d4 ♗g7 5 dxe5 ♘d7 6 ♘f3 ♘e7 7 ♘bd2 dxe5 is comfortable for Black, T.Alonso Martinez-A.Strikovic, Mondariz 2009.

Alternatively, 4 f4 ♗g7 5 ♘f3 ♘d7 6 ♗c4 ♘h6 7 0-0 0-0 led to a double-edged game in E.Bacrot-M.Adams, Moscow (blitz) 2007. In neither of these lines will Black be hurrying to play ...f7-f5, but at least we have the 'feel' of the Dutch mobile pawn centre.

Index of Variations

Index of Games

Printed in the USA
CPSIA information can be obtained
at www.ICGtesting.com
JSHW012137011123
51246JS00004B/18